EIGHT THEORIES OF ETHICS

Is it possible to study ethics objectively, or are moral judgements inevitably subjective? Are ancient theories of ethics of any contemporary relevance? Which ethical theory offers the most convincing explanation of how best to live one's life?

Eight Theories of Ethics is a comprehensive introduction to the theories of ethics encountered by first-time students. Gordon Graham introduces the fundamental concepts that underpin ethics, such as relativism and objectivity, and then devotes his attention to each of the eight major theories of ethics:

- egoism
- hedonism
- naturalism and virtue theory
- existentialism
- Kantianism
- utilitarianism
- contractualism
- religion

Throughout the book, the exposition draws on examples from great moral philosophers such as Aristotle, Kant and Mill, as well as contemporary debates over human nature, the environment and citizenship.

Eight Theories of Ethics is written in an engaging and student-friendly style, with detailed suggestions for further reading at the end of each chapter – including original sources and contemporary discussions. It is ideal for anyone coming to this area of philosophy for the first time, and for those studying ethics in related disciplines such as politics, law, nursing and medicine.

Gordon Graham is Regius Professor of Moral Philosophy at the University of Aberdeen. He is the author of *The Internet: A Philosophical Inquiry* (1999), *Philosophy of the Arts* (second edition, 2000), and *Genes: A Philosophical Inquiry* (2002), all published by Routledge.

EIGHT THEORIES OF ETHICS

Gordon Graham

Routledge
Taylor & Francis Group

LONDON AND NEW YORK

First published 2004
by Routledge
11 New Fetter Lane, London EC4P 4EE

Simultaneously published in the USA and Canada
by Routledge
29 West 35th Street, New York, NY 10001

Routledge is an imprint of the Taylor & Francis Group
©2004 Gordon Graham

Typeset in Sabon and Frutiger by Keyword Typesetting Services Ltd.
Printed and bound in Great Britain by MPG Books Ltd, Bodmin.

British Library Cataloguing in Publication Data
A catalogue record for this book is available from the British Library

Library of Congress Cataloguing in Publication Data
Graham, Gordon, 1949 July 15-
Eight theories of ethics/Gordon Graham.
p. cm
Includes bibliographical references and index.
1. Ethics. I. Title.

BJ1025.G675 2004
171–dc22
2003021375

ISBN 0–415–31588–3(hbk)
ISBN 0–415–31589–1(pbk)

CONTENTS

CONTENTS

CONTENTS

PREFACE

Most people who come to philosophy for the first time know rather little about it. Nonetheless they often have a preconceived idea that philosophy ought to raise and answer fundamental questions about how to live, about what things are good and evil, and about what the 'meaning' of human life is. Yet, the philosophy books they read at the start of their studies rarely seem to have a direct bearing on these topics and from this they conclude that their preconceptions about philosophy were mistaken. Sometimes the result is that the newcomers discover a new interest in 'academic' philosophy and leave their previous interests behind; alternatively they abandon philosophy with a feeling of disappointment, and turn to more 'popular' works that come from writers with little or no training in formal philosophy, or to works of literature that throw light on their original interests in a different way.

Both these outcomes are regrettable and unnecessary. It is indeed wrong to think that philosophers are solely, or even primarily concerned with the questions philosophy is commonly supposed to address. Yet the popular conception of philosophy is not wholly mistaken. Many of the greatest figures in Western philosophy from Plato to Wittgenstein have wondered what the good life for a human being consists in, what makes it good and whether its being so has any cosmic significance. At the same time, these questions are not well answered by simple personal reflections, however sincerely meant, such as one finds in books where the author merely aims to set out 'my philosophy'. Two thousand years of philosophical inquiry has shown that surrounding the topics of value and meaning there is a large set of complex questions whose understanding takes considerable intellectual effort. The same period, of course, has produced philosophical works on these themes from some of the finest minds in human history.

The purpose of this book is to help readers grapple with these questions while keeping clearly in view the concern about how we ought to live and whether our lives have any ultimate meaning, while at the same time familiarizing them with the ideas of the 'big' names in philosophy. Its aim, in other words, is to show that philosophy proper is the best way to investigate matters of ethical importance.

Early versions of several of the chapters were written and published as a textbook over a decade ago. At the suggestion of Tony Bruce of Routledge these have now been completely revised and others added to make up what is in effect a new book with a different title. I am grateful to him for the stimulus to undertake this and for the opportunity to introduce a wide readership to moral philosophy as I think it ought to be done.

Gordon Graham
King's College, Aberdeen
August 2003

A NOTE ON FURTHER READING

Each chapter is followed by suggested further reading. The items listed are divided into original sources, commentaries and contemporary discussion. I have tried to cite the most 'reader friendly' editions of original sources. The commentaries generally include some fairly introductory material, but also some in-depth commentaries that will provide material for more advanced study and some of these may prove less easy reading to the new-comer. The works listed under contemporary discussion are meant to direct the reader to up-to-date material that professional philosophers are currently engaged with.

Full details of all the items of suggested further reading, together with works quoted from or referred to in the text, will be found in the bibliography at the end of the book.

1

ETHICS, TRUTH AND REASON

This is a book about ethics, about right and wrong and good and bad in human life. But can we really tell moral right from wrong? Morality, many people think, is not like science, which deals in facts, but a matter of values, about which we can only have personal opinions. According to this point of view, there aren't any moral facts, and this explains why people disagree so much over ethical questions. While science is objective, morality is essentially subjective.

This is a very common view of ethics. It is also a very ancient one. Indeed, moral philosophy as an intellectual inquiry may be said to have its origins in a debate about its truth or falsehood. The question of the subjectivity or objectivity of morality provides the focus for the earliest complete works of philosophy – Plato's dialogues. In several of these dialogues, Plato constructs dramatic conversations between his teacher Socrates and various figures well known in ancient Athens. Many of these people were called 'Sophists', a group of thinkers who held that there is a radical difference between the world of facts and the world of values, between *physis* and *nomos* to use the Greek words, the difference being that when it comes to matters of value, the concepts of true and false have no meaningful application. By implication, then, in ethics there is no scope for proof and demonstration as there is in science and mathematics; ethical 'argument' is a matter of rhetoric, which is to say, of *persuading* people to believe what you believe rather than *proving* to them that the beliefs you hold are true.

We know relatively little about the historical Socrates outside the pages of Plato's dialogues, but it seems likely that Plato represented his famous teacher accurately when he portrayed him as arguing vigorously against the Sophists. Certainly, whatever about Socrates, Plato himself believed and argued with great subtlety that there are indeed right and wrong answers about good and bad, and that we can use our powers of reasoning to discover what these are. He further believed that it takes a certain measure of expertise to get the answers right, and that philosophy plays an important part in acquiring that expertise.

One way of describing the issue between Socrates (or Plato) and the Sophists is to say that it is a disagreement about the objectivity of morality. While the Sophists believed that good and bad, right and wrong, reflect *subjective* opinion and desire – how we as human beings and as individuals feel about things – Plato and Socrates believed that good and bad, right and wrong, are part of the objective nature of things – how the world around us really is. And it is with this debate that moral philosophy in the Western tradition began.

There is more to the historical dispute between Plato and the Sophists than this short summary implies (the Sophist Protagoras is more properly described as a relativist than a subjectivist, for example) but the point of referring to it is not to introduce a study of the ancient world, but to draw a connection between the origins of thinking about ethics and a contemporary debate along very similar lines. When modern day students (and others) first begin the business of thinking about ethics, they generally incline to the view that morality is essentially subjective. This is in contrast to other historical periods when most people would have taken the opposite view, and held that just as there are scientific laws, there are moral laws that lay down right and wrong quite independently of the likings or dislikings of human beings.

This is an oversimplification, of course. As the existence of the Sophists shows, in times past there were people who were subjectivists, and at the present time there are plenty of people who are objectivists, implicitly if not explicitly – human rights activists and environmental campaigners for example, both of whom generally think that human rights and environmental values generate universal and inescapable obligations. So, subjectivism and objectivism are both 'live' philosophical options, and this means that if we are to make a rational decision between them, we have to consider reasons

2

for and against either position. Once we do so, we have begun to engage in philosophical thinking. But the crucial question is: which view *is* correct?

RELATIVISM AND SUBJECTIVISM

A lot of people think that the subjectivity of morality is obvious. If so, it should be relatively easy to produce good reasons in support of the subjectivist point of view. What might these reasons be? Among the most commonly cited are three. The first is that people hold all sorts of conflicting moral opinions; the second is that they do so because of the impossibility of proving the superiority of one moral view over another; and the third is that proof is impossible since there are no observable moral 'facts'. One way of assessing the plausibility of subjectivism, then, is to ask about the truth of these claims and what, if they are indeed true, they actually imply.

Now the first proposition – that there are serious moral disagreements between people – can hardly be denied. Nor is this just a matter of individual disagreement; from ancient times it has been noted that such differences are to be found between entire cultures. The ancient Greek historian Herodotus, for example, recounts an episode in which the King of Persia induced horror on the part of both Greeks and Callatians by asking them to adopt each other's funeral practices. What the Greeks took to be right and proper – burning their dead – the Callatians regarded as utterly abhorrent. But since, by contrast, fire burned just the same in both Greece and Persia, Herodotus's implication is that moral practices are unlike physical phenomena in being relative to cultural contexts. While the laws of nature remain the same everywhere, rules of conduct differ from place to place.

This example has often been used to illustrate the position known as 'ethical relativism', the belief that ethical views are always relative to some particular culture or other. What this says (continuing with this example) is that cremation of the dead is *right for the Greeks*, but *wrong for the Callatians*. By implication, there is nothing right or wrong per se, or universally. But why stop at differences between *groups* of people? There are also differences of this kind to be found between individuals. Something that truly horrifies one person, another can find quite acceptable. What is called 'subjectivism' is really just an extension of relativism from the level of the social group to the level of the individual. But if moral differences are relativized to individuals, this seems to suggest that, when it comes to ethics, there is no truth of the matter to be discovered.

It is not hard to find examples from our own time and culture that lead people to this subjectivist conclusion. One of the most vexed moral issues of the modern Western world is abortion. While everyone can easily agree what medical procedures will result in an abortion, there does not appear to be anything like the same agreement on whether abortion is morally right or wrong. That is to say, when it comes to abortion, agreement is easily reached on matters of medical *science*, whereas on matters of medical *ethics* it is not. Moreover it seems that the examples can be multiplied very easily. For instance, everyone can agree on the relative effectiveness of different methods of capital punishment – lethal injection versus the electric chair say. What they cannot agree about is whether either method is morally *justified* or not.

So, at any rate, it appears. But appearance is not reality. Is it really the case that there is far more difference of opinion on moral than on medical or scientific matters? One point worth making is that, while moral *disagreement* hogs the headlines, so to speak, there is actually a lot of moral *agreement* in the contemporary world. It would be difficult to find anyone who thought rape, murder or theft a good thing, or believed honesty, loyalty and generosity to be evil things. Everyone condemns slavery, the sexual molestation of children and cheating at sport. This is not to say that there are no cheats and child molesters, or even that there are no slaves. But there is no one who openly owns up to these things as a matter of pride. This marks these off from the sort of example that impressed Herodotus. The Athenians and the Spartans were proud of the way they did things, and horrified by the practices of others. Often child molesters are not suitably horrified by what they have done; but they are never openly proud of it as an alternative lifestyle, and in those relatively rare cases when they do not seem to be at all ashamed of their deviant behaviour, this is usually some indication of mental illness.

Moral differences of opinion can be exaggerated, then. While abortion, euthanasia and capital punishment are indeed the subject of much dispute and disagreement, there is in fact a very large range of issues on which there is little moral disagreement. A similar point can be made in the opposite direction; the degree of scientific or factual *agreement* can be exaggerated. At every stage in its history, including the present, natural science has been marked by radical disagreement between expert practitioners. The greatest names in science – Bacon, Newton, Darwin, Einstein – generally had difficulty in getting their ideas accepted and the everyday practice of science is one in which people are constantly claiming to refute and disprove each other. Even more importantly, the history of science reveals dramatic disagreements *across time*. The mechanics of Sir Isaac Newton completely displaced the Aristotelian physics that had dominated science for many centuries, and then Newtonianism in its turn was displaced two centuries later by Einstein's theory of relativity. This is par for the course, in fact. Science lives by one generation disputing the hypotheses of the generation that preceded it.

Even so, it might be said, there is still a striking difference between science and ethics. Einstein didn't just disagree with Newton; he *disproved* him. Science does not merely change; it *progresses*. In ethics and morality, by contrast, though opinions *change*, they don't progress. This is because there is no possibility of proof or disproof, just disagreement. Moral opinions can't be conclusively proved or refuted. Here we encounter the second of the reasons subjectivists tend to advance in favour of their view – that there is no such thing as moral proof.

Sometimes philosophers have felt challenged by this claim to produce some moral proofs, but this rarely accomplishes much because such 'proofs' are invariably contentious and generally unconvincing to most of the people to whom they are offered. A more telling reply to this second subjectivist point is to draw attention to the fact that proof properly so called seems in short supply, not just in morality, but in almost *every* context. It is only an especially notable feature of morality that it doesn't admit of proof, if most other spheres of human discourse do. But they don't. It may be the case that in mathematics and logic there is scope for formal proofs (though it is worth noting that even mathematicians and logicians can, and do, disagree), but once we pass beyond mathematics and logic, conclusive proof seems very hard to come by. In the law, for example, where there is certainly *talk* of proof, the actual standard is not absolute or conclusive proof, but simply establishing a case beyond reasonable doubt, in criminal cases, and even more weakly in civil cases, showing that the balance of probability is in favour of the claim you are making. Now if we were to apply a similar concept of 'proof' in morality, it would not be so obvious that there could be no moral 'proofs', because there are often occasions when individuals who are determined to dispute some moral view or other do seem to go beyond the realms of 'reasonable doubt'. It may be impossible to prove some moral belief to be false. This does not mean that it cannot be shown to be unreasonable.

That the absence of proof is not unique to ethics is even clearer when we look beyond logic and the law to other areas of factual inquiry, notably history. Consider just a simple example. It is impossible to prove, i.e. demonstrate beyond doubt, on which day of the week Henry VIII married Anne Boleyn. The sort of evidence that would clinch the matter – church records, etc. – no longer exist. However, there is unquestionably a fact of the matter on which day it was, and from this we should conclude that even simple straightforward factual matters cannot always be proved.

The general point is that ethical or moral beliefs and propositions are only striking by not admitting of proof if they differ dramatically in this respect from other sorts of belief. But as we have just observed, this is not the case. There are plenty of factual matters that don't admit of proof. The example just given of Henry's marriage to Anne Boleyn is only one instance, and the study of history provides indefinitely many more. But so do such natural sciences as geomorphology, climatology and physiology. Just where the last ice cap extended, whether the hypothesis of global warming is true and what the cause of motor neurone disease is are all matters of perplexity and dispute. It is not only false but facile to think that, in contrast to moral issues, these are matters of fact upon which informed and disinterested minds are sure to agree. People who are equally well informed and experienced in the subject often disagree profoundly, and even the best minds frequently admit to uncertainty and ignorance.

Faced with these reminders of how different avenues of human inquiry actually proceed, moral subjectivists are unlikely to concede defeat however. There is still a crucial difference, they will contend. While it may indeed be the case that in history, geomorphology, medicine and so on, there are irresolvable disagreements, this is a contingent matter, something that just *happens* to be the case. Historical and scientific facts could *in principle* be uncovered to prove the case one way or another. *As it happens* we don't know on which day of the week Henry married Anne, but we *could*. In morality, on the other hand, disagreements are unprovable in principle. This is because there are no moral facts.

MORAL REALISM

It is on the basis of this third claim that subjectivism is sometimes called, in more technical language, 'non-cognitivism', which means 'not a matter of knowledge'. What some people believe to be right, others believe to be wrong, and of course, both sides may well speak of their moral disagreement as though it was a dispute about matters of fact, how things really are. But according to the non-cognitivist, it isn't. In the history of philosophy this view was most famously expressed and endorsed by the eighteenth-century Scottish philosopher David Hume.

> Take any action allow'd to be vicious: Wilful murder, for instance. Examine it in all lights, and see if you can find that matter of fact, or real existence, which you call vice. In which-ever way you take it, you find only certain passions, motives, volitions and thoughts. There is no other matter of fact in the case. The vice entirely escapes you, as long as you consider the object. You can never find it, till you turn your reflexion into your own breast, and find a sentiment of disapprobation, which arises in you, towards this action. Here is a matter of fact; but 'tis the object of feeling, not of reason. It lies in yourself, not the object.
>
> (Hume, 1739, 1967: 484)

The view that Hume is opposing here is often called 'moral realism', the theory that moral values, such as wicked and generous, are real properties of people and their actions in the way that hard and soft are properties of physical objects. Now such a view faces a major problem: if there actually were such moral properties, compared with ordinary everyday physical properties they would be decidedly 'queer' (as the philosopher J L Mackie famously put it).

Three aspects of this 'queerness' are usually cited. First, while properties like light and dark, hot and cold, loud and soft, sweet and sour, can be discovered through the senses of seeing, hearing, touch and taste, we can't see

7

or hear or feel right and wrong, good and bad. Second, as Gilbert Harman once pointed out, even if we could observe moral properties, they would still differ from physical properties like hot and cold. For, while physical properties figure in explanations of why we observe them, this doesn't seem to be true of moral properties.

> Observation plays a role in science that it does not seem to play in ethics. The difference is that you need to make assumptions about certain physical facts to explain the occurrence of the observations that support a scientific theory, but you do not seem to make assumptions about any moral facts to explain the occurrence of so-called moral observation.... You need only make assumptions about the psychology... of the person making the moral observation. In the scientific case, theory is tested against the world.
>
> (Harman 1977: 6)

Harman's idea (and example) is this. Suppose I see boys setting a cat on fire. To explain my feeling the heat of the flames, there has to be heat there. To explain my feeling of moral revulsion, on the other hand, it is only necessary to appeal to my moral beliefs; there doesn't have to be any 'moral horror' out there in the world for me to feel.

The third objection to supposed moral properties is one that Hume makes, and more recently J L Mackie. Hume thinks that the perception of properties is 'inert'. That is to say, merely seeing or hearing something will not of itself lead to action. But the essence of ethics is action – recommending and following courses of conduct. From this it would seem to follow that moral 'properties', if they did exist, would be lacking in the very thing we want – what philosophers sometimes call 'action guiding force'. Mackie puts the point this way. Moral reasoning has to yield 'authoritatively prescriptive conclusions', but if 'we ask the awkward question, how can we be aware of this authoritative prescriptivity... none of our ordinary accounts of sensory perception ... will provide a satisfactory answer' (Mackie 1977: 39). You cannot literally *see* what you ought to do.

This third point is closely related to a problem widely referred to as 'the naturalistic fallacy'. Once again, it is David Hume to whom we owe one of the most famous articulations of the problem. Towards the end of that section of the *Treatise* from which the passage quoted earlier comes, he says:

> I cannot forbear adding to these reasonings an observation, which may, perhaps, be found of some importance. In every system of morality, which I have hitherto met with, I have always remark'd, that the author proceeds for some time in the ordinary way of reasoning... ; when of a sudden I am surpriz'd to find that instead of the usual copulations of propositions, *is*, and *is not*, I meet with no proposition that is not connected with an *ought*, or an *ought not*. This change is imperceptible; but it is however, of the last consequence.
>
> (Hume 1739, 1967: 469)

Hume thinks that trying to derive an 'ought' from an 'is' is logically invalid; statements of fact cannot of themselves have prescriptive implications. If so, then propositions referring to 'real' moral properties could provide no rational basis for action since, being descriptions of how the world *is*, we could not infer from them how the world *ought* to be. Actually, the position is worse than this for the moral realist, because according to another version of the naturalistic fallacy, we cannot even infer good and bad from is and is not. This can be shown by what is known as the 'open question argument'. For any natural property, it always makes sense to ask 'Is it good?', and the fact that this question always makes sense shows that 'good' and 'bad' cannot be the names of natural properties in the way that 'hard' and 'soft' are. For example, suppose someone claims that happiness, say, is a naturally good thing. We can always wonder about this, can always ask '*Is* happiness good?' Now if happiness were good in and of itself this question would make no more sense than the question 'Does happiness make people happy?'. But it does make sense, and so we have to conclude that goodness is not a property of happiness.

This version of the naturalistic fallacy was formulated by the twentieth-century Cambridge philosopher G E Moore in a very influential book entitled *Principia Ethica* (The Principles of Ethics). Not everyone has been persuaded by the 'open question' argument, but even if it is a good one, it does not necessarily amount to a refutation of moral realism. Curiously,

Moore was himself a kind of moral realist who believed that there are moral properties. His response to the difficulty that he himself formulated was to declare that goodness is a 'non-natural' property, indefinable in the way a colour like 'yellow' is. We can't give a definition of 'yellow' that will enable us to class all yellow things together; we just *see* that yellow things have the property of yellowness in common. In a similar fashion, Moore thought, by a special faculty of moral intuition, we just 'see' that things have the indefinable property of goodness, and in *Principia Ethica* he lists some of the main things that he believed to have this non-natural property.

For a time, Moore's view was found persuasive, but most philosophers would probably agree that having identified a major difficulty for moral realism in his analysis of the naturalistic fallacy, Moore simply dug himself in deeper with the appeal to non-natural properties and a faculty of intuition. If the naturalistic fallacy shows that we cannot infer value judgements from natural facts by means of ordinary perception, the introduction of 'non-natural' facts and a special evaluative 'intuition' simple shrouds the whole issue in mystery.

MORAL RATIONALISM

There is, however, a different tack to be taken. In the *Treatise*, Hume allows for two spheres in which reason can operate – 'matters of fact' and 'relations of ideas'. The first of these is the one we have been concerned with so far. Are there matters of moral fact that we can perceive and refer to? The moral realist wants to say 'yes' but there seem to be major obstacles to doing so. What, though, about 'relations between ideas'? In his use of this expression, Hume clearly has in mind mathematics and logic. It is true that '$2+2=4$', for example, and yet this is not something we can open our eyes and see, or put our hands on and touch. Now Hume assumes that moral judgements could not be like this, but it is an assumption we might question. Consider this little argument.

1 You promised to pay back the money you borrowed.
2 Promises ought to be kept.
  So
3 You ought to pay back the money you borrowed.

From the point of view of logic, this argument is valid. That is to say, anyone who accepts the premises (propositions 1 and 2) is logically obliged to accept the conclusion. But since the conclusion (proposition 3) takes the form of a moral prescription – a proposition that tells us what the morally right thing to do is – it seems, contrary to Hume and subjectivists in general, that we *can* arrive at moral conclusions on the basis of reason.

Of course, it will be replied that this type of example doesn't prove very much because while the first premise (You promised to pay the money you borrowed) is factual, a claim about something that happened, the second (Promises ought to be kept) is not. It is a moral principle to which the person to whom the argument is addressed needs to subscribe before he or she is obliged to accept the conclusion.

Now this seems plausible. 'Promises ought to be kept' does sound like a moral principle, and if the arguments against moral realism are sound, we have to agree that it cannot be construed as a factual claim about some special sort of moral property – 'to-be-keptness' – that promises have. It can nevertheless be argued that this second premise, in something like the manner of a mathematical proposition, is true in virtue of 'relations between ideas'. That is to say, if you understand the concept of a promise and if you understand what 'obligation' means, you will have to agree that promises ought to be kept. In other words, the ideas of promising and being obliged to keep your promises are related, and accordingly the principle 'Promises ought to be kept' can be said to express a relation between ideas.

This is not quite the relation Hume had in mind. He thought that relations between ideas always took the form of analytic truths, or propositions that were true by definition. But the relation between making a promise and being obliged to keep it is more complex than this, and has been explored in detail in a very famous essay by the American philosopher John Searle – 'How to derive "ought" from "is"'. Searle draws a distinction between regulative rules and constitutive rules.

Some rules regulate antecedently existing forms of behaviour. For example, the rules of polite table behaviour regulate eating, but eating exists independently of these rules. Some rules, on the other hand, do not merely regulate but create or define new forms of behaviour; the rules of chess, for example, do not merely regulate an antecedently existing activity called playing chess; they... create the possibility of... that activity.... The institutions of marriage, money and promising are like the institutions of baseball or chess in that they are systems of such constitutive rules...

(Searle 1964, 1967: 112)

The ideas of making a promise and be obliged to keep it are related not by linguistic definition, but by a constitutive rule. By this account then Hume is partly right – reason does range over relations between ideas – and partly wrong – moral matters *can* be reasoned about, because at least some moral principles concern relations between ideas. The moral realist models moral reasoning on perception and Hume is right to reject this model. But there is an alternative model, which we may call 'moral rationalism' which construes moral reasoning on something like the model of mathematics. Now the advantage of this account is that it regards reasoning about morality as no different from reasoning in general. Whereas moral realism requires a special kind of moral seeing or intuition, moral rationalism need only hold that in morality as in anything else, we have to pay attention to facts (you did actually promise), we have to understand concepts properly (promising to do something puts the promiser under an obligation), and we have to combine our knowledge of the facts and our understanding of the concepts in logically valid patterns of reasoning. All three considerations are illustrated in the example just outlined, and though this is a simple instance of reasoning, much more complex cases can be analysed in the same way. On this conception, then, moral reasoning is no different from the sort of reasoning that goes on in a court of law, say, where advocates on either side try to construct good and convincing arguments based upon both factual evidence and legal concepts, and no different from the sort of reasoning that goes into public hearings or planning inquiries when people are ranged on different sides.

There are of course differences. One straightforward difference is that most laws and legal principles are established by law-making bodies – Parliaments and so on – for which there is no obvious moral equivalent. (The idea that God might be the source of the moral law will be discussed in a later chapter.) Even so, the parallel is enough to provide an answer to

12

the Sophists and other subjectivists. Morality is an aspect of human life that can engage our rational faculties as well as our feelings, in just the way that many other aspects of life can. I cannot reason about whom to fall in love with, but I can reason about whether it would be right to cheat on the person I love.

The parallel with law is instructive in another way. We can construct good and less good legal arguments that have clear conclusions about right and wrong and about what ought to be done. These arguments never amount to conclusive proof beyond all possibility of doubt or disagreement, but only proof beyond reasonable doubt or in accordance with what seems most probable. In this way legal reasoning falls short of logic and mathematics. Even so, as the existence and persistence of legal systems throughout the world demonstrate, legal argument is a good way of resolving disagreements, a good way of deciding what to believe about the allegations that are made against people, about what principles we ought to subscribe to, and what decisions it would be right and proper to take. Of course this is not the case in every instance. There are intractable legal disputes, both at the level of particular cases and general legal principles. But it would be an unwarranted counsel of despair to claim that because not *every* issue admits of rational resolution and reasoned agreement, we should never entertain the slightest hope of doing so. On the contrary, the reasonable position seems to be that we should set out in every case with the *hope* of rational resolution, doing the best we can, and accepting that we may not always succeed.

Exactly the same can be said for morality. Moral rationalists need not hold that reason has the means to answer every moral question at every level, and thus the power to resolve every disagreement conclusively. Rather, they need make only the following relatively modest claims. First, there are no grounds to declare reason powerless with respect to morality *from the outset*, which is to say, before even we start to think about the issues. Second, provided we accept that our conclusions will in all likelihood fall short of absolute proof or incontrovertible demonstration, the most plausible and intelligent approach to moral questions and disagreements is just to see how far clear and cogent reasoning – assembly of the relevant facts, analysis of the relevant concepts and adherence to the rules of logic – can take us.

13

OBJECTIVISM

Moral rationalism is a form of objectivism. This chapter has been concerned with the ancient philosophical dispute between objectivists and subjectivists. Although usually construed as a straightforward opposition, we can in fact distinguish not just two but *four* positions here. We might label these four positions: 1 hard subjectivism; 2 soft subjectivism; 3 hard objectivism; 4 soft objectivism. *Hard* subjectivism holds, as the Sophists are generally thought to have held, that in moral and evaluative questions there are never any 'right' answers. *Soft* subjectivism holds that in many such questions there are no right answers. Hard objectivism holds that for *every* moral question there is a right answer, and soft objectivism holds that for *any* moral question there may be a right answer. Now set out in this way we can see, I think, that the combination of moral rationalism and soft objectivism is the most plausible philosophical position to adopt. Why rule out in advance, as hard subjectivism does, the very possibility of resolving moral questions rationally? But if we don't rule it out altogether, then the claim of the soft subjectivist becomes irrelevant. It is of no consequence to know that some moral questions do not admit of rational resolution unless we know what these are, and without investigation we can't tell whether the questions that interest us are among those that have no answer. Hard objectivism, on the other hand, seems scarcely less dogmatic than hard subjectivism. It too is a pronouncement about what *must* be the case. But just as there can be legal cases (and historical investigations for that matter) that ultimately prove intractable, so too some moral disagreements may be too deep and difficult to admit of resolution.

On these grounds the first three positions are unattractive. That leaves soft objectivism as the best position to endorse – which is to say, the position that for any moral matter reason may be able to point us to a resolution that (remembering the legal parallel once more) is clearer and more cogent than any other and which it would be logically possible but unreasonable to dispute.

Soft objectivism is the underlying philosophical position of the remainder of this book. A few further observations are in order, however. To begin with it is worth noting that even if we don't come up with very clear-cut answers to the questions with which the rest of this book is concerned, there is still point in investigating them. Sometimes, it is more important to travel than to arrive, and mostly what we gain from tackling a philosophical problem lies in a better understanding of the issues than in an answer to the question.

Second, moral reflection proceeds on different levels. The most contentious questions in morality tend to be first-order ones, that is to say explicit moral problems – the rights and wrongs of abortion or capital punishment, say. Often disputes at these levels presuppose ideas at a higher or second order level, ideas about rights and values in general, about freedom, well-being and happiness, for example, and though philosophers can usefully contribute to debates about first-order moral problems, it is when we turn to consider underlying values that moral philosophy proper begins.

The course of life presents us with both possibilities and constraints. Some of these arise from our nature, others from the circumstances of life – 'the human condition' as it is sometimes referred to. Given these possibilities and constraints, what is the best sort of life to aim for? What values should we focus on and cling to? How should we strive to live, given the facts of human nature and the human condition? It is these second-order issues with which most of this book is concerned, and these issues to which we now turn.

SUGGESTED FURTHER READING

Original sources

Plato, *Republic* Bk I and *Gorgias*
David Hume, *A Treatise of Human Nature*
G E Moore, *Principia Ethica*

Commentaries

Nickolas Pappas, *Plato and the Republic*
James Baillie, *Hume on Morality*

Contemporary discussion

J L Mackie, *Ethics: Inventing Right and Wrong*
Gilbert Harman, *The Nature of Morality*
Michael Smith, *The Moral Problem*

2

EGOISM

The previous chapter ended with the question: What is the best sort of life to aim for? There is a familiar, almost commonplace answer to this question – to be rich and famous. This is a conception of the best life to have that is echoed in, and reinforced by media coverage of the life of the stars. It is also the idea that induces very large numbers of people to spend money on national lottery tickets when there is only a tiny chance of winning. Yet, as an answer to the philosopher's question, the idea that the best life is a rich and famous one does not take us very far, not so much because it is an unworthy ambition (though it may be) but because it is *logically* incomplete, and necessarily so.

INSTRUMENTAL AND INTRINSIC VALUE

Consider first the aspiration to be rich. If being rich means having a lot of money to spend, the belief that it is good to be rich in an important sense turns out to be vacuous. This is because, strange though it may sound, money in itself has no value whatever. If it were not exchangeable for other, quite different things – food, clothing, entertainment, i.e. goods and services that are independently valuable – we might as well throw it away. This point is not always easy to appreciate. So accustomed are we to thinking of the notes and coins in our pockets and purses as valuable, that the essentially valueless character of money itself can elude us. Yet, we only have to remind ourselves how worthless the currency of one country is in another country where it cannot be spent on the things that we want.

In fact, the *only* thing that makes money valuable is its usefulness as a medium of exchange for goods and services that are valuable, in themselves. When it cannot be used in this way, it has no value at all.

One way of expressing this feature of money, a feature it shares with many other things, is to say that money has *instrumental* but not *intrinsic* value. That is to say, it is valuable only as a *means* of obtaining something else; it has no value *in itself*. We could have lots of money in our possession, and still be unable to get the things we need and value. Perhaps we find ourselves in a desert with thousands of dollars, yet lacking the food and water we desperately require because there is nowhere to buy them. What this shows is that money is only as valuable as the things it is a means to. It follows from this that to say that the best life is one in which we have lots of money is not really an answer to the question 'What is the best life for a human being?' because it does not tell us what to spend our money on.

A related, though somewhat different point can be made about fame. If being famous means being well-known to a great many people, it too leaves unanswered the basic question because it does not tell us what we ought to want to be famous for. Is it equally good whether we are famous for the invention of life-saving drugs, like Alexander Fleming who discovered penicillin, for having killed more patients than any doctor in history, like the mass murderer Harold Shipman, for being the first person to conquer Everest like Sir Edmund Hillary, or for having amassed an absurd number of pairs of shoes like Imelda Marcos, wife of the Filipino dictator? Since we can be famous for quite different kinds of things – some good, some evil, some momentous, some trivial – and since such differences are obviously important, fame in and of itself does not seem to be specially worth striving for.

Someone who longed to be famous might reply that he or she valued fame regardless of what it was for, and therefore, unlike money, fame *can* be valued in itself. Not everyone will so value it, of course, but unlike the miser who mistakenly values money in and for itself, the seeker after fame is not making any kind of logical error. At one level, this is correct, but there is still something about fame that makes it insufficiently valuable by itself. Suppose someone sets out to be famous without caring what he is famous for. Even so, he has to choose *something* to be famous for – whether good, evil, momentous or trivial. But having done so, failure to achieve his chosen goal is a possibility. Now let us imagine that he not only fails, but fails *spectacularly*. In fact, so extraordinary is his unfailing ability to 'snatch defeat out of the jaws of victory', that he becomes famous as the world's greatest failure. (The skier Eddie the Eagle is a plausible instance of this. He set out to become famous as a skier, and became famous because he was so *bad* at it.) In this roundabout way the seeker after fame has, curiously, accomplished his aim. But we can see that, whatever it was he was aiming at, it would have been more desirable to him to have won fame through success than through failure. From this it follows that, whatever our aims, there are better and less good ways of becoming famous, and this shows that to the question 'What should we aim at in this life?' the answer 'fame' by itself is insufficient. Just as we need to be told what is worth spending our money on, we need to be told in which way it is best to become famous.

The example of the spectacular failure may suggest an answer. The disappointment he suffered, despite the fame he achieved, arose from the fact that he did not achieve fame in the way that he *wanted* to. This seems to imply that what we need to add in order to make the answer to our question complete is some reference to individual *desires*, some reference to what the person seeking fame *wants*. The same point might be made about money. If it is true that money has value only instrumentally, as a way of getting something else, so that being told to seek riches is not all we need to know, then the further necessary step seems obvious: money is valuable because it enables you to get whatever it is you want, and by implication it's good to be rich because this enables you to satisfy your desires.

In the light of these considerations we might, then, amplify the original suggestion in this way: the best human life is one in which you are rich enough to do whatever you want and famous for achieving it.

Even this formulation is not altogether satisfactory however. If what gives riches and fame their value is their connection with helping you to get what you want, and getting what you want is the essence of the good life, there is no reason to make special mention of riches or fame. Most people do want things that require quite a lot of money and many want to engage in activities that attract fame (or at least a reputation). Even those who do not have expensive tastes will require something in the way of wealth to lead the sort of life they do want. 'Riches' is a relative term, and everyone who wants anything needs to be rich to some degree. Even St

Francis who abandoned all his riches in the conventional sense, still needed the means to pursue his life as a mendicant friar. This only shows, however, that riches are not independently desirable. The position is not quite the same with fame, but those who have no interest in achieving things that impress large numbers of people may still have a good life according to this line of thinking. They don't want fame, but they may still be successful in getting the sort of life they do want. It seems then that if we regard the good life as 'getting what you want', we need not make special mention of either of the things with which we started, namely fame and riches.

EGOISM, SUBJECTIVISM AND SELFISHNESS

The idea that the best life is one in which I succeed in getting what I want is sometimes called egoism (from the Latin *ego* for I). It is an idea with an ancient history in philosophy, and figures prominently in several of the Platonic dialogues referred to in the previous chapter. Indeed, though the dialogues don't always do so, it is important to distinguish clearly between the claim that values are by nature subjective (the topic of the previous chapter) and the claim that what makes something valuable for me is that I want it (the topic of this chapter). This is a distinction that it is not always easy to grasp and hold in mind. Yet, though often connected, philosophically speaking, subjectivism and egoism are in reality two quite different positions. While subjectivists hold that moral and evaluative language must be rooted in feeling rather than fact, the feeling in question could be human feeling in general, not yours or mine in particular. By contrast, egoism holds that, whatever other people may think or feel, *I* have reason to accept advice and prescription, seek things and perform actions, only in so far as I want to. If I do not want to, the fact that they are objectively 'valuable' does not give me reason to do so.

Egoism is most powerfully represented in two of Plato's dramatic dialogues, the *Gorgias* where Socrates argues at length with (amongst others) a character called Callicles, and the *Republic*, in the earlier part of which the egoistic point of view is articulated by a character called Thrasymachus. Both Callicles and Thrasymachus argue that it is our desiring things which makes those things valuable to us, and that the good life, consequently, consists in being successful at getting what you want. If this requires the domination of others and the suppression of their aims in pursuit of your own, so be it. I lead the best life when I get what I want, regardless of how this affects others.

One way of putting the point is this. Suppose I face the choice of pursuing my career dishonestly and advancing my career (as many people do in countries where corruption is widespread). Why should I be honest? To ask this question is not to invoke the subjectivist idea that, so to speak, honesty is in the eye of the beholder. I may well accept that the action I am contemplating is objectively dishonest. Indeed, it is only if I do accept this that I can be conscious of a dilemma. Yet, faced with that dilemma, I may still wonder *why* I should prefer honesty to career advancement. In other words, the conflict is not between subjective and objective interpretations of 'honest', but the claims of altruism (obligations to others) and egoism (self-interest). It is easy to see that I have reason to advance my career. But what reason do I have to be honest when it is not in my interest to do so?

This example makes the difference between subjectivism and egoism clear, but it might lead us to overlook another important distinction, that between egoism and selfishness. The distinction between egoism and selfishness is not always easy to grasp, partly because the word 'selfishness' can be used in different ways. For example *The Virtue of Selfishness* is the (somewhat paradoxical) title of a book by the American woman philosopher Ayn Rand, where what she really means is 'self-interest', a concept to be discussed later in this chapter. What I mean by selfishness here is the tendency to seek and promote my own comfort and satisfaction before that of anybody else. Selfish people in this sense are people who (for instance) always try to get the best seat, or the finest steak, or the largest glass of wine for themselves. By contrast, egoism is the belief that I only have reason to do what matters to me. But other people can matter to me. For instance, I might well work with might and main for the sake of my children, and even be quite self-sacrificing on their behalf. So my action is not selfish; I am not preferring my comfort to theirs. But my motivation is egoistic rather than altruistic if the crucial factor in my doing so is that they are *my* children.

The difference between selfishness and egoism may be made clearer by recalling an episode from the life of the English seventeenth-century philosopher, Thomas Hobbes. Hobbes's philosophy was notorious in his day as the philosophy of an egoist and an atheist. On one occasion a clergyman saw him giving money to a beggar and thought this inconsistent with Hobbes's professed view. Surely, he asked, the only reason we have to give to beggars is Christ's commandment to relieve the poor. But Hobbes replied that he gave to the beggar both to relieve the beggar's distress and to relieve his own distress at the sight of the beggar. In other words what moved Hobbes to action was his own sense of pity. This made him an egoist, but the fact that he had pity for others shows him not to be selfish. A selfish person is someone who is not moved by the plight of others, who is caused no distress by the distress of others; an egoist is someone who insists that it is his own pity, and not the condition of the poor, which provides a reason for acting.

Once we make the distinction between egoism and selfishness we can begin to see the outline of an argument that might be used in egoism's favour. If 'getting what you want out of life' is an ideal that carries with it no implication whatever about what it is right or wrong to want (and thus may include highly altruistic wants such as the desire to work for the greater benefit of others), then how could we fail to subscribe to it? To be sure, from the point of view of determining actual behaviour it is uninformative, because it leaves so many detailed questions unsettled. But since we can only pursue those things we want to, we must therefore accept that 'getting what one wants out of life' is a principle to which everyone, automatically, subscribes. At least so it might be thought. But is it true? Can we strive only for those things we want? If so, it certainly follows that getting what we want is, necessarily, a fundamental part of a good life.

PSYCHOLOGICAL EGOISM

The thesis that people only do, and can only do, what they want is usually called psychological egoism, because it makes egoistic desire the most fundamental psychological explanation. That is to say, it says that all human actions must, ultimately, be explained in terms of the desires of the people whose actions they are. If people didn't want to do what they do, they wouldn't do it.

It is often thought that this last sentence has the status of a truism, something it is impossible to deny. Yet at first glance psychological egoism appears to be false. Surely there are countless examples of people doing something other than what they want? These range from simple domestic examples – I continue to make polite conversation with guests when what I really want to do is go to bed – to momentous events – the torture victim persists in his silence out of loyalty to his comrades when he longs for the pain to stop. If these are instances of people doing *other* than they want to, then the claim that people *always* do what they want is false. It cannot therefore be used as an adequate ground for egoism.

Confronted with examples like these, those who are sympathetic to psychological egoism usually reply that the sorts of instances given are not counter-examples to the thesis at all. There must be some sense, they say, in which I do want to be polite, and some sense in which the torturer's victim wants to be loyal to his comrades *more* than he wants the pain to cease, otherwise I would go off to bed and he would answer his tormentor's questions. This reply has two important features. First, it makes a claim about what must be the case and not merely what is. What started out as a claim about human psychology – that as a matter of fact the actions of human beings are always to be explained as the pursuit of some desire – turns out to be a claim about necessity – that all actions *must* flow from desires, otherwise the agent in question would never have performed them. But a response of this sort to the counter-examples is unsatisfactory, since it *assumes* the truth of psychological egoism, and thus cannot provide a defence of it. Only if psychological egoism is true are we entitled to assert that all actions must exhibit the wants of the person who performs them. If psychological egoism is false, this assertion is groundless. Secondly, the response shows that psychological egoism is not quite the thesis we might have thought it was, because it uses 'want' in a special and somewhat idiosyncratic way. This second point needs a rather fuller explanation.

Psychological egoism claims that people only do what they want to do, and that behind every action there must lie a desire to perform it on the part of the person whose action it is. At first this seems to conflict with experiences of our own and in the lives of others where other motives besides that of wanting can be called upon to explain actions. For instance, we normally think that as well as wanting to do something I may do it because it is advantageous, or fashionable or kindly or polite. Or sometimes I do it because I think it is the right thing to do from a moral point of view. We further think that these other motivations can actually *conflict* with what I want, and may take precedence over it. If so, what I want does *not* always explain what I do.

Now the egoist's response to this line of thought is to say that each of these other motivations is a sort of wanting. I do what is morally right because I want to do what is morally right; I do what is polite because I want to be polite; and so on. However, to analyse other motivations in this way is to alter the normal meaning of 'want' so that it comes to mean not 'have a positive desire for' so much as 'be motivated towards'. But interpreted in this way, psychological egoism becomes an empty claim. 'Wanting' here means having some motivation, and it is true by definition that every action must have *some* motivation behind it, if by 'motivation' we just mean 'whatever it is that explains it'. But this is a far cry from the claim (which psychological egoism appears at first to be making) that out of all the different kinds of motivation that could lie behind human actions only one, namely 'wanting' in a narrow sense, is ever effectual. This last claim is a substantial and challenging one. On the other hand the counter-examples show it to be false. In responding to the counter-examples in the way described, psychological egoism retreats from this substantial claim about human psychology, to an abstract claim about motivation, one which is true but empty. It relies on using 'want' in a way that is tailor-made to fit the egoist's claims. In short, psychological egoism is either false, or it is *trivially* true, true in virtue of its own idiosyncratic definition of 'want'.

RATIONAL EGOISM

It might be thought that in all this argument we have lost sight of the dispute between Callicles and Socrates and the central question about a good life. Psychological egoism was called into play in an attempt to support the claim that the good life consists in getting what you want, whatever that may be, by showing that in fact wants lie at the heart of human motivation. We have now seen that this is true only if we understand 'wants' in a special and quite trivial sense. If we understand them in the more full-blooded sense as meaning 'what I would find most pleasing', it appears to be false. People have other reasons for action besides desires of this kind.

But the egoist, especially the sort of egoist represented by the character of Callicles, has another response available at this point. He could abandon the concern with how the human psyche works and assert more baldly that, whatever may be true of human beings as we find them, we *ought* to consider the fulfilling of personal desires as the centrepiece of a good life, because the only really good reason for doing something is that you want to. This is the doctrine known as rational egoism, which is indeed a doctrine more in keeping with the dispute between Socrates and Callicles, since it is normative. That is to say, it is concerned with what we ought to do and why we ought to do it.

Why ought we to act only on the basis of our own desires? In answering this question there is a problem about the onus of argument. Upon whom does the burden of proof rest? Does the egoist have to prove to the rest of us that living by our own desires is the best way of living? Or do those who want to reject egoism have to prove that there are better ways of living? Who has to prove what to whom? Unless we have some idea of how to answer this question, we cannot have an idea about where the argument should begin.

This is a common problem in philosophy. Whereas in the law-courts the burden of proof (on the prosecution) is laid down by a legal principle – the presumption of innocence – there is in philosophy no easy general way of settling it. In the particular case of egoism, egoists have often thought that it is clear where the burden of proof lies. Since they appeal solely to the individual's own desires and nothing more, and since everyone has some reason to pursue his or her own desires just because they are their own, anyone who wants to appeal to other considerations (let's call them 'moralists') must explain why we should pay any heed to these other considerations.

To put the same point another way: rational egoists *recommend* that I should always do whatever I want. Since *ex hypothesi* (by the very nature of the case) I already want to do it, there is no logical space, so to speak, to ask what reason I have to do it. But moralists, who appeal to considerations other than my personal desires, must explain what reason I have to override those desires. For example, suppose I am on my way to the theatre because I want to see the play that is being performed and I come across an accident. A moralist might claim that I ought to stop and assist, and so perhaps I ought. But the reasons I can rehearse to myself in favour of stopping or not stopping are not on a par. Since I *already* want to go to the theatre, I do not need reasons for continuing in that intention. I need reasons for *not* doing so, and this shows that the burden of proof is on the moralist.

Of course, this is not to imply that there has to be some difficulty in meeting it, any more than the presumption of innocence means that it is always difficult to prove people guilty. Some court cases are, as we say, open and shut. Neither does this claim about the burden of proof imply that reasons of the right sort, moral reasons, cannot be given. Most of us will agree that in the imagined case it is easy to find the right sort of reason to persuade me that my intention of going to the theatre must be set to one side because something far more important has cropped up. This is compatible with the view that the burden of proof falls on the moral arguments, and this confirms the idea that in general it falls on those who reject rational egoism rather than those who accept it. By the very nature of the claim it makes, rational egoism gives us reason to accept it, something that is not true of alternatives to it.

However, though rational egoism may enjoy this advantage, it also has weaknesses. The first, though not the most important, is that it is repugnant to most minds. The idea that we should give pride of place to getting what we want just because we want it runs counter to a great deal in the Greek, Jewish and Christian ethical traditions which have shaped so much of our thinking. From a philosophical point of view, this is not an important weakness, because it cannot be turned into a conclusive objection. Someone persuaded of the desirability of egoism as an ethical creed will not be moved by the idea that it is in conflict with other, opposing creeds. It is true of any moral view that it runs counter to the views that oppose it. Hence this cannot, by itself be an objection to rational egoism.

Of course, it would be an objection if the ethical beliefs of the Judaeo-Christian tradition were true. But this is precisely what is brought into question by rational egoism. If I should love my neighbour as myself, it is not enough to love myself alone. But of course what the rational egoist is looking for is a convincing reason for loving one's neighbour as oneself. And this is all the more necessary because, I have suggested, we don't need

26

an argument for loving ourselves. This is something we automatically have reason to do.

NIETZSCHE AND THE 'WILL TO POWER'

Conflict with the Judaeo-Christian tradition, then, though it may make rational egoism unattractive to many people, is not an intellectual objection to it. Indeed, some philosophers have positively embraced the rejection of Judaeo-Christian morality. The most famous of these is undoubtedly the German nineteenth-century philosopher Friedrich Nietzsche. Nietzsche thought Christian theology was intellectually bankrupt. 'The Christian conception of God' he said, 'is one of the most corrupt conceptions of God arrived at on earth: perhaps it even represents the low water mark in the descending development of the God type' (Nietzsche 1895, 1968: 140). Nor was he any more sympathetic to the moral implications of Christianity. 'Nothing in our unhealthy modernity is more unhealthy than Christian pity' (Nietzsche 1895, 1968: 131). In short, 'Christianity has been up to now mankind's greatest misfortune' (Nietzsche 1895, 1968: 181). Someone who thinks this is unlikely to be impressed by the claim that egoism conflicts with Christian morality. So much the better, he will say.

Nietzsche's own philosophy of value is not quite egoistic in the way we have characterized egoism, but it is probably the closest that can be found expressly endorsed by a major philosopher. Whereas the egoism of Callicles and Thrasymachus is something Plato invents in order to refute, Nietzsche means to elaborate and defend his version of egoism. That is what makes it specially worth examining here.

Nietzsche was Professor of Classical Philology at the University of Basel in Switzerland, a post he was appointed to at the unusually early age of twenty-four. His great reputation, however, has little to do with philology, nor was it made chiefly in academic circles. Indeed Nietzsche's writings defy any straightforward classification and though he is now widely regarded as an important philosopher, he is a thinker with wide-ranging concerns and interest, as well as a powerful writer from a literary point of view.

To Nietzsche the most important fact about the period in which he was living was the destruction of the Christian religion at the hands of science.

The theory of natural selection developed by Darwin, he thought, had ended forever the possibility of rational belief in God (though in places Nietzsche is very critical of Darwinianism). It was Nietzsche who coined the celebrated slogan 'God is dead', and who claimed that '"Pure spirit" is pure nonsense'. But he also held that most people had not registered the enormous significance of the collapse of religion, and in a famous passage from one of his many books (*The Gay Science*) he imagines a scene in which the man who thinks that God is dead is regarded by his fellow citizens quite literally as a madman.

If God and the supernatural in general have been irrevocably expelled from human thought, then on Nietzsche's view, the whole foundation on which traditional values are built has been destroyed. Consequently everything having to do with values and the meaning of human existence has to be thought out completely afresh. The title for a last great book that Nietzsche proposed but never managed to write was *The Revaluation of All Values*, the first part of it (which was completed) being called significantly 'The Anti-Christ'. It was this total restructuring of human thinking that Nietzsche saw as his special task, a task so enormous that some people suspected him of megalomania, a suspicion confirmed for them by the fact that he did finally go insane and remained so for the last eleven years of his life. (The explanation of his insanity is still uncertain, and some believe that it was more likely the result of syphilis than of grandiose ideas.)

Now, however we regard Nietzsche's intellectual ambitions, the idea that traditional ways of thinking about good and bad are exhausted or outmoded is not so strange. Darwinian theory (as well as some very important developments in historical scholarship) did present Christianity with serious intellectual challenges, and whether for this or for some other reason, religious belief and practice in Western Europe did indeed undergo a major decline in the course of the twentieth century. Moreover, though the impact of this change is not always appreciated, the truth (if it is true) that the Judaeo-Christian basis for moral and ethical beliefs is no longer cogent or plausible, does leave contemporary society with many questions waiting for answers. Nietzsche's own writings, though very extensive, are not primarily an attempt to provide these answers, and certainly they do not do so in any sustained or systematic way. His chief purpose, rather, is to bring home to his readers the importance and urgency of the philosophical questions with which he is concerned. Nevertheless, it is possible to construct an outline of the sort of answers that his approach implies. In doing so, three ideas are specially important. These are 'the will to power', the *Übermensch*, and 'eternal recurrence'.

Since the question of what human beings ought to aspire to could no longer be answered in traditional religious or moralistic terms, Nietzsche began his rethinking by asking what it is that does move people, and his answer was 'the will to power'.

> What is good? – All that heightens the feeling of power, the will to power, power itself in man.
> What is bad? – All that proceeds from weakness.
> What is happiness? The feeling that power increases – that a resistance is overcome.
> Not contentment, but more power; not peace at all, but war; not virtue but proficiency.
>
> (Nietzsche 1895, 1968: 127)

It is this answer that makes his philosophy a variety of egoism. By 'the will to power' Nietzsche meant the desire to prevail in the circumstances of struggle that are an essential part of the human condition. (We can see the further influence of Darwin at work here and perhaps a precursor of Richard Dawkins' famous conception of 'the selfish gene'.) The will to power is more than just the will to live; it is the will to dominate and overcome the competitive challenges of existence. This conception has been widely misunderstood both by supporters and detractors, but it is easiest to see in what way it ought to be understood if we turn to the second of his three leading ideas, the *Übermensch*.

The German word *Übermensch* is literally translated 'overman', but usually rendered 'superman'. Neither translation is a happy one. The first means nothing in English. The second not only has comic book connotations but arouses ideas of Frankensteinian attempts to engineer physically and intellectually superb human beings. It is partly this understanding of *Übermensch* that gave rise to an association between Nietzsche's ideas and the Nazis' adulation of the supposedly superior Aryan race. This is an association that is strongly resisted by Nietzsche's contemporary admirers and commentators, who see it as something deliberately created by the forerunners of the Nazis. These included Nietzsche's own sister, who was responsible for publishing a posthumous collection of his diary entries under the title *The Will to Power*, a considerable part of which, there is reason to think, Nietzsche himself rejected for publication. But the association has undoubtedly been assisted by Nietzsche's own intemperate language, especially in his last publications. The passage quoted above, for instance, is taken from one of these, and continues 'The weak and ill-constituted shall perish: first principle of our philanthropy. And one shall help them to do so' (Nietzsche 1895, 1968: 127).

In substance, however, Nietzsche's views have very little to do with Nazism. Indeed it is worth noting that Nietzsche is repeatedly on record as denouncing both anti-Semitism and German nationalistic fervour. Nietzsche's *Übermensch* is not the tall blond-haired Aryan dreamt of in Nazi mythology but the man in whom the will to power is brought to perfection. (Nietzsche took a view of women that would not be popular today.) Indeed, he compares most Germans unfavourably with the poet Goethe, 'not a German event but a European one', 'the last German before whom I feel reverence', and for whom the ideal type was

> a strong, highly cultured human being, skilled in all physical accomplishments, who, keeping himself in check and having reverence for himself, dares to allow himself the whole compass and wealth of naturalness, who is strong enough for this freedom; a man of tolerance, not out of weakness, but out of strength, because he knows how to employ to his advantage what would destroy an average nature; a man to whom nothing is forbidden, except it be a weakness, whether that weakness be called vice or virtue.
>
> (Nietzsche 1889, 1968: 114)

The *Übermensch* is someone completely self-contained as far as the value and meaning of his life is concerned, someone who determines for himself what the values of his life will be and who has self-mastery over his intellect and emotions sufficient to make those values a reality in his own life. Having abandoned every inclination to look towards the supernatural, such a person asserts his own will and prevails against the pressure of conventional morality and unthinking conformity to social norms – 'a stronger species, a higher type, the conditions of whose genesis and survival are different from those of the average man ... superman' (Nietzsche, 2003, 177).

In addition to Goethe, Nietzsche's own declared models of 'supermen' included Julius Caesar and, for a time, the composer Richard Wagner, with whom he was personally acquainted. Though in the end they fell out, in many ways Wagner provides a good illustration of what Nietzsche had in mind when he talked of *Übermensch*. Wagner was a composer of opera on a very grand scale. His famous Ring cycle of operas was so large a conception that it was finally performed only when Wagner was able to construct a purpose-built theatre of his own at Bayreuth in southern Germany. The idea of opera on this scale sprang from an equally large artistic ambition, namely to set Art on the right path by creating an art form, grand opera, in which all the fine arts – the visual, the musical, and the dramatic – would be united. In advancing this conception Wagner was breaking through the conventional and practical limitations in the art world in which he worked. He was, in his own eyes at any rate, establishing his own artistic values.

As an individual Wagner had an enormously dominant personality. He attracted to himself many devoted disciples, and in the pursuit of his ambitions trampled over many others. For a time Nietzsche was one of his most ardent followers, till, perhaps, he himself became a victim of Wagner's overbearing personality. But, he says,

> let us remain faithful to Wagner in what is *true* and original in him .... Let us leave to him his intellectual tempers and cramps; let us, in all fairness, ask what strange kinds of nourishment and needs an art like his may *require* in order to be able to live and grow! It doesn't matter that as a thinker he is so often wrong; justice and patience are not for *him*. Enough that his life is justified before itself and remains justified – this life which shouts at every one of us: 'Be a man and do not follow me – but yourself! Yourself'.
>
> (Nietzsche 1887, 2001: 98, emphasis original. The final sentence is a quotation from Goethe.)

In a moment we will look again at Nietzsche's attitude to Wagner for the light it throws on his thought about values. But first we must consider the third of his principal ideas – eternal recurrence. Nietzsche was much struck by the thought that the matter in the universe is finite and the number of configurations it can assume is finite, while time is infinite. It follows that any configuration of matter will eventually recur and, since time is infinite, will recur again and again for all eternity. This is the belief in 'eternal recurrence'. If it is true that any configuration of matter will, given time, recur, it is true that we ourselves, being configurations of matter in time, will recur again and again. The perception that this is so gives us a standard by which to judge the actions we perform and the characters we develop. We can ask not merely whether they meet up to the standards of the day, but whether they are fit for eternal recurrence. In this curious way, the Christian conception of life as a preparation for eternity makes a reappearance in the writings of the anti-Christian Nietzsche.

This is a very brief summary of Nietzsche's voluminous writings and to set them out in this simple way disguises the fact that a great deal of what he wrote was more poetry than philosophy, aphorism rather than argument, and that his books contain many conflicts and contradictions. Nevertheless enough has been said to allow us to examine the fundamentals of his thought. Nietzsche saw supreme value in the individual's 'will to power'. The basis of this belief was his conviction that the foundation of traditional values – religion – had been destroyed. In a sense nothing could replace it, but the *Übermensch* rises above this calamity by recognizing it, accepting it and creating value and meaning for himself through his own 'will to power'. We will have to examine the idea of individual creation of value more closely when we come to the discussion of existentialist writers in Chapter 4. Here it is important to note that clearly what impressed Nietzsche was the idea of a solitary individual making sense of fundamental chaos and uncertainty by relying on nothing other than his own will and strength of purpose. It is for this reason that his thinking may be said to be egoistic.

Yet it is never entirely clear just why the exercise of the will to power is to be valued. It thus remains unclear what mode of human existence best exemplifies it. Nietzsche speaks frequently of 'life' (usually italicised) and 'strength' and 'power' and his tone implies that these are what we might call heroic values. The trouble is that they all appear to fall the wrong side of the distinction between instrumental and intrinsic value that was drawn in an earlier section of this chapter. They leave us asking 'the value of life *for what?*', 'the value of strength and power *to do what?*'. Some of the things he says suggest that Nietzsche would deny that 'the will to power' is of purely instrumental value. It is the will to power for its own sake that is to be valued. But why should we value the will to power if it expresses itself in meanness or triviality? Nietzsche himself loathed and despised many of the attitudes of the Germans of his generation but nothing that he says reveals a logical barrier to these despicable attitudes being themselves expressions of the will to power.

To see the force of this point we should consider the case of Wagner once more. Nietzsche for a time admired Wagner enormously because of the great force of his personality and his apparent disregard for those German values which Nietzsche thought small minded. But after some years he came to think that Wagner had succumbed to the parochial values he had earlier transcended. In short, he became a typical German of the sort Nietzsche greatly despised. Now there is reason to think that Nietzsche's view of Wagner was heavily influenced by personal factors, but whatever the historical truth, it is easy to see that this change on Wagner's part does not in itself warrant a change of assessment from the Nietzschean point of view. This is because, even if it is true that Wagner's work came to embody values he had hitherto disregarded (German patriotic fervour expressed in mythology and so on), it could still be true that he did this in the clear knowledge of the historical crisis of which Nietzsche made so much, and by virtue of his own will and personality. In short, *whatever* values Wagner's work represented, or came to represent, they could be a result of 'life', an exercise of 'strength' and 'the will to power'. It is the heroic character of Wagner's personality and way of life that impressed Nietzsche, but the trouble is that the 'will to power' need result in nothing heroic and can light upon those very things that Nietzsche loathed. In other words, there can be radically different but equally authentic responses to the injunction from Goethe that Nietzsche quotes so approvingly – 'Be yourself!'

Of course, it might be said that this leaves out of the picture the idea of eternal recurrence. Not every expression of the will to power is fit for all eternity. Why not? Whatever the answer to this question, it must be found, not in references to the will to power, but to the sorts of thing that 'will' results in. The idea of fitness for eternal recurrence seems intended to apply to people like Julius Caesar whose life stands as an example of great generalship across the centuries, but it can as easily be applied to examples of great indolence or fraud. Nietzsche says that the *Übermensch* is 'a man to whom nothing is forbidden, except it be a weakness'. But he himself wants to forbid some things – endorsement of bourgeois German piety for instance. What he does not appear to see, however, is that these things need not arise from weakness, but could be chosen as an exercise of 'life' and 'strength'. In short, Nietzsche's philosophy of value suffers from precisely the same fault as all forms of egoism. The rational egoist admires the exercise of individual will, especially when it goes against the flow of conventional moral opinion. But since the individual will can as readily be exercised in *affirming* conventional morality, his admiration is groundless and his preference for the unconventional groundless. This is because rational egoism can only give an account of instrumental value, yet requires some account of intrinsic value as well.

By pursuing Nietzsche's philosophy this far, we have in fact returned to the dispute between Socrates and Callicles. In the *Gorgias* Socrates is able to refute Callicles by the use of counter-examples. He invites him to consider the case of sexual predators on children, who get what they want in opposition to conventional moral scruple, and invites Callicles to endorse their way of life. He cites the example of a bird that eats and excretes simultaneously as the perfect desire satisfaction machine, and asks if this is not an ideal exemplar of the sort of 'good life' Callicles is commending. Callicles angrily rejects these counter-examples and declares that this is not at all the sort of thing he has in mind. But in doing so he is clearly inconsistent. The doctrine 'the best life is the one in which you get what you want' does not tell you what to want, and so it must rank the life of the drunkard whose desire is no greater than lying drunk among the garbage of the city along side that of a ruler, through whose strength of will and visionary purpose law and order are brought to a vast empire. Callicles is, of course, deeply reluctant to make this equivalence, and this is how Socrates forces him to abandon the egoistic principle on which he had built his argument. But it is an equivalence that logic obliges him to make.

In a similar fashion we have seen that anyone who views human will as central to the creation of value in the way Nietzsche does, can be forced into conceding that what matters is not just the assertion of will and desire but the assertion of *heroic* will and desire. This amounts to a concession that rational egoism – we ought to strive for what we want – is an inadequate answer to the question of how we ought to live.

It has to be acknowledged that the argument by counter-example that Socrates brings against Callicles is not and cannot be logically conclusive. Callicles could accept the requirements of consistency and accept that the life of the drunkard is as good as the life of the statesman, just as Nietzsche could accept that Wagner's endorsement of bourgeois German values was as much an exercise of the will to power as his former rejection of them was.

But this sort of argument can be given a further twist. Since what lies at the heart of rational egoism is the value of self-assertion, surely there is at least one 'life style choice' that it cannot endorse, namely self-denial. If we hold, not only that people are so constituted they will only do what they want (psychological egoism) but also that one *ought* to strive for what one desires (rational egoism), then we must regard those who do not follow their heart's desires as making a mistake of some sort, and regard this is as a mistake *whatever* their state of mind. Thus, faced with the way of life chosen by Buddhist monks, for example, who make every effort to suppress and conquer their fleshly desires, and who (let us suppose) are so successful that they come to be without anything we commonly call desires, the proponents of rational egoism are bound to say that the monks' life is, objectively speaking, less good than another, more self-centred human life. Their motto is the exact opposite of 'Be yourself'; it is 'Deny yourself', a motto that can also be said to characterize the Christianity Nietzsche so despises.

This implication – that the life of self-denial is less good than the life of self-assertion – follows from the fact that ethical egoism is a doctrine. It recommends the pursuit of personal desires and must therefore rule out their renunciation, even if those who deny themselves come to like the life they lead. 'Buddhism', Nietzsche remarks, 'is a religion for the fatigue and end of a civilization' (Nietzsche 1895, 1968: 144). It might be replied that Buddhist monks are not a proper counter-example to the egoistic ideal because though they alter their desires, they still end up doing what they want to do. To reply in this way, however, provides only a temporary respite. A Buddhist monk might say: My question is, What *should* I want, if I am to find the path to peace and happiness? It is dogmatism for egoists to argue that getting *whatever* I want *must* make me happy. Many people have hurtful or even self-destructive desires (drug addicts for instance). But if getting what I happen to want, or even what I desperately want, does not necessarily lead to happiness, why should I adopt the egoistic principle as the basis of my life and conduct? At the very least I need to be told what wants are good for me.

DESIRES AND INTERESTS

One response to this and to other objections says that rational egoism has been misrepresented. The most plausible version is not about desires but about interests. The difference between desires and interests is this. My desires are those things I experience as longings or inclinations. My interests are those things that are of vital importance to my life and well-being. Something is in my interest if it promotes that well-being. But what is in my interest need not always coincide with what I want or desire at any given moment. For instance, suppose I am a cigarette smoker who develops early signs of respiratory disease as a result of which I decide to give up smoking. For some considerable time I may experience a powerful *desire* to smoke, but I recognize that it is not in my interest to do so. Or, to change the example, I may be the sort of person who feels strongly inclined to spend the morning in bed. But if doing so would put my job at risk, it would be contrary to my interest, and I would have good reason to resist the inclination. It follows that if I am an egoist about my *interests*, there will be occasions when I have good (egoistic) reason not to do what I want or feel like doing.

There is thus an alternative version of rational egoism to the one we have been considering. It says not that you always have reason to pursue your own desires, but rather that you always have reason to promote your own interests. The best life, on this conception, is not one in which you succeed in getting what you want whenever you want it, but in which you succeed in securing what is in your interests over the longer term.

This revised form of egoism has two advantages over the simple desire version. To begin with, it supplies the basis of a reply to the sorts of counter-example that Socrates uses against Callicles. We can now say that it is not in the interests of the drunk or the paedophile to give into immediate desires. Consequently egoism is not committed to commending these modes of life. In the second place, we can acknowledge without difficulty that this sort of egoism employs the idea of objectively demonstrable, intrinsic values. Some things are as a matter of fact in my interests, and other things are not. I can be mistaken about these and desire all the wrong things. So to the question 'What ought I to want?' this version of egoism *does* have an answer; you ought to want what is in your interests. If anyone were to raise the further question 'Why should I do what is in my interests?' the egoist can reply 'Because it is in your interests' and insist that there is nothing more to be said.

Now this line of argument is a very plausible one, and many philosophers have supposed that it can provide all the elements we need for thinking about good and bad, right and wrong. Although it clearly excludes altruism – namely direct *concern* for the interests of others – it does not necessarily exclude morality conceived of as the recognition of *duties* to others. This is because – as philosophers such as Thomas Hobbes (1588–1679) and John Rawls (1921–2002) have argued in their different ways – it can be in our own best interests as individuals to observe common moral rights and civil obligations. In fact, on this way of thinking, rational egoism provides the best possible basis for morality precisely because it appeals to self-interest, which everyone acknowledges, rather than a moral sense or conscience which some people conspicuously lack.

These are topics to be returned to, but for the moment let us concede the following points. First, the version of egoism that refers to interests rather than desires can cope with simple counter-examples like the drug addict or the smoker. Second, it provides a conception of objective value – what really is good or bad for me – and not just a subjective feeling of approval. Third, by connecting good and bad with my self-interest, it explains their *rational* appeal. Fourth, it can provide a rational foundation upon which duties to others besides ourselves may be built.

These are impressive strengths, but there remains this all-important question: what *is* in my interests? It can be argued that while this question remains unanswered, all the important questions about the good life remain to be settled. We can see this by noting that Plato who (through the mouth of Socrates), argues so vigorously against the egoism of Callicles and Thrasymachus, could actually agree with this revised version of egoism, since he too believes that it is rational to do what is in my best interests and that the best possible life I can lead is the one that is in my best interests. His dispute with Callicles and Thrasymachus is about what this life consists in and how (what we would call) morality enters into it.

Plato thinks that it is directly and not just indirectly in my interests to do what justice requires of me, because the failure to do so is not emotionally or materially detrimental, but damaging to what colloquially we refer to as 'the real me'. My interests have to do with mind and soul, not with physical and psychological feeling.

Here another strand of thought in the dialogues comes into play. It is implicit in what many people, including Callicles, say that what they really mean by 'in my interest' is those things I find most pleasing or gratifying. Thus egoism becomes confused with or at least intertwined with the view that gratification and pleasure (and the avoidance of pain) are the essential ingredients of a good life. But this is in fact a distinct philosophy of value, known as 'hedonism' from the Greek word for pleasure. It is a philosophy that Plato also wants to reject, and the arguments surrounding it are well worth exploring. But it requires a chapter to itself.

SUGGESTED FURTHER READING

Original sources

Plato, *Gorgias*
Friedrich Nietzsche, *Twilight of the Idols and The Anti-Christ*
Friedrich Nietzsche, *The Gay Science*

Commentaries

Brian Leiter, *Nietzsche on Morality*

Contemporary discussion

Julian Young, *The Death of God and the Meaning of Life*, Chapters 7–8

3

HEDONISM

In Chapter 2 we saw that egoism, defined as getting what you want, is not an adequate conception of the best sort of life for a human being. Its strength is supposed to be that it locates the motive for the good life in subjective desire and not in any abstract conception of 'the good'; but try as we might, we cannot avoid questions about the relative value of the various desires that human beings have. In other words, we cannot avoid asking what we ought to want, and it is this question that a desire based egoism fails to answer.

In order to overcome this and other difficulties we considered a redefinition of egoism in terms of interests – the good life is one in which you successfully promote your own interests. This version does tell us what we ought to want – we ought to want what is in our own best interests, but it is not difficult to see that this answer does not take us much further forward. We now need to know what *is* in our best interests. What are the best things to want? In the history of philosophy an answer to this question is provided by a doctrine closely associated with the egoism we have just discussed. This is hedonism – the belief that the point of living is to enjoy life and that accordingly the best life is the most pleasurable one. So close is the association between egoism and hedonism that it is not always easy to distinguish the two views. In the *Gorgias*, for instance, the dialogue discussed in the previous chapter, the views Callicles espouses are both egoistic and hedonistic.

THE CYRENAICS

However, the ancient school of philosophy which first advocated the philosophy of hedonism was not the Sophists (the label usually given to Gorgias and Callicles) but the Cyrenaics, named after the birthplace of their founder Aristippus of Cyrene, a Greek town in what is now Libya. The Cyrenaics held that pleasure is the only natural good there is. That is to say, pleasure, and pleasure only, is universally recognized by all human beings to be desirable. Conversely, pain is a natural evil, something acknowledged the world over as undesirable. Consequently, to commend as the best life one which has as much pleasure and as little pain as possible in it, is to speak in terms that human beings of all cultures and periods can appreciate. This is the force of saying that pleasure is a *natural* rather than a conventional good and pain a *natural* evil.

In this respect, pleasure and pain differ markedly from such things as honour and disgrace. The difference has two aspects. In the first place honour is not universally regarded as something good or disgrace as something bad. In some cultures people have a very strong sense of family honour, for instance, and regard with horror anything that sullies the family name. In other cultures people have no such sense. In the second place, just what counts as honourable and which things are to be regarded as disgraceful are matters that differ from culture to culture. Whereas the things that cause pain cause it anywhere, the things that cause disgrace in one context may be quite without significance in another. For example, in some societies it is a terrible thing for an unmarried woman to become pregnant. But in *any* society it is a terrible thing to be found to have a cancerous growth. One effect of this is that, unlike pleasure and pain, ideals based upon the pursuit of honour and avoidance of disgrace often disintegrate in the face of quite different and competing conceptions of what life should be like. We can deliberately reject the idea that unmarried pregnancies are disgraceful, whereas we cannot reject the fact that cancerous growths are painful. Another effect is that honour and disgrace are values highly dependent upon the customs and practices of particular times and places. Nathaniel Hawthorne's novel *The Scarlet Woman*, which recounts the story of an unmarried mother in Puritan New England, describes a degree of shame and social ostracism that simply does not occur in contemporary Britain, say, where 40 per cent of children are born out of wedlock. By contrast the world of *natural* values remains constant.

In these two ways pain and pleasure differ from other values. This is what is meant by calling them 'naturally' good and evil, a feature that seems to put hedonism at an advantage over other possible philosophies of value. Or so the Cyrenaics and others thought. It is a question to which we will return, but first there are other problems to be raised. If we accept for the moment that pleasure is the only natural good and that this gives us reason to make the pursuit of pleasure and the avoidance of pain our main aim in life, we are still faced with this question: What mode of life will supply the greatest amount of pleasure? According to the Cyrenaics, who held the popular version of hedonism, the best life is one as full as possible of *bodily* pleasures – food, drink, sex and the like. This is a vision of the good life that still has its devotees. But if we were to take it seriously, we should soon discover that though pleasure and pains may be opposites, the one good the other evil, in the most straightforward contexts they commonly accompany each other. The result is that in the pursuit of bodily pleasure it is virtually impossible to avoid bodily pains.

For example, the pleasure of a good meal is in part dependent upon appetite, which is to say hunger. It is only by suffering (at least to a small degree) the pangs of hunger, that we can really take pleasure in the feast that follows. Similarly, many people find it pleasurable to get wildly drunk, but drunkenness is usually followed by nausea, headache and hangover. Or again, the injection of heroin is said to induce a bodily and mental sensation of unsurpassed pleasure. But it also numbs the senses so that those under its influence often injure themselves and suffer considerable pain and discomfort later on. Nor is the pleasure of sex unalloyed. Some people (all of us at some moments perhaps) find what is commonly regarded as illicit sex alluring. But to engage in it in the world as it is, would be to run the risk of VD, herpes, AIDS and other painful, sometimes fatal ailments. Even relatively safer forms of sexual gratification – pornographic shows and movies, for instance – usually bring some downside with them, if only the exhorbitant price of compulsory drinks and the tawdry accommodation in which they are customarily offered.

The Cyrenaics' ideal of the good life, therefore, is more attractive in theory than it is likely to be in real life. If we take it seriously we shall see that it is unrealizable and hence worthless as an ideal. This is a point worth stressing. Those who do not take easily to the injunctions of moralizers, or feel uncomfortable with the religious 'joy' of the pious, often have the sneaking suspicion that if it were not for the constraints of upbringing and convention, we would all opt for a life of pleasure of the most straight-forward kind. But in fact, as we have seen, it is far from clear that such a life would indeed be possible, regardless of social convention and constraint. There are many clear examples of this. One is gluttony. This is no longer regarded as a sin, but those who indulge too much in the pleasure of eating become obese and subject to all the ailments obesity commonly brings. Another is cigarette smoking. Most people smoke for the pleasure it gives, but again excess not infrequently leads to painful, sometimes incurable diseases of the heart and lungs. Occasionally those who suffer life-threatening illness as a result of smoking or overeating think that the pleasure they have had more than compensates even for such a dreadful end, but this does not alter the point that the pursuit of a life filled with pleasure and devoid of pain proved, in these cases, impossible.

THE EPICUREANS

This impossiblity, however, is not a logical one but a contingent one. There is no *necessary* connection between drunkenness and hangovers or sexual promiscuity and AIDS. These pleasures bring pains just because of the way the world happens to be. What this implies is that the flaw in the Cyrenaics' conception of the good life is not that it gives pride of place to pleasure, but that it gives pride of place to some *kinds* of pleasure, namely straightforward bodily ones. This is a point observed by, amongst others, the ancient Greek philosopher Epicurus who gave his name to an alternative version of hedo-nism – Epicureanism. (From what we know of Epicurus this is something of a misnomer, since his own philosophical interests seem to have been chiefly concerned with quite different questions.)

This version of hedonism is to be found reflected in common speech. An 'epicure' is someone who savours the finer things of life – good wine, good food, good company, urbane literature, elegant dress and so on – and this use of the word faithfully reflects the Epicureans' view that if life is to be filled with pleasure it can only be filled with those pleasures that, gener-ally, do not have accompanying pains. Now these, we should observe, will be relatively mild and gentle pleasures – good wine but not too much of it, delicately flavoured light meals of the sort that will appeal to the gourmet but not the gourmand, music and drama that delight but do not stir debilitating emotions, and so on. In fact, as this range of examples indicates, the Epicureans' philosophy of pleasure and the good life is to be contrasted quite sharply with popular conceptions of hedonism, since it contains very little that would commonly be described as an indulgence. Indeed it actually requires its adherents to forswear many of the things that people generally find most pleasurable.

It does so, of course, because it is only these refined and gentle pleasures that are without accompanying pains and hence only these pleasures that are capable of filling a life. But at the same time it is rather evident that these are acquired pleasures, the pursuit of which would require a good deal of constraint on the part of those who sought pleasure in this way. We do not naturally restrict ourselves to a glass or two of the best wine. Left to their own devices more people will take pleasure in the noise and rhythm of Rock 'n' Roll or Heavy Metal than will savour the delicate harmonies of Boccherini's *Minuet*. This raises an important question. If Epicureanism advocates a life of pleasure of the sort we must *learn* to acquire, can it continue to claim the 'natural' appeal that seems to be hedonism's great advantage over other philosophies? The excesses of Cyrenaic hedonism are mitigated in the Epicurean version. But if Epicureanism requires us to relinquish 'natural' pleasures and pains, the gain would appear to be more than outweighed by the loss.

JOHN STUART MILL ON HIGHER AND LOWER PLEASURES

Hedonism is the view that pleasure is a natural good and the only natural good there is, and that pain is, correspondingly, the only natural evil. We have now seen, however, that were we to seek to maximise the pleasure in our lives and minimise the pain, we would end up leading a certain sort of life, an Epicurean one, and a sort of life different to that which hedonism is commonly thought to recommend. Hedonism is, then, a real philosophy of life – it gives us clear guidance about the best way to live. But the style of life it prescribes will not appeal to everyone. Those who aspire to moral endeavour or artistic achievement, say, will find it unworthy, and those who seek passion and excitement will think it dull. This means that it is not universally appealing, which is what pleasure is supposed to be. The fact is that the life of pleasure recommends only some pleasures. Whatever may be true of pleasure in the abstract, it is not true that any given set of pleasures, including the set of pleasures hedonism ends up recommending, are in any sense naturally good.

This is shown in part by the fact that we can, apparently, make intelligible discriminations between pleasures. This was a possibility with which a much more recent philosopher was greatly concerned. John Stuart Mill (1806–1873) was a nineteenth-century English philosopher. Like the Cyrenaics and the Epicureans he believed that pleasure was a natural good and pain a natural evil and consequently in Mill's moral philosophy it is in terms of pleasure and pain that the good life is to be assessed. But Mill also thought that there are important differences between the various lives that people can lead, differences that cannot be straightforwardly explained in terms of pleasure.

An example he made famous is this: We can imagine a pig whose life is pretty well filled with swinish pleasures and we can imagine a Socrates whose intellectual achievements, though enormous, have resulted in the frustrating perception that his greatest achievement is to appreciate just how little he knows. The pig is satisfied and Socrates dissatisfied, so that hedonism would appear to commend the life of the pig. But Mill thought it obvious (as most of us will probably agree) that the life of a Socrates dissatisfied is better than the life of a pig satisfied. This must lead us to wonder how any appeal to pleasure as the sole thing which is good in itself could explain this difference. In an attempt at explanation, Mill introduced a distinction between higher and lower pleasures. Pleasure is indeed the touchstone of value, he thought, but some pleasures are better than others.

How can this be? Surely, if we declare some pleasures better than others, we must be invoking a standard of 'better' other than the standard of pleasure itself. If so, this shows that pleasure is not the only good there is. Two moves are commonly made in an effort to avoid this conclusion. First, it is sometimes said that the difference between higher and lower pleasures is to be explained in terms of quantity of pleasure. A higher pleasure brings *more* pleasure. However, such a distinction is entirely superficial. It cannot establish any fundamental difference between pleasures because it makes higher and lower pleasures commensurable. That is to say, we can arrive at a pleasure equivalent to the highest of pleasures if only we add up enough of the lowest pleasures. For instance, suppose we take the reading of Shakespeare to be a higher pleasure, and the eating of doughnuts to be a lower one. If the only difference between the two is quantity of pleasure, we can attain the equivalent of a pleasure in great drama if we eat a large enough quantity of doughnuts.

Of course someone might accept this conclusion and agree that pleasures are commensurable, that the pleasures of Shakespeare or Beethoven can be compensated by sufficient numbers of doughnuts or episodes of *Dallas*. But agreeing that this is so is tantamount to denying that there are different kinds of pleasure. From this it follows that *quantity* of pleasure cannot provide us with the means to discriminate between pleasures in the way that Mill wanted to.

Mill himself, however, did not appeal to quantity but to quality. He thought that higher pleasures brought a different and better *quality* of pleasure. Yet, it is difficult to know whether this appeal provides any solution at all. Does the idea of a better quality of pleasure not already invoke a standard of better and worse other than pleasure itself? Even if it does not, the suggestion is unhelpful in another way, because the way Mill explains it, we cannot actually tell higher quality pleasures from lower quality ones.

We can see this by exploring the method for discriminating between pleasures that Mill proposed – namely asking those who have experience of both higher and lower pleasures which of the two they prefer. On the face of it this seems a sensible procedure; who could be a better judge between two things than the person who has experience of both? But in reality the method establishes nothing. Suppose we ask someone who has listened to both opera and country music which is the higher pleasure and her answer is 'opera'. There are two possible explanations of this answer. It could be that the two sorts of music generate different qualities of pleasure, that the person who has experienced both has the sensitivity to discriminate between them, and that she has found the pleasure opera gives her to be of a higher calibre than that generated by country and western. However, an alternative and equally good explanation is that her musical tastes are such that she simply finds opera more pleasurable than country and western. Now it is obviously crucial for those who want to distinguish between higher and lower pleasures that her preferential judgement is to be explained in the first and not in the second way. Yet how could we ever know that this was so? Whichever is true, her verdict will always come out the same. But if we cannot know that the second is the true explanation, we do not have a 'method' of discriminating between quality of pleasures. The result is that we could call upon the testimony of any number of 'judges', and still we would not be accumulating evidence in any significant way, because each and every verdict would be open to this same ambiguity of interpretation.

Nor did Mill (or anyone) ever actually use this method. Indeed Mill thought he knew which pleasures were higher pleasures in advance of any method, so that if someone who had tried both had actually told him that warm baths were a higher pleasure than philosophy, he would have dismissed this as the judgement of an ignoramus. This suggests that Mill regarded the appeal to the authority of competent judges, not as evidence of higher pleasures, but as a criterion or test. In declaring some pleasure to be of a higher quality, the competent judge does not provide us with evidence. Rather, the pleasure in question is a higher one just because competent judges prefer it. So, for instance, we can say that a piece of music gives a higher quality of pleasure, if it is a fact that those who know a great deal about music prefer it, just as we can declare a wine to be of higher quality if it is preferred by those who have done a lot of wine tasting.

There are several problems with this alternative interpretation. Is there in fact sufficient unanimity between competent judges, or would we find that the 'quality' of a pleasure varies depending upon whom we ask? Must competent judges prefer on grounds of pleasure, or are there other grounds upon which their preferences might be based? Even if these questions can be answered satisfactorily, there remains the same question as before. How do we know that those who have listened to a lot of music or done a great deal of wine tasting have *more refined* tastes, and not merely *different* tastes from those who have not? Until this question is answered, Mill's account of higher and lower pleasures, whichever way we interpret it, remains a piece of arbitrary stipulation.

The appeal to higher and lower pleasures, then, accomplishes little and raises more questions than it settles. It is important to stress, however, that nothing that has been said so far runs counter to the view, which Mill obviously shared, that some of the activities in which human beings take pleasure are better than others. All that has been shown is that the mark of their being 'better' cannot be that they are productive of a higher pleasure. We can indeed take pleasure in 'higher' things, but what makes them 'higher' is not the pleasure they give us, but something else about the activities themselves. From this it follows that there must be some other good than pleasure, and hence that strict hedonism is false.

SADISTIC PLEASURES

Hedonists might reply that this refutation of their philosophy succeeds only if we first accept one of the premises from which Mill's argument began, namely that the life of a Socrates dissatisfied is better than that of a pig satisfied. But perhaps we need not accept this. Indeed a consistent hedonist ought not to. If pleasure is the only natural good, then *any* life filled with pleasure is as good as any other and better than a life with pain and dissatisfaction. To accept this is to accept that, contrary to what Mill and perhaps most people think, Socrates has reason to envy the pig, since the pig leads a better life. The fact that neither we nor Socrates, given our abilities and interests, would find pleasurable the sort of life the pig likes misleads us into thinking that the pig's life is not a good one. But from a persistent hedonist's point of view, it *is*, because it is filled with pleasure, and pleasure is the sole natural good. Of course, a human life filled with pleasure will contain many activities different from that of the pig, but it will not contain any more pleasure, and hence will not be any better. Thus, it can be argued, hedonism avoids the difficulties which Mill's appeal to higher and lower pleasures encounters, by denying that there are any differences in the merits of different kinds of pleasures.

Such a denial brings us back, in fact, to the dispute between Socrates and Callicles. Socrates, it will be recalled, drew Callicles attention to the fact that, as far as satisfaction of wants goes, there is no difference between those who succeed in the demanding and enobling tasks they set themselves, and those who succeed in the lazy and vulgar lifestyles with which they are content. The point can as easily be put in terms of pleasure. If pleasure is all that matters, we cannot justify a preference for the pleasure which a surgeon takes in saving the life of a child by means of an immensely demanding operation, over the pleasure a sadist takes in the sufferings of the animal he is torturing. Yet it seems obvious to most people that there is a crucially important difference between the two.

This particular example is mine, but Callicles, it will be recalled, when presented by Socrates with a contrast between heroic and vulgar pleasures, accepts that there is indeed a difference to be explained. It is this acceptance which provides the means for his defeat. Had he not accepted this difference, the argument would have had to take a different direction. Similarly, if thoroughgoing hedonists insist that, in so far as it is true that a torturer gets just as much pleasure from her trade as does a healer, the torturer and the healer lead equally good lives, then an appeal to alleged differences between the two cannot provide a counter to their thesis. A consistent hedonist does not have the problem Callicles does.

To some minds this just shows how depraved a philosophy hedonism is. But in terms of philosophical cogency, this is not so evident. In the first place, we should note that hedonists are not recommending torture as a way of life. Neither is hedonism necessarily egoistic, which is to say, concerned only with one's own pleasure. Hedonists need not deny that the lives of the torturer's victims are about as bad as can be. On the contrary, given the hedonist view that pain is a natural *evil*, they will positively assert this. Their view is rather that, if someone, whose psychology is highly abnormal no doubt, were to enjoy torture in exactly the way that most of us enjoy our favourite activities, then his life would be as enjoyable as ours. Now even hedonists might hesitate to expressly commend the life of the torturer, since she has caused a lot of pain and suffering. But it is difficult to see that they can avoid regarding it as having this much to be said for it; she got a lot of pleasure from it.

It is this last point that flies in the face of received wisdom. Whereas hedonists may think that the sadist's getting pleasure from her hurtful activities does not shift the overall balance from negative to positive, they have got to regard it as a point on the plus side; it would have been even worse if there was no pleasure to offset the victims pain. By contrast, to most people the very same fact makes the sadist's activities *worse*, not better. Applied to this sort of case, then, hedonism is sharply in conflict with conventional wisdom and highly unpalatable to normal sensibilities. Yet the mere fact that some view or other is unconventional or unpopular does not in itself show it to be false. Those who first advanced the view that the earth is not flat were also denying conventional wisdom. To refute hedonism as a philosophy of value something more is needed than appeal to counter-intuitive examples of the sort we have been considering. In order to find a most substantial objection we should now turn to another Greek philosopher, Aristotle.

ARISTOTLE ON PLEASURE

Aristotle (384–322 BCE) was a student of Plato, for a time tutor to Alexander the Great, and director of the Lyceum at Athens where he lectured on and conducted original research into almost every branch of human knowledge. Most of his thought has come down to us by means of the notes of his students, and it is in one such set of lecture notes, called the *Nicomachean Ethics* (hereafter *NE*) that his thoughts on pleasure are to be found. Aristotle was not averse to the view that pleasure is a good. In fact, in the *NE* he expressly says that 'necessarily pleasure is a good', and even describes the chief good as 'a kind of pleasure' (*NE* VII 13). But he thought that we cannot adequately assess the merits of hedonism unless we inquire closely into what is meant by pleasure.

When hedonists recommend pleasure just what are they recommending? We began with an opposition between pleasure and pain. It is in terms of this opposition that the Cyrenaic and Epicurean versions of hedonism are formulated. Yet it is clear that there is an important asymmetry between the two. The word 'pain' can be used to refer both to a particular kind of bodily sensation, and to any unwanted experience in general. A knife can cause a pain in my leg, and an unkind remark can give me pain also. But the two sorts of pain are not the same. The first is a locatable sensation, the other a psychological experience.

When we speak of pleasure, however we cannot be referring to a locatable sensation. I can have a pain in my leg, but never a pleasure. Of course, some bodily sensations can be pleasurable – the sensations associated with food, drink and sex for instance – but this does not make pleasure itself a sensation. The right thing to say is that food, drink, sex and so on are productive of pleasurable sensations, not that they are productive of pleasure. This is an important point to grasp for two reasons. First, it throws a different light on the idea that pleasure is a natural good. Let us agree that there is reason to call physical pain a natural evil because it is a sensation which humans and other animals instinctively seek to avoid. (It should be noted that not all philosophers accept that pain is in this sense a natural evil, partly because human beings do sometimes appear positively to value pain – in initiation ceremonies, for example.) But if there is no sensation of pleasure corresponding to that of pain, then there is nothing that is a natural good in quite the way that pain is a natural evil. The most we can say is that there are sensations which are pleasurable – those associated with sex are an obvious example – and that people naturally seek these sensations. Whether they seek them *because* they are pleasurable is another matter. Consequently, even if we agree that human beings naturally seek sexual gratification, we cannot straight off conclude that they naturally seek pleasure. At the very least the picture is more complex than it is with pain.

A second implication of the asymmetry between pain and pleasure is this. While there are indeed pleasurable sensations, other things can be pleasurable also. A warm bath may be pleasurable, but so can a conversation, or a game of tennis. Because they were specially impressed with the pain/pleasure distinction, the early hedonists tended to overlook the fact that other things besides sensations can be pleasurable, and when they spoke of pleasure, they thus focused upon pleasurable sensations. As Aristotle remarks:

> Since neither the best nature nor the best disposition either is or is thought to be the same for all, neither do all pursue the same pleasure, though all do pursue pleasure.... It is the bodily pleasures, however that have taken over the title to the name pleasure, because these are the ones we most often encounter, and because everyone shares in them; so because they are the only ones they recognize, people think they are the only ones there are.
>
> (*Nichomachean Ethics* VII 13)

In other words, pleasure is not one thing. Consequently, though it is true (on Aristotle's view) that human beings seek pleasure, this does not imply that they all seek one type of sensation. In fact,

> there are actually pleasures that involve no pain or appetite... pleasures [include] activities and ends...; and not all pleasures have an end

50

different from themselves... this is why it is not right to say that pleasure is perceptible process.

(Nichomachean Ethics VII 12)

What Aristotle means to emphasize here is that activities that are engaged in for pleasure may differ in important respects. Someone may engage in sexual intercourse for the pleasurable sensations it produces. In this case, in Aristotle's language, the pleasure resides in the end of the activity, the sensations it produces. But not all pleasurable activities are like sex. Golf, for instance, gives great pleasure to many millions of people, but to play golf for pleasure is not to play for some end independent of the activity itself. The pleasure does not lie in a special sensation of the nervous system that swinging a golf club produces. It lies in the game itself. This is what Aristotle means by saying that 'not all pleasures have an end different from themselves'.

In short, there are different kinds of pleasure, and it is a mistake to suppose, as crude versions of hedonism do, that looking for pleasure is a matter of seeking the means to induce pleasurable sensations. Sometimes it does, but more often it doesn't. In most cases pursuing pleasure means engaging in enjoyable activity. To enjoy what you are doing is to be thoroughly absorbed in it. This is what Aristotle has in mind when he says that pleasure is not a 'perceptible process' but 'unimpeded activity'. To be absorbed in an activity is to engage in it for its own sake, to regard it as a source of interest and value. If I enjoy restoring antiques, this means that I find the activity full of interest and worth engaging in irrespective of what other benefits, such as money, it may bring. But this is to say that the activity itself has value, independently of the pleasure it gives. It is not that I enjoy the activity because it gives me pleasure. Rather, it gives me pleasure precisely because it is an activity I enjoy. Aristotle elsewhere says the same thing about victory. To be victorious, and to be honoured for it, gives pleasure because these are themselves good things. Their goodness does not arise from the fact that they give pleasure.

This understanding of pleasure casts a rather different light on hedonism. If we take hedonism to be the instruction to seek pleasure and enjoyment, we can see that this is not the simple injunction we might have supposed. Any such advice should really be expressed in the plural: 'Seek pleasures'. But this leaves us with the question 'Which ones?' Aristotle, like Mill, will say 'Good ones', but unlike Mill he sees that the mark of their goodness must arise from something other than their merely being pleasures. At the most general level, Aristotle would say, the hedonists are right to want a pleasant life, and the pleasantest life is a happy one. The value of such a life is twofold – pleasure and happiness. But the pleasure arises from the happiness. So, if we want to know what a good life is, that is, the sort of life we ought to take pleasure in, we need to know more about happiness than pleasure.

SUGGESTED FURTHER READING

Original sources

Diogenes Laertes, *The Lives of the Philosophers*
John Stuart Mill, *Utilitarianism*

Commentaries

J C B Gosling, and C C W Taylor, (eds), *The Greeks on Pleasure*
Richard Taylor, *Good and Evil,* Chapters 6–7
Roger Crisp, *Mill on Utilitarianism*

Contemporary discussion

J L Mackie, *Ethics: Inventing Right and Wrong*

4

NATURALISM AND VIRTUE THEORY

One of the most compelling arguments against hedonism emerges from Aristotle's analysis of pleasure, but it would be quite wrong to infer from this that Aristotle rejected hedonism outright. On the contrary, he agreed with the hedonists in believing pleasure to be a highly desirable aspect of life. Their mistake did not lie in valuing pleasure, but in a mistaken conception of what pleasure is. They thought of pleasure as an experience of a special kind produced by certain activities, an experience that explains why we value those activities, just as the fact that some activities cause us pain explains why we view them negatively. In other words, the hedonists construed pleasure as a kind of sensation, the positive counterpart to pain.

However, this is a mistake, and it leads us to think that activity is valuable if it is pleasure producing, whereas on Aristotle's account, the relationship is the other way round; an activity is pleasure producing if it is valuable. So, I get pleasure from golf, for example, because I think it a good game to play, and I find it even more satisfying when I manage to play it well. If we apply this analysis to the good life in general, then, the focus of our aspiration should not be pleasure in the sense of entertainment or bodily gratification, but the pursuit of activities whose value is such that engaging in them will give us pleasure and satisfaction. Taken in combination, the outcome of a good and rewarding human life is not *hedos* but *eudaimonia*.

Eudaimonia is usually translated 'happiness', but this is not an altogether helpful translation. It comes from the Greek words meaning 'good' and 'spirit' and while in English the expression 'being in good spirits' does capture one aspect of a flourishing existence, perhaps the best translation of *eudaimonia* is the rather more general term 'well-being'. But whatever English equivalent we settle on, the point to stress is that the Greek word carries with it the idea of being actively engaged in things rather than simply experiencing them passively. The happy man, on Aristotle's picture, is not the man whose life is filled with passive pleasures, but the person who excels at all those activities and aptitudes that are characteristic of human beings. Happiness is not mere contentment with one's lot, but the exercise of healthy appetites, the imaginative and productive use of one's mental faculties, and the establishment of good personal, professional and public relationships. It is this concept of happiness or well-being that this chapter will explore.

THE RATIONAL ANIMAL

For Aristotle, human beings are simply one type of animal, the species *Homo sapiens*. Now this is incontestably true, however liable we are to forget it, and given this fact, we can expect to learn important things about ourselves by considering our natural constitution and our distinctive place in the natural world. The first step in learning these lessons is to see that the question 'What is a good life?' can be asked for a very wide range of living things. Consider for instance the simple case of a potted plant. We know that there are conditions under which plants flourish and others under which they wither and die – too wet, too dry, too light, too dark, too warm or too cold. Furthermore, just what these conditions are differ according to the type of plant – conditions that suit a cactus will not suit a tropical orchid, for example. From this it follows that we can say that there are good and bad living conditions for plants.

In a similar way, animals sicken and die under different conditions – a horse cannot live on meat, a lion cannot live on oats, a fish cannot live on land, a bird cannot survive under the water. But the good life for an animal is not just a matter of survival. A plant or an animal might survive, but in a weak, sickly or malformed condition, so we must speak of *flourishing* and not merely survival if we are to distinguish what it is for a plant or an animal to live well. Now the conditions under which a plant or an animal flourishes we can call, along with Aristotle, the 'good' for that thing, and given those conditions we can describe the thing in question as living well and being a good instance of its kind. A regime in which a lion, for instance, has the right amounts of the right sort of food, exercise and company, will produce a lion that is both physically in excellent shape, and whose behaviour is just what is natural to lions. Conversely, as we know from the treatment of animals in zoos and circuses, if a lion is caged, isolated from its own kind and fed without having to hunt, its physique will deteriorate and its behaviour become neurotic.

In just the same fashion Aristotle thought that we could discover the 'good for man' and hence what it is for a person to live well. That is to say, it is possible to delineate both the sorts of activities that constitute human flourishing, i.e. those things that it is natural for human beings to excel in, and the conditions which make this possible. In this way Aristotle arrives at a view of the good life importantly different from that of his predecessors. Whereas the hedonists and Plato looked for the one thing that was good above all else and good in itself (though of course each came up with a very different answer and further differed about how 'the good' was related to 'the good life'), Aristotle's view carries the implication that there is no *one* good, that what is and what is not good must always be relativized to some natural kind or other. There is no such thing as 'good *full stop*', we might say, only 'good *for*'. What is good for a cactus is not good for an orchid, what is good for a horse is not what is good for a lion, and so on indefinitely, including what is good for a human being.

The good, then, is not some abstract object or property that, as it were, radiates its goodness independently of human beings and other creatures. Rather it is a mode of existence determined by the natures of different creatures. At the same time, to make good relative in this way is not to make it subjective in the style of Callicles, Thrasymachus and so on, because whether something is or is not good for a horse, or a lion or a sycamore tree, is a matter of ascertainable fact. We cannot *decide* that oats are good for a lion, because lions either do or do not flourish on a diet of oats. So too with human beings. We cannot decide that parental care is good for children, and that psychologically stable human beings are better than neurotics and psychotics. These are matters of discoverable fact.

Philosophers sometimes mark this difference by distinguishing between 'attributive' and 'predicative' uses of the word 'good'. An example of the attributive use is when I say 'This cake is good'. Now it is evidently possible to interpret this use (as subjectivists do) as declaratory or expressive – to say 'This cake is good' just means 'I really like this cake'. On this interpretation, the word 'good' very often does no more than to express personal liking or preference. But when I say 'Aspirin is a good painkiller' I am using the word 'good' *predicatively*, and what I say makes a claim about the world, and does not merely express a preference. I may like the taste of aspirin (if it has a taste), but all the liking in the world will not make it *true* that aspirin is a good painkiller if as a matter of fact it is not.

On the Aristotelian conception the expressions 'a good person' and 'a good life' use the word 'good' predicatively. Accordingly we can ask in any particular case whether it is used truly or not. Our ability to answer the question, however, depends upon our understanding the proper basis for such judgements. Just as a good (specimen of an) orchid, is one that exhibits all the things that make for excellence in a plant of that kind, so a good person is someone whose life exhibits those features that are distinctively human excellences. Thus, answering the question 'Is X a good person?' requires us to know what human beings at their distinctive best are like, and answering the question 'What sort of life ought we to want?' will consist in describing such a human being.

THE GOOD FOR HUMAN BEINGS

But what *is* the good life for a human being? In the *Nichomachean Ethics* it is said to be 'activity of the soul in accordance with virtue', a pious sounding expression scarcely illuminating as it stands. Its meaning, however, is actually not so difficult to discern. Despite the initial impression this phrase may make on modern minds, Aristotle's conception of the good life for a human being has almost nothing to do with religion, or even with morality as we normally understand it. The Greek word translated 'soul' is '*psyche*', from which we get our word 'psychology' and refers to the mind or rational faculty that human beings possess rather than any spiritual essence. 'Virtue' is a translation of the word '*arete*' meaning 'excellence' so that 'in accordance with virtue' just means 'in the best possible way'. Thus, Aristotle's conception of the good life is one in which we use our minds to make, and act, and think, in the best possible ways. This is of course the good life in the abstract. It needs to be given content by appeal to the actual nature of human beings.

It is important to emphasize here that Aristotle's appeal to the activities of the mind does not imply that intellectual endeavour or academic inquiry makes up the good life. Rather, it is intelligence in the full range of human activities that he has in mind, intelligence of the sort that potters, politicians and parents may employ in their respective tasks and occupations, no less than scientists and philosophers. Indeed, Aristotle puts *phronesis* or practical wisdom rather than intellectual brilliance at the heart of a good life, because even the highest forms of intellectual inquiry need to be guided by good sense if they are to be pursued fruitfully and well.

The picture of the ideal human life that emerges from Aristotle's conception of the good is a moderate rather than a heroic one. It is bound to strike us as sound and sensible rather than exciting or inspiring. Aristotle thinks that those who can be shown to lead good lives are middle aged, well educated, financially secure and socially respected. Neither slaves nor the poor nor the ignorant nor the stupid could lead good lives, for to be any of these things is to be deficient as a human being, much in the way that a tree may be stunted or an animal deformed. Moreover, those who single-mindedly pursue some one goal or strive to excel in just one thing – in sport, music or politics say – and who do so to the detriment of economic prosperity, making friends, having a family, attaining social standing or getting a rounded education, also lead impoverished lives. For Aristotle, it is all round general excellence that matters, and not super excellence in just one or two things.

One implication of Aristotle's moral philosophy – that the lives of slaves, the poor and the handicapped are not good lives, and that a humanly good life is the preserve of the talented and successful – sometimes has an offensive ring to modern ears. This is because in the contemporary world the expression 'the good life' has a moral connotation (to be discussed in a later chapter) which it did not have for Aristotle. His conception implies only what most people would agree upon, that it is better to be free than to be someone else's slave, better to live in reasonable prosperity than in poverty, better to be talented (or at least accomplished) in some things than in nothing. These judgements, for Aristotle, are not fundamental moral or evaluative opinions with which others may or may not agree. Nor are they the expression of subjective preferences such as form the basis of egoism, or even natural preferences of the kind to which the hedonists appealed. Rather they are statements of fact. This raises our next question: On what are these 'facts' based?

ETHICS AND SOCIOBIOLOGY

Aristotle, in common with most Greeks, thought that everything has a *telos* or end at which it naturally aims, and that depending upon the mode of existence of the thing in question, this end will be reached more or less well. Thus 'oak tree' is the end or *telos* of every acorn, and given the right conditions, an acorn will develop into a tree of a certain shape, size, colour and so on. The *telos* of the acorn, then, is to be found in the sort of picture of an oak tree that appears in botany books. Such a picture does not show us what some particular oak tree looks like, but what *any* oak tree *ought* to look like. Given abnormal conditions – not enough water, too much exposure to sea breezes – individual trees will deviate from this end; they will be stunted or deformed in some way.

Judgements about the maturity or deformity of an oak tree are based on the biological nature of the species *quercus*, something about which we think we now know a lot more than Aristotle did, thanks largely to evolutionary biology and the science of genetics. But though we are here in the realms of genetics and biology, we can still refer to the *right* conditions and employ evaluative terms like 'stunted' and 'deformed'. This gives us a clue to answering normative or evaluative questions about human beings. Facts about right and wrong, good and bad, on Aristotle's account, are derived from facts about the biology of things. Thus our knowledge of human good is a function of our biological knowledge of the species *Homo sapiens*.

Aristotle was one of the greatest thinkers of all time, and by the standards of the ancient world his biological understanding was highly advanced. He thought that each natural kind, including human kind, has a distinctive, and discoverable function, i.e. a *telos* peculiar to that kind, and from that *telos* we can derive the good for that thing. Under the inspiration of this conception Aristotle himself produced work that made him both the founding father of biology and a major influence upon its development for centuries to come. But more recent biology, especially since Darwin, has made such advances that, however great in its own day, Aristotelian biology has now been completely superseded. Does this mean that the ethical and evaluative implications of Aristotelianism are outmoded also?

For a good many years it was thought so, partly because modern biology no longer believes in the existence of radically separated species that have been distinct from the beginning of creation. Furthermore, biologists no longer see any sense in studying the physiological character of plants and animals in terms of overall function. In modern biology we can describe the function of some part of the anatomy – the function of the heart in the anatomy of a lion, for instance – but we cannot sensibly talk about the function of the *lion*. The heart serves an end in the body of the lion, but the lion does not serve any end. Even if careful observation of lions reveals characteristic patterns of both physiology and behaviour, modern biology holds that the explanation of these will be found, not in some *telos* towards which all lions naturally strive, but in their genetic structure, of which these characteristics are a manifestation or expression. Thus modern biology, rather than pointing us towards the study of individual species with a view to discovering their distinctive *function*, points us to the study of a microbiological structure that will reveal a distinctive *genome*.

It seems then that modern biology is not the sort of study that could allow us to derive facts about right and wrong, good and bad in the way that Aristotelian biology could. And yet Aristotelianism has undergone something of a revival in recent years. This is because alongside biology there has grown up a study much closer to Aristotle's, one which may allow us to speak in some of the ways that he did. This is the study of ethology. The very name 'ethology' indicates the connections of this relatively new science with the concerns of the ancient Greeks, because it is derived via Latin from Greek words meaning the study and depiction of character. In its modern sense ethology can be described as the study of animal behaviour in its natural environment, and among its first well-known exponents was Konrad Lorenz, whose famous book *On Aggression* was based on an ethological study of wolves.

If we set ourselves to study not the physiology but the behaviour of animals in their natural environment, we come to see, ethologists tell us, that there are conditions under which animals cannot thrive and in which their natural behaviour may undergo destructive and even self-destructive alteration. For instance, the male of one species of fish is armed with a sting whose purpose is to protect the egg-carrying female from predators. But if a male and female are removed to the safety, but confinement, of a small tank in which there are no predators, the male will eventually turn its sting upon the female herself. This behaviour is clearly abnormal since it works to the destruction of the fish and its progeny, and it comes about because of the unnatural conditions in which they have been placed. These conditions are simply not good for the fish.

Examples of this sort can be multiplied very easily, and our understanding of natural function is further enriched by evolutionary biology. It is possible to show, in many cases, that functions like the protective sting just described, have emerged in the course of evolutionary adaptation. Plants and animals have developed the traits they possess because this equips them better for survival. Darwin's expression 'survival of the fittest' is well known for the important part it has played in the advancement of the biological sciences. But 'fittest' is a normative term that aims to describe what is naturally good and advantageous.

Can the sciences of ethology and evolutionary biology be extended to human beings? The combination of the two, together with explorations from the social sciences, has resulted in 'sociobiology', the name of an inquiry specially associated with the Harvard entomologist E O Wilson who wrote a famous book with the title *Sociobiology: The New Synthesis*. Wilson's idea is that we

> consider man in the free spirit of natural history, as though we were zoologists from another planet completing a catalog of the social species on Earth. In this macroscopic view the humanities and social sciences shrink to specialized branches of biology; history, biography and fiction are the research protocols of human ethology; and anthropology and sociology constitute the sociobiology of a single primate species.
>
> (Wilson 1975, 2000: 547)

This study of human beings as socially interacting higher animals with an evolved biology aims to combine insights from evolutionary theory, genetics, ethology and sociology in a way that will generate an account of what is the most natural and hence most successful mode of existence for human beings. Wilson's later, much shorter book *On Human Nature* is perhaps the most straightforward account of this approach, but something of the same sort can be found in Desmond Morris's *The Naked Ape*, and later editions of Richard Dawkins spectacularly successful book *The Selfish Gene*.

VIRTUE THEORY

Sociobiology is a modern equivalent of Aristotelian biology, and it holds out the promise of answering the question 'What is the good life for human beings?' Its philosophical importance is further underlined by the fact that Aristotelian ideas have made a significant comeback in moral philosophy also, as is evidenced by the titles of recent books by Alasdair MacIntyre – *Dependent Rational Animals* – and Philippa Foot – *Natural Goodness*. These philosophers (among others) think that there is much to be gained by focusing on the predicative rather than the attributive use of 'good', and they further believe that too much attention has been given to what are called 'thin' moral concepts such as good and bad, right and wrong, and not enough to contrasting 'thick' moral concepts, such as generosity, cowardice, foolhardiness and prudence.

This approach to moral philosophy, often called 'virtue theory' has three important attractions. First, it provides a plausible alternative to both ethical subjectivism and the kind of moral realism discussed in Chapter 1. As Alasdair MacIntyre writes:

> Whatever it means to say of some particular member of some particular species that it is flourishing, that it is achieving its good, or that this or that is good for it, in that it conduces to its flourishing – assertions that we can make about thistles and cabbages, donkeys and dolphins, in the same sense of 'flourishing' and the same sense of 'good' – it is difficult to suppose either that in making such assertions we are ascribing some nonnatural property or that we are expressing an attitude, an emotion, or an endorsement.
>
> (MacIntyre 1999: 79)

The point applies equally to human beings as to other creatures. Words like 'healthy', 'intelligent', 'outgoing' and 'lazy' have real descriptive content. To call someone 'good' or declare their actions 'right' tells us almost nothing about what they are like or have done. But to describe them as lazy or intelligent is to convey a good deal of information about them.

Secondly, such descriptions are determined not by our liking or disliking, but by the facts of what they actually did. When people run away from danger, it is simply false for me to describe their behaviour as brave, however sympathetic I may be. And if they hold their ground and confront the danger, this fact obliges me to describe their action as brave, whether I like them or not. So too with all the other virtue words. I may care nothing about other people's feelings, but I still cannot be kind by laughing at their distress. I cannot avoid the charge of laziness if I neglect my work to stand around doing nothing.

Thirdly, the descriptive content of virtue words is such that it has a normative element 'built in' so to speak. While 'good' and 'bad' seem to say no more than 'nice' and 'nasty', words such as 'generous' and 'cowardly' are more like 'nutritious' and 'poisonous'. To call something nutritious is both to describe it *and* to recommend it; to say that something is poisonous is to describe it *and* to warn against it on the basis of that description. In both cases fact and value come together, and they do so because nutrition is a function of the properties of the food and the nature of the creature for whom it is nourishing. Oats are not nutritious to a lion, but they are to a horse, and this is because of the natural properties of oats, lions and horses. In a similar way, virtue theory holds that generosity, bravery, kindness and the like are character traits that count as virtues, not because people happen to applaud them, but because of the facts of human nature – our vulnerability and dependence on others.

What then is human flourishing? The answer to this question will provide the naturalist's account of the good life, but it is an answer that will only be arrived at with systematic and extensive investigation. That investigation may not follow exactly the sort of path described in Wilson's sociobiology, but it is clear that since human beings are complex creatures around whose lives impressive social, political and cultural structures have arisen, any plausible account of their flourishing will have to take the social and the psychological into account as well as the biological more strictly interpreted. This is Wilson's ambition for sociobiology: 'In the process it will fashion a biology of ethics, which will make possible the selection of a more deeply understood and enduring code of moral values' (Wilson 1978, 1995: 187). If so, then perhaps the questions of moral philosophy will finally be answered by the sciences of anthropology and evolutionary biology, in a way that is different from but nonetheless much in the spirit of Aristotle.

Yet there are further philosophical difficulties in the way of completing that programme.

THE NATURAL AS A NORM

Ethology is defined as the study of the behaviour of animals in their natural environment, and this definition raises the first question: what *is* the natural environment of man? Wilson remarks: '*Homo sapiens* is ecologically a very peculiar species. It occupies the widest geographical range and maintains the highest local densities of any of the primates' (Wilson 1975, 2000: 547). That is to say, unlike almost all other species – bears or tigers, for example – human beings live in strikingly *different* environments – compare the environment of the Inuit of the Arctic Circle with that of the Kalahari desert dwellers. And the point about densities also directs our attention to the fact that human modes of existence can differ enormously. Compare the environment and lifestyle of someone resident in New York or London with that of an East African tribesman, or the life of a Tibetan monk with that of a Parisian socialite. These are differences far greater than those that obtain between any other primates. Gorillas and chimpanzees live in only a few parts of the earth, and the size of the groups they live in are pretty much the same wherever they live. So which of the vastly different environments that human beings live, if any, is their natural environment and which is the mode of existence that is natural to them?

One response to these questions is to look past all the variety to some underlying unity. According to Wilson 'Human nature . . . is a hodgepodge of special genetic adaptations to an environment largely vanished, the world of the Ice-Age hunter-gatherer' (Wilson 1978, 1995: 187). The underlying unity on this account is a distant evolutionary history in which human nature was formed, a nature human beings share and can be seen to reveal in the many environments in which they have made their home.

This idea – that the natural behaviour of human beings is more easily discerned in relatively 'primitive' societies such as those of contemporary hunter-gatherers – is one that many people find attractive and plausible. They have a sense that life in the modern city is a kind of cultural accretion on top of a more basic mentality. Moreover, it is on the strength of this idea that judgements of relative superiority are often made. It is commonplace to hear the 'naturalness' of the life of the North American Indians, say, commended and contrasted with the 'artificiality' of the life of the commuter in a modern city. And there is a quite widespread belief that, for instance, the European nuclear family is not as 'natural' as the extended family which still persists in less developed parts of the world.

This use of 'natural' as a term of commendation is widespread – think of the expressions 'natural childbirth' or 'natural remedy' – and for that reason extensively used by advertisers: '100% natural', whether applied to food or fibres, is a selling point. Its negative counterpart – 'unnatural' – is not so commonly used nowadays (though at one time certain sexual practices were described as 'unnatural'), but the term 'artificial' often serves much the same purpose. But whichever terms we use, any naturalistic account of value requires us to be able to do two things – to draw a distinction between the natural and the unnatural, and explain why the former is preferable. Neither task, as we shall see, is easily accomplished.

How are we to know what is and what is not natural? The sociobiologist's answer is straightforward enough in outline. What is natural is what suits human beings as they have evolved, their 'special genetic adaptations to an environment largely vanished, the world of the Ice-Age hunter-gatherer', to quote Wilson again. The problem with this criterion is that our knowledge of that distant history is very limited indeed. If, in order to determine what is and what is not natural for human beings we need to know about Ice-Age hunter-gatherers, the truth is that we are largely limited to speculation. Nor will it do to appeal, as sociobiologists and evolutionary psychologists sometimes do, to contemporary hunter-gatherers, because as far as fitness to survive is concerned, the New York stockbroker is as well *fitted* to survive as the Kalahari bushman, for the obvious reason that both *have* survived. Judged by the standard of ways in which it is possible for human beings to live given their evolved genetic inheritance, the two ways of life are at least equally good, and that of the New York stockbroker probably better.

Suppose then that we were presented with a choice between such radically different styles of life and thus have the opportunity to ask 'which way should I choose to live my life?'. The appeal to 'naturalness' interpreted as suitability for creatures with our genetic inheritance will not provide an answer. And this is true, not just for this relatively stark choice, but for almost all the other choices we might try to make on these grounds. There may well be many reasons to favour what is called 'natural' childbirth over induction or caesarian section, but these cannot be explained by or rooted in a sociobiological explanation of their 'naturalness'. Similarly, a 'natural' diet cannot be shown to enjoy any special relationship to our biological nature or our environment. When people speak of a 'natural' diet, they often have it in mind to draw a sharp contrast with what are called 'junk' foods. Now there may well be reasons for recommending foods high in fibre and low in fat (though this is now contentious), but one of them cannot be that these are 'natural' foods, because in the first place many people 'naturally' (i.e. left to their own devices) choose junk food, and in the second place, a low fibre/high fat diet does not inevitably lead to death or ill-health, and 'healthy' eaters can die young.

But there is an even more important objection to the attempt to make 'natural' a norm. The relationship between those who choose a 'healthy' diet and the food they eat is not like the relationship between a tiger and the animals it hunts. Still less is it like that between a plant and the nutrients it extracts from the earth and the atmosphere. A crucial difference is this. Human beings can and do *think* about what they should eat and drink. They are not driven by natural instinct alone, nor, in adult life does it drive them very much. So, while a cow will simply turn away from meat, we can decide whether or not to eat it. In deciding we can certainly take into account the fact that this food serves some useful biological function, but we can take other factors into account too, such as its taste. All human beings do this in fact. It may be fashionable to suggest that less industrialized societies have more 'natural', additive free diets, but the fact is that the poorest peasants in remote parts of India and China have since time immemorial added a wide variety of spices to their food. This serves many purposes, no doubt, but one of them is the enhancement of taste, an enhancement that children have a 'natural' reluctance towards and have to learn to like.

The philosophical point is this. We take to certain foods more easily than others and some of these foods serve essential biological ends. Both facts are important in considering what to eat, and there may be some reason to call a diet that gives them pride of place 'natural'. However, these are not the only facets of food that we can reasonably consider in constructing our diet. Nor are we obliged by nature or by anything else to lend them an importance above all others. We can *deliberate about* the merits of 'natural' foods. The point can be generalized. There may be patterns of behaviour and ways of life that we have some reason to call natural. But from this fact, if and when it is one, nothing automatically follows about the good life. We can ask ourselves critically, how much weight we are to give to it.

IS THE 'GOOD FOR MAN' GOOD?

In these last examples 'natural' has been taken to mean things that we are instinctively disposed towards and which are well suited to our genetic makeup. The possibility of raising critical questions about what comes naturally, in this sense, is in fact a very important one. So far we have been concerned to ask whether (when we replace his outdated biology with modern sociobiology) we should endorse Aristotle's conception of 'the good' as 'the good for (the species) man'. What we have found is that it cannot provide a basis for deciding between a wide range of competing lifestyles. This is because it cannot single out just one form of life as 'naturally' good for human beings, and even if it could, this would only be one consideration amongst others.

This last point leads on to a more profound criticism. Perhaps the way of life to which we take naturally is something we have reason to resist. Perhaps, some of the things that are *good for* human beings are not in fact *good*, viewed from a wider perspective.

For example, it may well be natural for human beings to hunt, and natural for them to take a real pleasure in the suffering and destruction of other animals. There is enough support for cruel sports in almost all times and cultures to suggest that the appetite for them, if not universal, is certainly widespread. Moreover, it is not difficult to imagine a story which explains how blood-lust of this sort has evolutionary advantages and hence is part of our evolved nature. But it is just as easy to see that from the point of view of the other animals involved, or from the detached point of view which concerns itself with pain and suffering wherever these are to be found, this impulse in human beings, however natural or good for them, is not to be applauded or encouraged.

Similarly, I do not find it hard to imagine that ethology and/or evolutionary psychology might show racism or xenophobia to be deeply entrenched in the unselfconscious behaviour of human beings. (There seems plenty of evidence for it.) Nor do I think, if such were found to be the case, that we would for long lack a plausible explanation of its place in our evolutionary development. But in such an event we would not necessarily have found reason to commend this natural human impulse, or to cease to strive against its manifestation.

In short, even if, despite earlier arguments it *were* possible, using the new sciences of ethology, sociobiology, evolutionary psychology, to outline with reasonable certainty and clarity a manner of life which we had reason to call the 'good for human beings', we would still be left with this question: Is the 'good for man' good? To put the issue like this is to separate two questions which have so far been run together, namely, 'what is a good life?' and 'what is good?'. But the two questions are connected. One answer to the first is that the good life consists in *realizing* the good.

NATURAL GOOD AND FREEDOM

At first it may sound implausible to think that what is natural to human beings – the conditions under which they thrive and the activities they instinctively delight in – might nonetheless be an unworthy way for them to live. Yet it is an idea with which the history of moral ideas is quite familiar. The Christian doctrine of original sin, for instance, holds that there is a powerful inclination on the part of human beings to do what they should *not* do. For the moment, though, we should notice another objection. Human nature and the natural are given. That is to say, our nature and what is natural to us is something we discover, with the help of ethology or some other science. It is a matter of fact, and from the point of view of Aristotle and many of the ancient Greeks that this is one of the things that makes it a fitting basis for a conception of the good life.

But from another point of view, this is just what makes human nature and the natural an unsuitable basis for human action. To appeal to facts about our nature, and to try to make them unalterable determinants of the way we live is to disguise from ourselves a fundamental feature of the human condition, namely its radical freedom. Faced with an account of the 'natural' way of life we are still free to choose it or reject it.

To see the full force of this point consider the position of zookeepers responsible for the health and welfare of the animals in their charge. We can well imagine that they would find ethological studies of great value, since those studies could be expected to tell them the sorts of conditions under which their animals would flourish. They might even tell them (as in the case of polar bears) that some animals simply cannot flourish in the conditions zoos can provide. In the light of this knowledge, the zookeepers will lay down a pattern of life for the different animals, a pattern the animals will unreflectively follow (or be made to follow) and which, if the ethologists have got it right, will be good for them. The animals themselves, however, are not involved in either the discovery or the implementation of the regime that is good for them. Nor could they be.

Now it should be obvious that ethology could not stand in the same relation to the life of human beings. The very simple reason is that, were such a way of life to be laid down for us, we would still have to decide whether or not to follow it. Either that, or some political 'zookeepers', who thought that their knowledge of human nature and the natural was superior, and for that reason authoritative, would deny us the freedom to choose. More importantly still, if we ourselves were to suppose that what is natural for us is authoritative, we would be denying our own freedom to choose.

One way of making this point is to say that we would be making our essence determine our existence, whereas 'existence comes before essence'. This is an expression coined by the French philosopher Jean-Paul Sartre, and it leads us to examine the next philosophy of value – existentialism. But before that a summary may be useful.

SUMMARY

We have been asking the question 'What sort of life would it be best to have and to pursue? Chapter 1 addressed the sceptical challenge presented by subjectivists who hold that this question is a matter of subjective preference and not one that we can meaningfully reason about. That challenge can be met by distinguishing between *moral realism* which falsely tries to base morality on a special moral sense, and *moral rationalism* that appeals instead to thinking about relations between ideas and concepts.

Chapter 2 then began with the rather mundane idea that the best life is one of riches and fame. But we saw that this answer confuses *intrinsic* values – things valuable in themselves – with merely *instrumental* values – things valuable only as a means to something else. What we need is an answer that will point us to intrinsic values, and this requirement is what led us to *egoism*, the doctrine that the good life consists in getting what you want, whatever that might be. However, detailed analysis showed egoism to be inadequate because it either rests upon a falsehood about the sorts of motives human beings have, or it recommends a policy of following desires without telling us which out of all the desires we can have we ought to follow. If, in order to answer this objection, egoism is amended to a version which recommends the pursuit of those desires which are in my own interests, this still leaves us asking which desires it is in my best interests to pursue.

At this point some ancient schools of philosophy appealed to *hedonism*: follow those desires that give you pleasure. This was the topic of Chapter 3 and once again we discovered problems and difficulties. There does not seem to be any compelling reason to give pleasure a specially important place in our lives. Indeed many possible aspects of a human life other than the pleasure it contains contribute to its value.

Just what are these other aspects and how might we hope to knit them into a coherent whole? This is the question Aristotle expressly addresses and he tries to answer it by giving an account of what is distinctively human, and thus defines 'the good' as 'the good for man'. The arguments considered in this chapter, however, showed that this appeal to human nature is not successful, even with the help of the modern sciences of ethology and sociobiology. First, it is impossible to specify a 'natural' good for human beings that will enable us to decide between competing styles of life.

Second, even if we could do so, this would not show that the attributes, attitudes and activities that add up to human flourishing are good in a wider sense. The conditions under which human beings do best as a species of animal might be (and probably are) conditions under which a wide range of other creatures, both plant and animal, might be put at risk. What comes naturally to human beings and what leads to the vigorous flowering of the species has its dark side (as the Christian doctrine of original sin holds), and in the absence of further argument we have no reason to regard this dark side as an aspect of life it would be good to promote.

In any case, Aristotelian naturalism overlooks one crucial respect in which human beings differ from other animals – their radical freedom. This is the concept from which existentialism takes its cue.

SUGGESTED FURTHER READING

Original sources

Aristotle, *Nichomachean Ethics* ed. Broadie and Rowe. This new translation has both a historical and a philosophical introduction

Commentaries

Gerard J Hughes, *Aristotle on Ethics*

Contemporary discussion

Phillippa Foot, *Natural Goodness*
Alasdair MacIntyre, *Dependent Rational Animals*
E O Wilson, *On Human Nature*

5

EXISTENTIALISM

KIERKEGAARD AND THE ORIGINS
OF EXISTENTIALISM

The author whose themes have been acknowledged by existentialist writers as formative was an obscure nineteenth-century Dane, Søren Kierkegaard (1813–1855). Kierkegaard was a very curious man as well as a prolific writer, but his fame is chiefly as a religious thinker rather than a philosopher in the normal sense. By upbringing and persuasion he was a Protestant Christian, and for a time aspired to be a country parson. Nonetheless he reacted fiercely against many aspects of the Danish Lutheran church of his day. This reaction was volubly expressed in a large number of writings. However, Kierkegaard was also reacting to the philosophy dominant in Northern Europe in the early and middle nineteenth century, namely the philosophy of one of Berlin's most famous professors, G W F Hegel.

Kierkegaard's objections to established Lutheranism and to Hegelian philosophy were at bottom the same. To his mind, both, in different ways, tried to make the demands of Christianity reasonable. In the case of the church, the Gospel was presented, not as a radical challenge to the customary intellectual and social order of the world, but as the sort of thing that reasonable and respectable men and women would naturally agree to. He instances the biblical story of Abraham and Isaac. In that story Abraham, under the belief that God requires it of him, is represented as willing to take an innocent child, his own son, and murder him, though in the end the boy lives. Kierkegaard was struck by the fact that church people could listen to this story with attention and respect, whereas if one of their neighbours actually acted in the way that Abraham did, they would be scandalized. Similarly, in the mouths of Protestant pastors all trace of the mystery of the Trinity or the absurdity of the Incarnation was smothered by sheer respectability, till both doctrines lost anything that could be called challenging. In Kierkegaard's view

> The point is rather to do away with introductory observations, reliabilities, demonstrations from effects, and the whole mob of pawn-brokers and guarantors, in order to get the absurd clear – so that one can believe if one will . . . [because Christianity] has proclaimed itself as *the paradox*, and has required the inwardness of faith with regard to what is an offence to the Jews, foolishness to the Greeks – and an absurdity to the understanding.
>
> (Kierkegaard 1846, 1992, Vol. 1: 212–13)

In the case of Hegel, the transformation of the Christian Gospel was more self-conscious. Hegel claimed that his philosophical system, with which he aimed to encompass and explain all aspects of human knowledge and experience, was nothing less than an encyclopaedic rationalization of the Christian religion. It was the truth of Christianity converted into a form to which all rational minds could assent. For Hegel, to bring about such a transformation was to do Christianity a great service, to put it beyond the vagaries of 'faith' or mere subjective opinion. But to Kierkegaard it was nothing short of its destruction. To make Christianity 'rational' was to turn it into a mere theory. As such it might elicit our intellectual assent but it would not demand and could not sustain what Kierkegaard calls the 'inwardness' that real religious faith requires.

Moreover, on Kierkegaard's view the Hegelian 'System' (which he mocks by spelling with a capital S) is worthless as a guide to life. 'Having to exist with the help of the guidance of pure thinking is like having to travel in Denmark with a small map of Europe on which Denmark is no larger than a steel pin-point' (Kierkegaard 1846, 1992, Vol. 1: 310–11). Philosophical systems are too lofty, too far removed from practical living to be of any use. The trouble with speculative metaphysicians like Hegel, he tells us in another place, is that they must turn aside from their contemplation of space and time in order to blow their nose!

Kierkegaard's writings are full of this sort of remark, and they abound in paradox. Much of what he writes is suggestive, but it is difficult to reconstruct Kierkegaard's polemic into a consistent and sustained intellectual critique of academic philosophy. Partly this is because he wanted to avoid all systematic philosophizing. He wrote many of his books under a variety of pseudonyms, intending them to be the presentation of differing, sometimes conflicting points of view. The result is that his writings are often puzzlingly inconsistent. For instance, his analogy of the map suggests that a philosophical system is the right *sort* of thing (namely, a guide) but on the wrong scale, whereas in countless other places what he writes implies that philosophy, or any form of thought which aims to arrive at demonstrable conclusions, is the wrong *kind* of thinking by which try to address the fundamental questions of human existence.

Understanding Kierkegaard is further complicated by two facts. The first is that he wrote his books under pseudonyms so that we cannot automatically identify the views expressed as his. The advertised author of the *Philosophical Fragments* (which are far from fragmentary) and their *Concluding Unscientific Postscript* (a postscript described as 'pamphlet' that runs to 630 pages) is Johannes Climachus and Kierkegaard himself referred to as the editor. Second, there is Kierkegaard's insistence that we cannot grasp thought in independence of the person whose thought it is. There is a unity of living and thinking which must be appreciated if we are to understand an author. In his own case this introduces another element of paradox. His writings are of a highly individualistic, anti-conventional character. Yet to outward appearances his life was no more remarkable than most of his middle-class Danish contemporaries. He lived quietly on a private income inherited from his father, and apart from a broken engagement and an unpleasant brush with the press later in life, there is nothing about his life that could be called historic or dramatic.

Still, for all this confusing abundance, Kierkegaard's writings contain certain abiding themes. In his earlier writings he describes three different ways of life – the aesthetic, the ethical and the religious. These are represented as mutually exclusive, and requiring the individual to make a radical choice between them. It is in the later writings, notably in the *Concluding Unscientific Postscript* that the philosophical underpinnings of this requirement are set out. Three of these form the basis of the existentialist point of view. First, the most fundamental questions facing a human being are essentially practical because the question 'How shall I spend my life?' is inescapable. Whatever interest there may be in purely intellectual questions, they can never take priority over practical questions of living. This is something it is especially important to grasp in the context of religion. Christianity (or any other religion) is a way of living, not a theoretical explanation of the world or of human experience. It follows from this that it is a deep mistake to try to substitute a theological doctrine or a philosophical system for a religious faith.

> Speculative thought is objective, and objectively there is no truth for an existing individual, but only an approximation, since by existing he is prevented from becoming entirely objective.
>
> (Kierkegaard 1846, 1992, Vol. 1: 224)

> Philosophy is perfectly right in saying that life must be understood backward. But then one forgets the other clause – that is must be lived forward.
>
> (Kierkegaard 1846, 1992, Vol. 2: 187)

Second, it is not only fruitless but misleading to try to demonstrate or prove the objective truth of the beliefs by which men and women are expected to live. This is because in matters of living, as opposed to questions of pure intellect (natural science for instance), 'truth is subjectivity'. What Kierkegaard means by this is that any religion or philosophy that we are meant to live by has actually to be *lived* by. Whatever the *objective* truth of Christian teaching, those who live by it have to accept its truth *subjectively*, that is, as true for them. Between the presentation of a doctrine and its acceptance by those to whom it is presented, there is an essential and inescapable gap, a gap that cannot be closed by still further objective evidence or proof, but only by a subjective 'leap of faith'. (It is from Kierkegaard that this famous expression comes.) The twentieth-century existentialist Albert Camus expresses the same thought when he writes: 'I understand then why the doctrines that explain everything to me also debilitate me at the same time. They relieve me of the weight of my own life and yet I must carry it alone' (Camus 1942, 2000: 54), (though it should be added that Camus is critical of Kierkegaard's analysis of the 'leap of faith').

But, third, though from the point of view of critical objectivity the 'truth which edifies' will always appear 'absurd', this does not imply that we are free to live by any old doctrine that takes our fancy. The attainment of practical, subjective truth is as at least as difficult as the intellectual effort involved in speculative theory.

> With regard, for example, to comprehension, a person of high intelligence has a direct advantage over a person with limited intelligence, but this is not true with regard to having faith. That is, when faith requires that he relinquish his understanding, then to have faith becomes just as difficult for the most intelligent person as it is for the person of the most limited intelligence.
>
> (Kierkegaard 1846, 1992, Vol. 1: 377)

The difficulty involved in the attainment of faith, however, is emotional rather than intellectual. Kierkegaard wrote several books with titles such as *Fear and Trembling*, *The Concept of Dread*, *Purity of Heart*, and he had a great deal to say in general about the emotional conditions under which a real living faith emerges. In his view, 'there is only one proof of the truth of Christianity and that, quite rightly, is from the emotions, when the dread of sin and a heavy conscience torture a man into crossing the narrow line between despair bordering upon madness – and Christendom' (Kierkegaard 1938: 1926).

Kierkegaard's overriding concern was with religious faith and with the demands of Christianity in particular. This emphasis upon Christianity continues to make him of interest as a religious writer. But many of the central elements in his thought can in fact be given a wholly secular treatment. Though some later existentialists have also been Christians, the most famous existentialist of all, the French philosopher Jean-Paul Sartre (1905–1980), was avowedly atheist. As we shall see, however, despite this important difference the fundamentals of his thought are strikingly similar to Kierkegaard's.

SARTRE AND RADICAL FREEDOM

It is Sartre who uses the expression 'existence comes before essence'. This is a succinct and memorable summation of what all existentialists, Christian and non-Christian, have in common. It means that in answering the basic question of existence – How should I live? – we must reject any appeal to the idea of human nature or essence, that is to say any appeal to a conception of 'human being' that will be found in every individual and of which each individual is an example. Part of the reason for rejecting this conception is the belief that human beings have no preordained, essential character. As Sartre puts it, 'Man is nothing else but what he makes of himself' (Sartre 1946, 1973: 28).

It is Sartre's atheism that leads him to reject the idea of human nature. There is no such thing as human nature on his view, because there is no God who could have created it. The only coherent way in which we can speak of a distinctive human nature is as a preconceived creative plan for human beings, similar to the plan an engineer draws up for a particular design of engine. Such a design – the essential character of the engine – precedes the existence of any actual engine, and each engine is a realization of that design. If there were a God, and He had conceived of human beings and then created them, we could speak of human nature, and could even say that human essence comes before existence. But there is no God and hence no preordained human nature.

Of course, if this were all there were to Sartre's argument, he could hardly claim that existentialists, both religious and non-religious, share the common ground he claims. For it would amount to no more than an assertion of the truth of atheism, an assertion Christians and others would equally deny. But Sartre also argues that, even if there were a creative God with a preformed plan for human beings, there would still be an unmistakable sense in which existence must come before essence. This is because, like Kierkegaard, Sartre thinks that the question of existence is more a practical than a metaphysical matter.

In the lecture 'Existentialism and Humanism' he too uses the biblical example of Abraham and Isaac to bring out this point. In that story an angel commands Abraham to sacrifice his son Isaac on an altar. Were we to treat the story in a purely objective mood as a piece of history, we would ask whether Abraham really was addressed by a supernatural voice. No doubt many people today reject stories like this, because they no longer believe in the reality of angelic voices. But Sartre's main point is not about the literal truth or falsehood of the story. He sees that, even if there were no doubt about the reality of the supernatural voice, Abraham would have to decide whether or not it was the voice of an *angel*, a real messenger from God, or only an imposter albeit a supernatural one. And this is a question that he must decide *for himself*, and he cannot be relieved of this necessity by the supernatural voice offering further assurances that it is indeed angelic.

In a similar way each one of us is addressed personally by the claims of any ethical standard or principle.

> If a voice speaks to me, it is still I myself who must decide whether the voice is or is not that of an angel. If I regard a certain course of action as good, it is only I who choose to say that it is good and not bad.
>
> (Sartre 1946, 1973: 33)

It is in this way that any answer to the question 'How shall I live?' is inescapably existential. However authoritative, however objectively 'provable' or 'unprovable', it requires the one whose existence it addresses to give it assent. Without this, Sartre thinks, any such answer is effectively silent, and thus is no answer at all.

It is in this sense that human beings are radically free. Nothing we can imagine – no God, no human nature and no science or philosophy – can decide for us the fundamental question of existence. Moreover, there is another side to this freedom. Because nothing determines the answer except ourselves, we alone are responsible for the decisions we make. Freedom liberates our will from the determination of any other agency, but it also leaves us solely responsible. This is why Sartre says

> Man is *condemned* to be free. Condemned, because he did not create himself, yet is nevertheless at liberty, and from the moment he is thrown into this world he is responsible for everything he does.
>
> (Sartre 1946, 1973: 34, emphasis added)

The argument so far might be taken to imply that humankind's inescapable freedom is a logical truth, something we come to understand through philosophical analysis. At one level this is true. Sartre thinks that radical freedom arises out of the nature of the human condition. 'There is no difference' he says, 'between the being of man and his being free' (Sartre 1943, 1957: 25). This remark comes from his largest philosophical work *Being and Nothingness*, in which he offers a full-scale metaphysical analysis of what it is for something to exist. There are, according to Sartre, two modes of existing, Being-in-itself and Being-for-itself. What this rather obscure terminology is meant to capture is the contrast between things, like stones and trees, that are just *there* and have no awareness of or value for themselves (Being-in-itself) and things, notably human beings, that are aware of themselves and whose consciousness of their own existence is central (Being-for-itself). The contrast has to do with a point about past and future that Kierkegaard also makes. Action, and thought about it, has to do with the future. Whereas the past is made and unalterable, the distinguishing feature of the future is that it is yet to be made. At present it is nothing, to be fashioned as we will.

It is the peculiarity of human beings that they are both physical objects, (and thus Being-in-itself), and self-consciousnesses, (and hence Being-for-itself). But the distinctive feature of Being-for-itself, or self-consciousness, is that it is a sort of nothingness, just in the sense that it can never be or become simply another object in the world. No matter how hard we try to think of ourselves as merely physical objects existing alongside all the other objects of the world, our consciousness always floats free, so to speak. It is always a subject, never an object. The point can be illuminated by this parallel. In order to have visual experience of anything, we need literally to occupy some point of view. But the point of view we occupy, though essential to sight, cannot itself figure as an object within the visual field. If I stand on a hillside, my position determines my field of vision. It is not within that field. If we are to see things at all, occupying some point of view is crucial. But the point of view is not itself something seen, and could not be. So too with the subject of consciousness. Subjective consciousness is an ineliminable precondition for the perception and understanding of objects, but never itself an object. It is not a *thing* at all.

Many people find this sort of philosophical analysis hard to understand and appreciate. Sartre himself did not suppose that his analysis would by itself be illuminating because he regarded the inescapability of freedom not merely as a conclusion from metaphysical analysis but as an actual feature of lived human experience. For this reason much of his thinking about freedom is to be found in novels rather than in formal philosophical works. In these novels different characters come to a deepening realization of just what a gulf there is between the way in which ordinary objects exist and the way in which human beings exist. As a result of this sort of reflection they come to appreciate what it means to be free.

The experience is not a pleasant one but one of anguish, since radical freedom is a difficult and painful condition to accept. This idea of an anguish which results from a true perception of the human condition is not dissimilar to Kierkegaard's 'Dread', and it has an important part to play in Sartre's philosophy of value. But in order to see this we have to go back a little.

ANGUISH AND BAD FAITH

Sartre's remark that it is I who must choose to say whether a given course of action or way of life is good or bad for me might lead us to think that each individual may do as he or she pleases. But this is not so; at least, if 'do as one pleases' means take whatever course of action is most agreeable. What is true is that a good human life is distinguished not by *what* is chosen, but by the *manner in which* it is chosen. A wholly authentic or truly human life is possible only for those who recognize the inescapability of freedom and its responsibility. (The terms 'authentic' and 'inauthentic' come from another existentialist, the German philosopher Martin Heidegger.) And this recognition can be achieved only at the cost of anguish. Consequently, a good life, the sort of life that has meaning and value, is not easy to achieve.

Anguish arises from two sources. The first is the perception that in recognizing our radical freedom as human beings we are acknowledging that we are nothing, literally no thing. As a result nothing can fully determine our choice of life for us, and hence nothing can explain or justify what we are. This sense of groundlessness was famously labelled 'the absurd' by the French-Algerian writer Albert Camus. According to Camus, 'there is but one truly serious philosophical problem and that is suicide' because confronted with their own absurdity human beings have to judge 'whether their life is or is not worth living' (Camus 2000: 11). Similarly, Sartre thinks that the existence of everything, being-in-itself as well as being-for-itself, is absurd. By this he means that existence is always a matter of brute, inexplicable fact. But the fact that we share our absurdity with everything else does not make us any the less absurd, or make the human condition any easier to accept. Indeed, as we shall see, Sartre spends a good deal of time exploring the ways in which human beings strive to hide from themselves their own absurdity.

The second source of anguish is this. Acknowledgment of our freedom to make choices makes us, literally, creators of the world of value, and as a consequence we bear all the responsibility that brings with it, and this turns out to be immense.

> When we say that man chooses himself, we do mean that everyone of us must choose himself; but by that we also mean that in choosing for himself he chooses for all men. . . . What we choose is always the bet-ter, and nothing can be better for us unless it is better for all. If, more-over, existence precedes essence and we will to exist at the same time as we fashion our image, that image is valid for all and for the entire epoch in which we find ourselves. Our responsibility is thus much greater than we had supposed, for it concerns mankind as a whole.
>
> (Sartre 1946, 1973: 29)

If Sartre is correct in this, by being radically free, that is free not merely to respond to values but to create them, the individual in acknowledging that freedom takes on the responsibility of legislating for all mankind. One way of putting this would be to say that in acknowledging our radical free-dom we must recognize the necessity of playing God, with the awesome-ness that comes with such a thought. In fact Sartre himself says 'To be man means to reach towards being God. Or if you prefer, man fundamentally is the desire to be God' (Sartre 1943, 1957: 556).

A true understanding of our condition as human beings, then, involves the recognition that at bottom our existence is absurd. To say that it is absurd is to say that it is without necessity or explanation. Human existence is a matter of brute fact and it is only by adopting God-like aspirations that we can bestow any meaning upon it. Not surprisingly, since as T S Eliot once wrote 'human kind cannot bear very much reality', ordinary human beings are strongly inclined to avoid the anguish by hiding the truth from themselves. Sartre distinguishes three characteristic ways in which this is done.

The first of these is the least interesting. It is the response of those who think that, faced with alternative courses of action and modes of life, they can simply fail to choose. But this is an illusion. The decision not to choose is itself a choice, and a choice for which the individual is no less responsible than any other. Indecision leads to consequences as certainly as conscious decision does; idleness is one form of activity.

The second kind of response to anguish is the way of the 'serious minded'. The serious minded are those people, often religious but not necessarily so, who assert that there is some objective source of value, God perhaps, or just Goodness itself, and who profess to direct their lives in accordance with this. The hedonists and Aristotle are 'serious minded' in this sense. So are Christians, Muslims and Jews and any others who purport to find the source of all that is good somewhere other than in their own decisions and commitment. What such people fail to see is that the only way these objective, external values can come to guide their lives is through their own commitment to those values as values. This is the point of Kierkegaard's stress upon the necessity of subjectivity. Alternatively, such serious minded people seek the advice of others. But even when they receive it, they have still to decide for themselves whether to accept it. And as Sartre points out in the famous case of a young man who sought his advice during the Second World War about whether to join the Free French Army or remain at home with his mother, the choice of adviser can in itself represent a decision. Often we preselect the people whose advice we seek.

The third avenue of escape from the anguish is bad faith. 'Bad faith' is perhaps modern existentialism's most famous concept, and almost as famous is the example of the waiter with which Sartre illustrates it. The idea is this: Faced with the terrifying realities of the human condition (its absurdity and responsibility), individuals may seek escape by ordering their lives according to some preordained social role. Instead of accepting their own subjectivity and freedom to choose, they may try to objectify *themselves*, adopt roles which they then act out, and think of themselves as mere functionaries. Such an individual is Sartre's waiter. He suppresses his personality and individuality and thinks of himself, not as the individual he is, but as a waiter whose every action is determined by the job. But of course, if existential freedom is inescapable, this attempt at objectification in a social role is doomed to failure. The best the waiter can accomplish is a sort of play-acting.

> His movement is quick and forward, a little too precise, a little too rapid. He comes towards the patrons with a step a little too quick. He bends forward a little too eagerly; his voice, his eyes express an interest a little too solicitous for the order of the customer. Finally there he returns, trying to imitate in his walk the inflexible stiffness of some kind of automaton while carrying his tray with the recklessness of a tight-rope walker. All his behaviour seems to us a game . . . the waiter in the cafe plays with his condition in order to realize it.
>
> (Sartre 1943, 1957: 59)

What such pretence involves is a measure of self-deception. The waiter pretends to himself that his every thought and movement is determined by what it means to be a waiter.

> He applies himself to chaining his movements as if they were mechanisms, the one regulating the other; his gestures and even his voice seem to be mechanisms; he gives himself the quickness and pitiless rapidity of things.
>
> (Ibid.)

But in his heart of hearts he must know that the role determines his behaviour for only as long as he chooses to let it. At any moment, he can turn on his heel and leave his customers standing and their orders unfulfilled. He only pretends to himself that he cannot.

Self-pretence and self-deception are puzzling concepts. When I deceive other people I know the truth and they do not. But how then can I deceive myself, for this requires me both to know and not to know the truth? This is an important question, but the explanation of bad faith can make do with something less than self-deception in the fullest sense. It is enough that we can avoid reminders of the truth. The waiter knows that he could adopt a quite different attitude to those who come to his café, but he refuses to think about it. In a similar way, but of course with much more grievous results, some Nazi commandants assumed the role of the obedient soldier, one who simply has to accept orders, and they refused to deliberate about any alternative. To describe these cases properly we do not need to say that those involved both knew and did not know what courses of action were open to them. We need only say that they knew but would not think about it.

Nazi commandants may or may not have acted in bad faith (there is more to be said about this shortly). Sartre's primary concern is with more mundane roles, those we adopt in an attempt to escape the anguish of radical freedom. Such attempts are futile because human freedom is inescapable. Acting in bad faith cannot accomplish what it is supposed to. Even so, it is still to be avoided since it constitutes an inauthentic way of living. This gives us a clue to the existentialist conception of the good life. It is the life lived in good faith. Though Sartre says relatively little about this ideal, we can see that it consists in the pursuit of consciously self-chosen values and purposes for which the chooser takes full responsibility. When it comes to fundamental moral and evaluative questions, he thinks,

> there are no means of judging. The content is always concrete and therefore unpredictable; it always has to be invented. The one thing that counts is to know whether the invention is made in the name of freedom.
>
> (Sartre 1946, 1973: 52–3)

There are four principal difficulties that the existentialist philosophy of value encounters. First we may ask whether human existence is absurd in a way that gives reason for anguish. Second, is it always, or even usually better to act in good faith? Third, in what sense, if any, is it true that individual human beings are the creators of value? And fourth, are we really so radically free? It is best to consider each of these questions in turn.

THE ABSURDITY OF EXISTENCE

As we have noted, in company with many other existentialist writers Sartre holds that human existence is absurd. What they mean by this is that there is no explanation of the existence of human beings in general or any individual in particular which will show that existence to be necessary.

All existence is a matter of brute, contingent fact. To take this view is to take sides in a long-standing philosophical dispute, a dispute that dominated seventeenth- and eighteenth-century intellectual debate. On one side were philosophers who subscribed to what was called rationalist metaphysics, notably Descartes (1596–1650), Spinoza (1632–1677) and Leibniz (1646–1716). They thought that there must be a reason for everything's being as it is. If there were not, the world would be unintelligible, a meaningless jumble of events. This belief that everything has an explanation is often called 'the principle of sufficient reason'.

In opposition to the rationalist metaphysicians were the philosophers generally called empiricists. Among these, John Locke (1632–1704) and David Hume (1711–1776) are the best known. They regarded the ambition to provide a sufficient reason for everything as a profound error. The empiricists were impressed by the results of experimental science, then still in its infancy. They saw that explanations of natural facts could be obtained by experimental inquiry into empirical facts (hence the name empiricist). To explain in this way, however, was to do no more than appeal to demonstrable contingencies – how things *are*, not how they *must* be. To the empiricists, the rationalists' mistake lay in supposing that matters of scientific fact could be explained in the same way as the propositions of logic or mathematics. Logical and mathematical theories can be demonstrated by abstract reasoning to hold by necessity. Scientific theories can only be shown by experimental reasoning to hold as a matter of contingent, i.e. non-necessary fact.

When Sartre and others say that human existence is absurd they mean to side with the empiricists and deny that it can have any rationalistic explanation. They differ from the empiricists, however, in the implications they draw from this. In seeing the absurdity of human existence as a cause of anguish they imply that the absence of a rationalistic explanation is an unfortunate deficiency, something that we need but cannot have if we are to make sense of our lives. From an empiricist point of view, however, to think this is to share the rationalist's mistake. The mistake lies in the false *hope* of supplying a logically sufficient reason for everything. But once we understand the contingency of existence, the right response is to abandon that hope, and once it has been abandoned, the fact that human existence is not the sort of thing that can be explained in terms of a logically sufficient reason will not trouble us. Human existence is not a matter of logical necessity. It is a matter of contingent fact. But why should anyone want more than this?

The language of absurdity can mislead us. To conclude that human existence is absurd seems to provide some reason for despair. But if 'life is absurd' just means 'there is no logically necessary explanation of the existence of human beings', we have no reason for anguish, unless we think there should be such an explanation. According to empiricists, this is just what we ought not to think. The existentialists, it seems, have not wholly discarded the rationalism with which they find fault. This is why they are sometimes described as 'disappointed rationalists'.

If this analysis is correct, there is a serious question to be raised about the basis of existentialist philosophy, as least as it has been expounded by more recent thinkers (though some of the same points can be made about Kierkegaard). However, it would be hasty to think that these important issues could be settled in a few brief paragraphs. The most we can do here is raise them in outline and then pass on to the other aspects of existentialism that ought to be examined.

ACTING IN GOOD FAITH

The chief implication of existentialism with respect to human conduct is this: what you choose to do, how you choose to spend your life, is not as important as the way you choose it. Whatever the choice, it is at least valuable in so far as it is made in good faith. This means it is made in full recognition of the freedom and responsibility that attach to all human choice.

The idea that value attaches to the manner and motive behind the choices we make is a very plausible one. The familiar expression 'it's the thought that counts' expresses this very idea. The value of a gift can lie almost entirely in the spirit in which it is given. A gift given in bad grace may cost much more but be of far less value than a simple present more gracefully given. Similarly, an inquiry made out of nothing more than a sense of professional duty will be valued much less than the same words spoken in friendship. On a larger scale the same thing applies. The poverty of St Francis of Assisi can be regarded as a blessing, the path to an admirable life because of the spirit in which it was accepted. But just the same degree of poverty would be a misfortune in most other lives because of the resentment and disaffection that would accompany it. What such examples show is that the motive and intention of an action and the spirit expressed in it can all be important factors in the evaluation of that action.

So much we might all agree with. But existentialists want to go further and claim first, that the *principal* value attaching to an action or a way of life is the mentality of those who have chosen it, and second, that of all the possible attitudes that might be taken into consideration, it is our attitude to freedom and responsibility that is crucial. Often we regard upbringing, or culture, or genes, as the formative influence in determining an individual's attitudes and personality, the things that make us what we are. To the existentialist, this is an important error. It is our own choices that determine who we are, and to pretend otherwise is bad faith. Consequently, to recognize our fundamental freedom to be self-determining is the only possible response of good faith. Such recognition is distinctively human, and for that reason good faith is the most important human achievement.

But necessarily, to recognize our freedom to determine for ourselves what we shall be places no constraints on possible choices. This means that any choice might be made in good faith. To choose to be a vicious criminal could be as much an expression of good faith as choosing to devote your life to those who suffer. The question then arises as to whether the fact that a vicious life is chosen in good faith makes that life any better.

A standard example used to explore this question is that of the sincere Nazi. No doubt many of those who served the Nazi Party and Hitler's government were mere time-servers, who joined the Party or supported it solely for personal advantage or monetary reward. Then there were others who chose to do what they did in bad faith, disguising from themselves the truth about the regime that they were serving, or pleading the necessity of following orders. But there were undoubtedly *some* true believers, who saw in Nazism a creed that they wanted to believe, and who freely chose to endorse it. Moreover, they willingly, even gladly, accepted the responsibility for fashioning a world built upon the values of *Mein Kampf*, even to the point of genocide, the destruction of an entire race of people.

What are we to make of this third category, the *sincere* Nazis? This is a question that has been asked repeatedly since the end of the Third Reich, by historians, theologians, philosophers, and above all survivors of the concentration camps such as Primo Levi and Elie Wiesel. Now the implication of existentialism would appear to be that though these people led wicked lives, the fact that they freely chose them and acknowledged their responsibility for this choice is a redeeming feature. But is it? It may be plausible to say on behalf of the sincere Nazi that at least he accepted responsibility and did not try to hide it. Is it any less plausible to say on behalf of the person who accepted his role in the Holocaust in *bad* faith, that at least had sufficiently decent feelings not to positively endorse it?

It is difficult to know how this disagreement might be resolved. One line of thought we might adopt on behalf of the existentialist says that the life of the sincere Nazi is objectively bad but subjectively good. If this means that, though his life was bad, it embodied those things that were values *for him*, we can hardly deny it. He did indeed choose those values; that is what is meant by calling him sincere. But this does not advance matters. We know what he freely chose. We want to know whether the fact that he chose freely made it any better or not.

THE CREATION OF VALUE

A more radical line of thought and one to which some existentialist writers have been drawn suggests that, at least in a range of cases, we cannot draw this contrast between subjective and objective value, because there is *only* subjective value. Kierkegaard says something like this about the decision to be a Christian: 'It is subjectivity that Christianity is concerned with, and it is only in subjectivity that its truth exists, if it exists at all; objectively, Christianity has absolutely no existence' (Kierkegaard 1964: 116).

In a similar vein Sartre says: 'Whenever a man chooses his purpose and commitment in all clearness and in all sincerity, whatever that purpose may be it is impossible to prefer another for him' (Sartre 1946, 1973: 50), and a little later on remarks: 'If I have excluded God the Father, there must be *somebody* to invent values' (Sartre 1946, 1973: 54, emphasis added). What this seems to imply is that, at least for a range of cases, it is wrong to think of the individual as choosing between values. Rather, the act of choice itself confers value. In other words, we are ourselves creators of value. (Elsewhere, it is true, Sartre says things which appear to deny this implication, and it will be appropriate to consider these other remarks a little later on.)

Are we creators of value? In asking this question we must be careful to ask who 'we' are. Once this supplementary question is raised two importantly different positions can be distinguished. One way of interpreting the question 'are we creators of value?', takes 'we' to mean a group of some sort – the particular society in which an individual lives, the general cultural milieu in which the question is raised, or even the whole human race. Taken this way, the question 'are we creators of value?' means, 'Are values pre-established for individuals by the group to which they belong, be it their race, culture or society?' Many people (including a significant number of philosophers) think the answer to this question is 'yes' and the philosophy of value they thereby accept usually goes by the name of 'relativism'. This is because, understood in this way, whether something is or is not of value is a matter relative to some context. This means that questions of human value cannot be intelligibly raised in the abstract. Prised free of some particular context, they simply do not make sense, and if so, since the context to which questions of value are relative is a human one, there is thus a sense in which human beings are the creators of value. It is in the context of the interests, preferences and goals of human beings that things come to have value.

A parallel to this kind of relativism is to be found in the law. Polygamy (marriage to more than one wife) is permitted in some legal jurisdictions, notably Islamic ones, and forbidden in others, notably Christian ones. To ask in the abstract 'Is it illegal to marry two women?' is to ask a senseless question. The only answer that can be given relativizes it to a context: 'It is in England, but not in Saudi Arabia'. The question only makes sense within the context of some body of law. Within such a context there will (usually) be a straightforward answer; outside such a context there is no answer at all. Similarly, relativists think, all matters of value can only be discussed intelligibly within a human context, and it makes no sense to think of values as transcending specific human interests and desires.

Other philosophers (Plato for instance) have construed matters differently and supposed that in matters of value just as in matters of scientific fact, there is mind-independent truth waiting to be discovered. Where true value lies is a question over which the whole of mankind could be confused and mistaken. Some of the issues here have already been dealt with in Chapter 1. But the 'slant' existentialism puts on them is somewhat different.

When Sartre declares that there are no independent values for the 'serious-minded' to follow, and when Kierkegaard says that the truth which edifies cannot be objective, both mean to reject the Platonic conception of value. This is a more radical contention than the legal relativism just outlined. Though most philosophers would draw a distinction between objectivism and relativism, from the existentialist point of view they are equally 'objective'. This is because both of them make matters of value true or false independently of the individual. It might be true (as relativism holds) that certain forms of sex and marriage are to be valued only because of the sorts of creatures human beings are and the kinds of social institutions that have grown up over the centuries. But if so, this does not make these values any more a matter about which the existing individual can pick and choose than if they had been established facts before the advent of any human beings at all. Existentialism seems to go further than this and interprets the question 'Are we creators of value?' as a question that refers to individuals. It means 'Is *each one* of us a creator of value?'. Sartre likens the situation of anguished choice in which every individual is placed to that of military leaders who by ordering an attack may be sending a number of men to their death.

> All leaders know that anguish. It does not prevent their acting, on the contrary it is the very condition of their action, for the action presupposes that there is a plurality of possibilities, and in choosing one of these, they realise that it has value only because it is chosen.
>
> (Sartre 1946, 1973: 32)

The final phrase of this quotation makes it clear that for Sartre the freedom of individuals extends beyond choosing their own values out of a pre-existent set, and in some cases at least includes the freedom to create value, to *make* things valuable.

To see whether this radical version of existentialism is plausible, consider the following example. Dr Samuel Johnson, the famous eighteenth-century wit and conversationalist, had some very odd physical habits.

On occasion, when he suddenly stopped in his tracks, he would perform with his feet and hands a series of antics so strange that a crowd would gather around him laughing or staring. As if oblivious to their presence, he would either hold out his arms with some of the fingers bent, as though he had been seized by cramp, or he would hold them high and stiff above his head, or, alternatively, close to his chest, when he would agitate them up and down in the manner of a jockey holding the reins of a horse galloping at full speed. At the same time he formed his feet into the shape of a V with either the heels together or the toes. Having twisted his limbs into the required postures, with many corrections and alterations of their relative positions, he would finally take a great leap forward and walk on with the satisfied air of a man who had performed a necessary duty and who seemed totally unconscious of having done anything odd.

(Hibbert 1988: 201)

As a matter of fact, extreme mannerisms of this type are not as uncommon as we might suppose, but even so we can reasonably be puzzled by them, in Johnson or in anyone else. 'Why do this sort of thing?' we want to know.

A little girl once had the courage to ask Johnson directly and he replied gently 'from bad habit. Do you, my dear, take care to guard against bad habits'. This, of course, is no real explanation at all and leaves his behaviour as mysterious as before. It is possible to imagine things that he might have said which would have gone some way to explaining his behaviour. For instance, he might have replied that people's lives were dull enough and that if he could give them a little harmless amusement, he was willing to spend the time and stand the cost to his reputation that this involved. No doubt we would still have questions to ask, but his story would be the start of an explanation because it would connect his behaviour with a pre-existent value, namely providing others with harmless amusement.

Suppose, however, instead of an explanation such as this, Johnson assumed the extreme existentialist point of view and said that gyrating in the manner described was something he did indeed regard as 'a necessary duty' and something to which he attached great value. Unlike the first explanation, this does not in fact make any sense of his behaviour, or give us a clue as to why he has, or we should, adopt it. Consequently, and despite his imagined assertion to the contrary, it does *not* bestow any meaning or any value. This is because it lacks any connection with values we can recognize.

It is of the utmost importance to stress here that recognizing values is not the same as sharing them. We may not be likely to share the desire to give harmless fun to complete strangers at our own expense, but we can recognize it as the sort of value we could have. Equally important is the observation that people can actually value things that are unintelligible or meaningless. To say that the individual cannot create values does not mean that Johnson could not really have attached importance to his little ritual. Presumably he did. What it shows is that his attachment, however deep, was not sufficient to *make* it valuable.

An existentialist might reply that his attachment to the ritual makes it valuable *for him*. There is reason to think Sartre would not reply in this way. He expressly denies that his version of existentialism is 'narrowly subjective'. He wants to reject the distinction between subjective and objective and appeals instead to 'inter-subjectivity' saying, 'In every purpose there is universality, in this sense that every purpose is comprehensible to every man' (Sartre 1946, 1973: 46). About the choice of an individual made in good faith, we can say both that it rests upon shared values and that no one but he or she can make it.

But to my mind this retreat from the radical position is made at the expense of clarity. There is an uninteresting sense in which only Bill can make his own choice, namely the sense in which if anyone else made it, it would not be Bill's. If this is what Sartre means by its being impossible 'to prefer another choice for him' we must agree. But the truth of this does not remove the possibility of saying that Bill ought to have chosen differently. If this is what Sartre means to rule out, then he has indeed embraced 'narrow subjectivity'.

Once again, there is more to be said, but here there is space only to review general lines of thought. What we have seen is this. Faced with the phenomenon of the sincere Nazi, the existentialist must either simply assert that the sincere Nazi's good faith makes his actions better than the same actions performed in bad faith (an assertion that many will feel inclined to deny), or else the existentialist must argue that in some sense or other subjective endorsement is actually creative of human value. It is this second claim that the example of Johnson puts to the test, and it is not easy to see how a satisfactory response to that sort of example could be formulated.

The arguments we have considered both for and against the existentialist's position are thus inconclusive. Despite these counter examples existentialists can continue to *assert* the individual's radical freedom from any natural or conventional values. This brings us to a fourth critical question.

RADICAL FREEDOM

The heart of existentialism is the doctrine of radical freedom. The human condition, we are told, is one of inescapable freedom (though not just this) and hence inescapable responsibility, the unceasing responsibility to choose our own values and commit ourselves to them. This idea conflicts sharply with familiar ways of speaking. We often say things like 'I cannot come because I must ...', and the 'cannot' and 'must' signify necessities which constrain our choices and our actions. They rule out courses of action as impossible. But if Sartre is right, such ways of speaking are deluded, since there are no practical necessities and everything is possible for us – to accept, reject or avoid.

Put like this, however, existentialism seems to be flatly false. It is not possible at every moment to choose any course of action if only because previous decisions may themselves have limited our present choices. If I eat my cake now, I am not free to have it later on. Nor is it only my decisions that limit my freedom of choice. The decisions of others may do so as well. I may not be free to buy the stereo system I want because you have just bought the last one in stock.

It might be replied that these sorts of example do not count against the general thesis of radical freedom because they are instances of *logical* impossibility – it is logic that determines that I cannot buy what is not for sale, and cannot eat what is already eaten. This says nothing more than that those courses of action that are not open to me are not open to me, a trivial truth of no interest. It places no restrictions upon my choice amongst those courses of action that *are* open to me. Within the boundaries of the logically possible I am still inescapably free.

However, even this amended version of the thesis also seems to be false. In Iceland I am not free to buy a bottle of whisky anywhere except at a government liquor store. Here is a restriction on my freedom that is not a matter of logic but of law. An existentialist might reply that I am free to choose to break the law. This is true, but not enough to show that I am wholly free. Let us leave aside the important fact that this requires others to be willing to break the law also (I cannot sell liquor to myself). In saying that Icelanders are not free to buy and sell each other liquor, I am of course speaking of legal freedom, and not of logical freedom. So though it is true that there is no logical bar to my buying liquor elsewhere, this does not show that I am free in the relevant sense. We can still distinguish between those logical possibilities that are legal possibilities and those that are not. It might be tempting to reply that, since the law can be broken, legal restraints are not restrictions on freedom properly so called. But this seems mistaken. A country in which I am legally free to speak out against the government is a freer country than one in which I am not, in a very straightforward sense of 'free'.

The general conclusion to which this example points us is that talk of 'freedom' always needs some qualification. To be free is to be free with respect to something – logic or the law in the examples just given. But once we have seen this we can also see that there are a good many important ways in which we can and cannot be free. For instance, I can invest wherever I want, but some investments are illegal and others are foolish. If my financial adviser were to say 'You can't invest in that!', only on one possible interpretation would he mean that such an investment is logically impossible (the company in question no longer exists). It is just as likely for him to mean that it is financially impossible (the funds are not available) or that the proposed investment is illegal (you can't invest in cocaine) or that it is foolish (there are shares in many far more profitable firms available). Or (more rarely perhaps) he might mean that it is unethical or immoral, that a morally decent investor could not invest in it.

All these reasons present investors with constraints upon what they can and cannot do. They rule out actions on the grounds that they are (respectively) logically impossible, financially impossible, illegal, imprudent, immoral. An existentialist might continue to insist, as in the liquor example, that it is only the first two of these that present real restrictions on freedom, since it is perfectly possible to act illegally, imprudently and immorally. For this reason only the first two can be said to be real constraints on our freedom. This is a thought that many people find compelling. What is logically or physically impossible does indeed seem to be impossible in a stronger sense than those things said to be legally or morally 'impossible'. But the important thing to observe is that logical and physical impossibilities are no more important than legal ones from the point of view of practical deliberation.

When we reason about what to do, we seek to restrict our choice of action; this is the point of the reasoning. We want to rule out certain courses of action. Of course, in order to be able to rule them out, we have to be able to consider them in the first place, so there must be a sense in which they are available to us. But in deciding against them on certain grounds, we are also acknowledging that there is reason to rule them out. The existentialist insists that all this 'ruling out' on legal, moral or prudential grounds cannot make the action impossible, and hence cannot eliminate our freedom to choose it. Sartre says that we are condemned to be free, because in the absence of God 'it is nowhere written that "the good" exists, that one must be honest or must not lie, since we are now upon the plane where there are only men' (Sartre 1946, 1973: 33). But this is just to confuse freedom from one point of view with freedom from every point of view. To be free of a divinely created natural law is not thereby to be free of every constraint or restriction.

If this is correct, the radical freedom of which existentialism speaks is at best a mere logical freedom. Within the boundaries of logical possibility there are many other ways in which freedom of action may be constrained. But more than this. These additional constraints are not to be rejected but *welcomed*, since the freedom we ought to want is not unconstrained possibility of choice but *rational* freedom. To see what this means consider the following example.

Suppose I am engaged in a piece of historical investigation, or am trying to arrive at a scientifically adequate explanation of some disease. In each case freedom is essential; I want to be able to arrive freely at the right answer. That is to say, I must avoid formulating my answer in accordance with what would please my professors, my political masters, those who fund my work, or with what would be fashionable and attract headlines. The only thing that matters is that I arrive at the right answer by the free process of rational thought. But to say that I must be free to arrive at my own answer is not to say that I am free to arrive at just any answer. Some answers will be ignorant and silly, however appealing they might be to my imagination, and worthless from the point of view of the study in question. Of course I am free to arrive at one of these worthless answers, in the sense that it is always possible for me to ignore the principles of good reasoning and falsify the evidence. But this freedom is not what we have in mind when we speak of freedom of thought. Conversely, when I am free of external pressure, the fact that I arrive at the truth by obeying the rules of argument and evidence is no restriction on my freedom. The freedom I want and that is worth having is not any less valuable because it is bound by rationality.

What the example shows is that some constraints, far from being restrictions on freedom, are just what make freedom valuable. When I check my calculations and say 'That answer can't be right' I am freely engaged in thought about necessity. It is of no consequence to be told that I am free (which in an uninteresting sense I am) to accept any answer I like. The same point may be applied to other kinds of freedom. We have seen that trying to arrive at the truth in mathematics, science or history does not represent any illegitimate constraint on human freedom. On the contrary, it allows human beings to engage in the sort of freedom that is valuable, namely rational freedom. Similarly to be free to choose your own values does not preclude an attempt to discover what is objectively good and evil. If in so doing we do discover the truth, this will no more be a fundamental rejection of freedom than the mathematician's pursuit of his subject.

This conclusion has important consequences for existentialist ways of thinking. To appreciate their full force we need to see them in the context of a general review of the argument.

RESUMÉ

Existentialists hold that we are radically free with respect to our choice of values and style of life. In some deep sense we *define* ourselves and what we stand for. One consequence of this radical freedom is that individuals have to accept full responsibility for what they do and are and believe. There is no God or external standard of 'the Good' to refer to, and no sociological or psychological conditioning to blame. This condition of radical freedom, however, is not one that everyone welcomes. Indeed for many it is a cause of anguish and there is a strong inclination to hide from it by disguising the origin and manner of human choice. In other words, it is common and easy to act in bad faith, and a real achievement to act in good faith. Moreover, since even our choice of fundamental values is radically free, whether we act in good or bad faith is the supreme test of our human worth and dignity, and this is true regardless of the values we choose and act upon.

At this point critics appeal to the case of the sincere Nazi. Doesn't existentialism oblige us to say that sincere Nazis were, at the very least, better than those who didn't really believe in the myth of the Aryan race and the desirability of the Holocaust? If so, it conflicts with a view at least as intelligible, that the clear-sighted endorsement of evil is *worse*, not better, than shamefaced duplicity.

Such an objection, of course, amounts to simple counter-assertion, but it is counter-assertion that existentialism needs reason to rebut. In pursuit of such a reason we explored a more radical line of thought, namely that the sincere clear-sighted individual is the source of value. That is why there is nothing further by which his choices may be judged good or evil. Yet closer investigation of this reply shows how hard it is to make sense of the idea that value and meaning can be bestowed by individual acts of will. To say that individuals are free to choose their own values is more naturally interpreted as meaning that they are free to choose *between* pre-existent values.

Even this choice cannot be said to be radically free in the sense that existentialists have intended. The previous section showed that there is no conflict between the idea of freedom and obedience to restrictions and constraints of certain kinds. Thought is not any the less free because it obeys the laws of logic. Similarly our choice of values is not any the less free because it seeks to follow the truth about good and evil. What this shows is that subjective choices can be guided by objective values without any loss of freedom. It follows that a search for objectively rational values by which to lead our lives and determine actions need not be an exercise in bad faith.

Of course, to say that the free pursuit of rational values is possible is not to give any guarantee of its success. Many philosophers, from Plato onwards, have approached the task with considerable optimism however. The philosopher who held out the greatest hope for a rational investigation into the good life was the German eighteenth-century philosopher Immanuel Kant. His ideas are the subject of the next chapter.

SUGGESTED FURTHER READING

Original sources

Søren Kierkegaard, *Concluding Unscientific Postscript*
Søren Kierkegaard, *Fear and Trembling*
Jean-Paul Sartre, *Being and Nothingness*
Jean-Paul Sartre, *Existentialism and Humanism*
Albert Camus, *The Myth of Sisyphus*

Commentary

Patrick Gardiner, *Kierkegaard: a very short introduction*
John Lippitt, *Kierkegaard and Fear and Trembling*
Christina Howells ed. *The Cambridge Companion to Sartre*

Contemporary discussion

Julian Young, *The Death of God and the Meaning of Life*, Chapters 9–11
Thomas Nagel, *Mortal Questions*, Chapter 2

6

KANTIANISM

Up to this point we have been thinking of the idea of the good life as the life it would be most desirable for a human being to lead. But it is time now to consider an important distinction that may be made between two senses of the expression 'the good life'. In one sense 'the good life' means the most desirable or happiest life. In another it means the worthiest or most virtuous human life.

VIRTUE AND HAPPINESS: 'FARING WELL' AND 'DOING RIGHT'

This is a distinction that plays no significant part in Greek philosophical thinking. It came to real prominence first in eighteenth-century Europe. Although it is only then that we can see the distinction self-consciously drawn, it is arguable that its origin is to be found much earlier with the emergence of Christianity. For one of the innovations of the Christian religion is the idea that the poor and the meek can be blessed, and, conversely (in the words of St Mark's Gospel), that even gaining possession of the whole world is not really profitable if we lose our souls in the process. As we shall see in a later chapter, these Christian ideas if they are to be discussed properly have to be examined within the larger context of religious conceptions of the good life. But there can be little doubt that they have had a large part to play in the formation of common moral ideas and in particular the widespread acceptance of the distinction that provides the focal point of this chapter.

98

This distinction may be marked in a number of ways. One way is to contrast 'faring well' with 'doing right'. It is a commonplace that even the most unprincipled men and women who never do right can fare well enough. Indeed, since at least the days of the Hebrew Psalmists people have been perplexed by the fact that it is often the wicked who prosper. Moral wrongdoing, it seems, is no bar to material success. Conversely, it is proverbial that the good (often) die young, so that doing right is no guarantee of faring well. In short the two senses of a good life easily and frequently part company.

Now the ancient Greek thinkers, though they did not formulate this distinction expressly, were aware of these familiar facts about happiness and virtue. In much of the philosophical writing that survives from that period, we can see attempts to accommodate such facts. Aristotle, it is true, is quite uncompromising in his belief that to be deprived of the social and material benefits of this life is to be deprived of a good life. But Plato sometimes advances the idea that such benefits are not the benefits that matter. In fact we can see this idea at work in some of the arguments we have considered already. When Socrates argues with Thrasymachus and Callicles, he several times suggests that those who get their own way and triumph over others only *seem* to get the best of it. In reality, he claims, they do almost irreparable damage to their own most fundamental interests – the good of their own souls. Accordingly, Socrates argues that, faced with a choice between doing and suffering evil, those most interested in their own true welfare will choose to suffer rather than to commit evil.

The contrast between material profitability and spiritual loss is made explicitly in the New Testament. 'What shall it profit a man' Jesus asks 'if he gain the whole world and lose his own soul?' (Mark 8:36). Often this utterance is used by Christians for purely rhetorical purposes. It is offered not as a challenging thesis so much as a reminder of something we all know, namely that 'Man does not live by bread alone', to use another biblical saying (Deuteronomy 8:6 and Matthew 4:4). But we lose the force of what Jesus is saying if we regard it merely as a pious sentiment which everyone in their less worldly moments will agree with. What we need to ask is just what contrast is at work in the question and just what is meant by 'the soul' here.

This is specially important because for many people (even if it is not always thought nice to admit it) the answer to the New Testament question is obvious: 'His profit is the whole world, and how much more could he want?'. It is this response and its implications which are explored in the famous story of Dr Faustus, the man who gave his soul to Satan in return for unlimited material wealth and power.

The story of Dr Faustus is based, probably, on a real sixteenth-century German magician Johannes Faust. However, the legend which grew up about this man is much more important than the man himself. According to the legend, Faust entered into a pact with the devil who promised, in return for his soul at death, to give him knowledge and magical power far surpassing that which human beings can normally attain and by which he might accomplish all his worldly desires. To ensure that both parts of the bargain were kept Satan sends one of his more devious servants, Mephistopheles. He it is who conveys the knowledge and power and is the instrument of Faust's death.

The original legend of Faust received much more sophisticated treatment at the hands of the English dramatist Christopher Marlowe in his famous play *The Tragical Life and Death of Dr Faustus*, and in the German poet Goethe's poem *Faust*. What is important about this story in all its versions is the distinction it forces us to make between the two senses of 'the good life'. If we are to find convincing reasons by which to persuade ourselves and others that Faustus has the worst of the bargain, we cannot appeal to his failure to achieve the good things that life has to offer. That is precisely what Satan guaranteed to supply. So the good that he loses out on, and the evil he brings upon himself, must be of a quite different order. There must be a difference in kind and not merely degree between the sorts of good and evil that are brought into question by the case of Faustus. This means that we must elaborate a distinction between senses of the expression 'a good life'.

In doing this we might appeal to the rewards and punishments of an afterlife, as generations of human beings have done. Indeed the story itself encourages us to do this. Such an appeal raises two distinct questions. First, is there an afterlife? And secondly, if there is, do its rewards outweigh everything in this life? Both of these topics will be left to the final chapter, though here we might observe that it is the second question which is the more important for a philosophy of the good life. For the moment, if we stick to this world, and if we construe Faustus's loss as contemporaneous rather than in the future, we need to show, first that the *materially* best life (which he undoubtedly enjoys) is not the *morally* best life, and secondly that there is more to commend morality.

In other words, any adequate reply to the challenge represented by the story of Faustus which aims to show that he makes a mistake must draw upon the distinction between material and moral goodness, between how we fare and how we behave, between a *having* good life and *leading* a good life. We should notice, however, that it is not enough to respond to Faust and those who think like him merely by drawing the distinction. We also have to show why one sort of good life – doing right – is preferable to the other – faring well. This means, as Plato saw, showing why, faced with the choice, we should prefer to suffer materially rather than do evil.

KANT AND 'THE GOOD WILL'

This is in fact the task which the eighteenth-century German philosopher Immanuel Kant (1724–1804) set for himself. Kant was one of the greatest moral philosophers of all time. He developed and refined the very idea of 'the moral life' precisely to provide rational answers to these problems. Kant's most celebrated work in moral philosophy is entitled *The Groundwork to the Metaphysics of Morals*. As this title suggests, Kant aimed to lay out the fundamental, rational character of moral thought and action. He begins the book with an argument similar to that we found Socrates using against Callicles, the argument that material benefits and personal talents may be used well or badly and hence cannot constitute the fundamental principle of good and evil.

> Nothing in the world – indeed nothing even beyond the world – can possibly be conceived which could be called good without qualification except a good will. Intelligence, wit, judgement, and the other talents of the mind, however they may be named, or courage, resoluteness, and perseverance as qualities of temperament, are doubtless in many respects good and desirable. But they can become extremely bad and harmful if the will, which is to make use of these gifts of nature and which in its special constitution is called character, is not good. Power, riches, honour, even health, general well-being,

and the contentment with one's condition which is called happiness, make for pride and even arrogance if there is not a good will to correct their influence on the mind and on its principles of action so as to make it universally conformable to its end. It need hardly be mentioned that the sight of a being adorned with no feature of a pure and good will, yet enjoying uninterrupted prosperity [i.e. anyone like Faust] can never give pleasure to a rational impartial observer. Thus the good will seems to constitute the indispensable condition even of worthiness to be happy.

(Kant 1785, 1959: 9)

Kant's point is this: however wealthy or talented we may be, such benefits can be abused. Great wealth can deliberately be squandered on useless trivia, or used to corrupt and belittle others. Criminals and terrorists sometimes show a great talent for electronics, money laundering or strategic planning. Kant sees that, unless we are prepared to say that even in this sort of case these good things are unqualifiedly good, we must look elsewhere for the most basic standard of good and bad, right and wrong.

If material goods and natural talents cannot be the fundamental standard, what can it be? The examples just given of the abuse of good things might incline us to think that what is important is the purpose to which wealth and talent are put. But according to Kant this cannot be so because, however carefully we plan our actions, it is impossible to guarantee their outcome (The Scottish poet Robert Burns expresses the same thought in a famous line 'The best laid schemes of mice and men, gang aft agley', i.e. go oft astray). If, Kant says, we have a good will or intention in what we try to do, but 'by a particularly unfortunate fate or the niggardly provision of a step-motherly nature' we are unable to accomplish the end in view, the good will that we had would still 'sparkle as a jewel in its own right, as something that had full worth in itself' (Kant 1785, 1959: 10).

An example may serve to make the general point. Suppose someone works for an international charity, collecting money and organizing supplies of medicines for refugee camps. In the wake of a great disaster, she makes a Herculean effort and manages to fund and to dispatch a massive quantity of much needed medicine. But through no fault of hers, the storage facilities fail, the medicines become contaminated. Unfortunately they are nonetheless administered in ignorance of their poor condition, and the result is that the death rate in the camps rises to a level far higher than it would have done if no medicines at all had been sent. This is of course a great tragedy. But even should the charity worker *feel* guilty, she would not actually *be* responsible for this terrible outcome. The real fault must be laid at the door of 'a particularly unfortunate fate or the niggardly provision of a step-motherly nature', and her efforts towards an end that failed to materialize, would 'still sparkle as a jewel ... that had full worth in itself'.

Kant would make the same point with respect to the reverse kind of case. Suppose I see someone I regard as my enemy crossing a lonely road on a wild night when I am driving home, and try to run him down. As luck would have it, the sound of my sudden acceleration alerts him to a falling tree and he leaps into the ditch just in time to avoid being crushed beneath it. By this curious route, my evil intention has saved his life. Nevertheless, this good outcome mitigates none of the wickedness of my action.

Intention and outcome, then, need to be separated, with the result that it does not appear to be *successful* action that matters ultimately. This is because, in the first example, the unfortunate consequences did nothing to sully the fine nature of the intention, and in the second example, the beneficial results did nothing to alter its evil character. Thus it seems to be the intention behind an action (what Kant calls 'will'), rather than the success or failure of that action, that is all important.

About intention and will, however, more needs to be said, because intentions can themselves have differing motives behind them. The charity worker whose case was considered a moment ago can fail to bring about her good intentions and remain (so to speak) morally unscathed. But if we were to discover that her reason for attempting the relief work in the first place had nothing to do with the welfare of those involved but was rather a way of trying to win personal fame and glory, this would seriously undermine the moral merit in what she was doing. The same point is illustrated by the real case of bounty hunters in the American Wild West. These were people who aimed to do a good thing – bring violent and vicious criminals to justice. But often they themselves cared nothing for justice. They did what they did partly for monetary reward and partly because they enjoyed hunting down human beings. Such motives, on Kant's and on most people's view, completely destroys the moral worth of their actions.

But much more contentiously Kant also thinks that motivations of which we approve do not themselves carry moral worth. He says:

> There are ... many persons so sympathetically constituted that without any motive of vanity or selfishness they find an inner satisfaction in spreading joy, and rejoice in the contentment of others which they have made possible. But I say that, however dutiful and aimiable it may be, that kind of action has no true moral worth.
>
> (Kant 1785, 1959: 14)

This is because it arises from *inclination*. Kant does not think, as some people have supposed him to, that you ought never to enjoy doing good. He does think, however, that there is an important difference between the actions of someone who spontaneously and with pleasure does what is right and the same actions on the part of someone who performs them, with difficulty perhaps, but solely *because* it is right. He invites us to consider the case of someone whose life has been easy and happy and who takes a great interest in others and attends to the needs of those in distress. Suddenly his life is clouded by some great personal sorrow. He finds that he can take no interest in the affairs of other people and is constantly overwhelmed by self-concern, though he still has the means to alleviate distress and the need to do so is as strong as ever.

> Now suppose him to tear himself, unsolicited by inclination, out of this dead insensibility and to perform this action only from duty and without any inclination – then for the first time his action has genuine moral worth.
>
> (Kant 1785, 1959: 14)

The reason Kant thinks that true moral merit and demerit attaches to actions regardless of the feelings of those who perform them lies in his belief that 'inclination cannot be commanded' whereas action can. Since people can only be praised or blamed where they can be held responsible, praise and blame can only attach to action, not to feelings. You cannot make yourself glad to see someone, but you can nonetheless *welcome* them. You cannot help taking pleasure in the failures of people you dislike (what in German is called *Schadenfreude*), but you can, despite your feelings, act in a sympathetic way towards them. It follows, on Kant's view, that it is action not feeling that determines moral worth.

We must combine this conclusion with the earlier contention that success is not morally important either. What matters fundamentally is that people should aim to do what is right because it is right. Whether or not their natural inclinations support or oppose this, and whether their good intentions come off or not are both irrelevant; the first because we cannot command our feelings, and the second because we cannot completely control the world about us. The only thing wholly within our control, and hence the only thing for which we can be praised or blamed from a moral point of view, is the *will*. This is why Kant says that it is only a good will that can be unqualifiedly good, and that the unqualifiedly good will is doing your duty for duty's sake.

Suppose we agree with this (for the moment at any rate). There remains this important question. If the only unqualifiedly good thing is a good will, and if the good will is not good because of what it results in, how are we to determine or demonstrate its goodness? In what does its goodness *itself* consist? Kant's answer is that the good will is a purely rational will. To see what he means by this, however, needs a good deal of explanation.

DAVID HUME AND PRACTICAL REASON

Philosophers have often elaborated a distinction between theoretical reason and practical reason. The distinction they have in mind is that between reasoning which is directed at telling you what to think or believe, and reasoning that is directed at telling you what to do. In fact, however, the distinction is rather hard to draw; even the way I have just put it is open to objection since it is quite correct to speak of beliefs about what to do. But that there is some difference or other is fairly plain, because generally speaking a piece of theoretical reason, by which we mean appeal to evidence and argument, ends with a conclusion about what is the case – for example, 'Smoking is a contributory cause of lung diseases'. Practical reason on the other hand, which also consists in a review of evidence and arguments, ends with a conclusion about what ought to be done – for example, 'You ought to take a course in accountancy before you leave college'.

Some philosophers have thought that the difference between theoretical and practical reason is this: practical reason requires some desire or other on the part of the reasoner before the reasoning has any force. To see why they have thought this we need only take the example offered a moment ago. Imagine an argument designed to convince you that you should take a course in accountancy before you leave college. It might run like this:

> The best paid jobs for graduates at the present time are to be found in the financial and commercial sectors. Employers don't want to recruit people who think they already know all about business. But at the same time, they want people who are not totally unfamiliar with business practice, and who can show that the intellectual abilities they have in history or philosophy will show themselves in ways beneficial to the company. So to have a course or two in accountancy is to make yourself a more attractive prospect in the job market than either a business graduate or a pure arts graduate.

As an argument, this has no doubt proved persuasive to many, but it is obvious that its strength is a function of two things. First, the facts it alleges about jobs in the finance sector and about company recruiters must be true. Second, the person addressed must want a well-paid job. If either of these conditions does not hold the argument loses its force. So, for instance, if the person I address this argument to has a private income and is thus not in search of a job at all, the conclusion 'You ought to take a course in accounting' doesn't apply.

In this respect the second example differs markedly from the first. If evidence and argument is mounted which shows that smoking contributes to lung disease, only the facts alleged need be true for the conclusion to follow and for me to be obliged to accept it. What I want or do not want does not come into the matter. Of course, people sometimes allow their desires to blind them to the truth, but the point is that when this happens their belief is irrational, contrary to reason. In the case of practical reason, on the other hand, your desire determines the applicability of the argument.

One way of putting this is to say that practical reason is hypothetical. That is, it takes the form 'If you want such and such, then you ought to do so and so'. If on the other hand you don't want such and such, nothing follows about what you ought to do. This means that practical reason, at least so far as the example we have been discussing goes, is not a very forceful guide to conduct, since we can escape its demands by abandoning or modifying our desires.

Some philosophers have in fact claimed that all practical reason is hypothetical and dependent upon desire in this way. The Scottish philosopher David Hume (1711–1776), who was mentioned briefly in a previous chapter, held this view. In a famous passage of his *A Treatise of Human Nature* he claims that 'Reason is, and ought only to be the slave of the passions, and can never pretend to any other office than to serve and obey them' (Hume 1739, 1967: 415). By this he means that the use of reason can only be practical in so far as it points the means to ends that we independently desire.

This view of Hume's has what some people regard as a curious consequence, namely that we cannot reason about desires and cannot therefore declare any desire to be irrational. Hume in fact accepts this.

'Tis not contrary to reason (he says) to prefer the destruction of the whole world to the scratching of my finger. 'Tis not contrary to reason for me to chuse my total ruin, to prevent the least uneasiness of an Indian or person wholly unknown to me. 'Tis as little contrary to reason to prefer even my own acknowledg'd lesser good to my greater, and have a more ardent affection for the former than the latter.

(Hume 1739, 1967: 416)

We need to be very clear about what Hume is saying here. He is not commending any of the attitudes that he describes. All three are abnormal, and may even be said to be unreasonable, if by reasonable we just mean 'what ordinary people would accept as sensible'. No doubt if we were to come across someone who thought so much of himself that he really did express a preference to see the whole world destroyed rather than have a scratch on his little finger, we would be appalled at his attitude. Similarly, anyone who sincerely preferred to go through agonies, rather than have someone quite unknown to him suffer the mildest discomfort, would no doubt be treated as odd to the point of madness. And those who are self-destructive, that is, those who seem positively to seek the things that harm them and belittle what is in their best interests are generally recognized as psychologically problematic. But none of these attitudes, according to Hume, is strictly irrational, since no intellectual error of any kind is being made. There is no fact of the matter, or mathematical-type calculation, or logically provable inference about which the person in question is mistaken. The difference between normality and abnormality lies entirely in the uncommon character of the desires these people have.

If this is true, it is clear that no appeal to reason could produce a conclusive ground for action because all such appeals come into play only in a subservient role to desire, and consequently Reason in the abstract is silent upon practical matters. This means that general principles like 'You ought not to murder' must sooner or later depend upon some desire or other, the desire not to rob others of their most valued possession (life), or the desire not to cause anguish and suffering to friends and relatives. But what if someone does *not* have any such desires? What if they are complete nihilists in the sense that they care for nothing? Does this mean that the principle does not apply to *them*? And is there here the further implication that the principle would cease to apply to me also, if only I could induce in myself a state of mind in which I too no longer cared about the lives and feelings of others?

On the face of it, this seems quite unacceptable. Most people would say of those who are callously indifferent to the feelings of others, not that they are free from obligations because they don't care, but that they *ought* to care? Yet if Hume is right, there is no further rational basis upon which this 'ought' is to be based. They don't care and 'tis not contrary to reason' that they do not. If Hume is right, how could feelings and desires be made subject to reason? You either have them or you don't.

HYPOTHETICAL AND CATEGORICAL IMPERATIVES

It was this question of practical rationality that caused Kant to try to provide an alternative account of practical reason to Hume's, although he does not expressly discuss Hume in the *Groundwork*. If we think of the conclusions of practical reason as imperatives (directives about what to do), these come, Kant argues, not in a single type, but in two different types. First of all there are those that Hume rightly identifies as hypothetical, which is to say, imperatives whose force depends on our having the appropriate desire. This can be seen from the following imaginary dialogue.

'If you want to run in the London marathon, you ought to start training,' (Hypothetical imperative).
'But I don't want to run in the London marathon.'
'Well in that case, you've no reason to start training.'

Hypothetical imperatives themselves fall into two kinds. This is an example of what Kant calls 'technical' imperatives, instructions that point to the technical means to chosen ends. Then there are assertoric imperatives. These imperatives also rest upon a desire, but not a desire that someone *happens* to have. Assertoric imperatives appeal to desires that human beings tend naturally to share – health and happiness, for example. Just because these are widely shared, their existence is usually assumed, and in the normal run of things this gives rise to the appearance of assertoric imperatives carrying more general force than hypothetical imperatives do. But despite this appearance, assertoric imperatives are not universally binding. For example the assertoric imperative 'You ought to give up smoking because it is ruining your health' is normally treated as a knock-down argument (assuming there really is a causal connection between smoking and ill-health). But in fact someone could reply 'I have no desire to be healthy', and though such a sentiment is highly unusual, when true, it is enough to dispel the force of the assertoric imperative. In cases like this the value we had reasonably supposed to be common to us – good health – is not in fact shared, and the recommendation to action fails to apply just as much as in the case of a technical imperative.

In contrast to both kinds of hypothetical, there are categorical imperatives. These have the very special property of resting upon no hypothetical condition whatever, and hence cannot be rejected by denying any conditional desire. It is imperatives of this sort that are supposed to block the move that Hume's account of practical reason leaves open.

'You ought to visit your neighbour in hospital, because you promised to.'
'But I don't want to.'

'Whether you want to or not, you ought to keep your promises.' (Categorical imperative).

With the discovery of categorical imperatives, Kant thought, we have reached the heart of morality. Categorical imperatives transcend our wants and desires by presenting us with rational principles of action in the light of which those desires themselves are to be assessed. Philosophers usually express this by saying that such principles of conduct are overriding, that is, they take precedence over other sorts of consideration when we are deciding what to do.

In fact this idea of overriding principles of conduct fits rather well with a view that many people have about morality, namely that it is a more important dimension to human behaviour than any other. If we show that some proposal is likely to be unprofitable, or unpopular, we are providing reasons against it, but not overriding reasons, because considerations of profit and mere popularity (or so it is commonly thought) should not take precedence over what is morally required of us. The profit motive is a rational one to have, but it must take second place to honesty. Making people laugh is a good thing, but not when it involves telling slanderous lies about others. In short, moral uprightness requires us to give second place to popularity, profitablility, convenience and all other sorts of personal advantage.

This common belief about the overriding character of moral considerations is what makes Kant's conception of *categorical* imperatives appealing. Or at least it does so, if there are such things. So far, in fact, we have simply drawn a contrast between two basic types of imperative (the technical and the assertoric are fundamentally the same). As yet, we have no clear indication as to how categorical imperatives are grounded in reason.

Now there is a real difficulty about this just because it is so easy to see that hypothetical imperatives are grounded in reason *precisely in virtue of their being hypothetical*. 'If you want credit for this course, you must sit the exam.' If you *do* want credit, you can test the rational basis of this recommmendation by checking the rules to see if it is true that credit is obtainable only by sitting the exam (and not by submitting an essay for example). The rationality of the recommendation is simply a function of its truth. Or again 'If you want clear skin, you ought to use perfume-free soap'. If you *do* want clear skin, it is open to you to test the truth of this recommendation by examining the effects of soap with and without perfume.

But in the case of a categorical imperative, there does not seem to be any truth to check. 'You ought not to steal, if you don't want to end up in jail' can be checked by looking into facts about detection and conviction rates. But what facts can we look into to check the categorical 'You ought not to steal'? Actually, it is no part of Kant's strategy to appeal to any realist moral 'facts'. Rather, he thinks that we can check the rationality of categorical imperatives by examining them in the light of what he calls 'pure practical reason'. Kant calls it *pure* practical reason because on his view it involves no appeal to matters of empirical fact or sensory experience but to principles of intellectual reasoning alone.

PURE PRACTICAL REASON AND
THE MORAL LAW

Imagine a world of perfectly rational beings (for brevity's sake let us call them 'angels'). To say that such beings are perfectly rational is to say that they always *do* what we, being less than perfect, always *ought to do*. Kant expresses this by saying that what is *objective law* for angels (demonstrably the right thing to do) is also *subjectively necessary* for them (just what by nature angels are inclined to do). This is not true for us. What is objectively right is usually experienced by us as a constraint on action, something we ought to do, because our natural inclinations often lie in other directions. By contrast, for a perfectly rational creature there is no sense of constraint, no sense of being bound or required, and from this we can see that in a world of angels the laws of rationality would be like the laws of nature are in this one. We could explain and predict the behaviour of the angels by appealing to moral laws, laws of right and wrong, just in the way that we can explain and predict the behaviour of liquids, gases and solids by appealing to the laws of physics. Angels do what is morally right as automatically as water runs downhill.

Now this supplies us, in fact, with a way of determining what the moral law is. Suppose I propose to perform an action for a reason (what Kant calls a maxim). I can now ask myself 'Could acting on that maxim be a law of nature in a world of perfect beings?' If it could not, I have shown that the proposed action is not in accordance with pure practical reason and therefore not morally right. Consequently it is contrary to a rational will to perform the proposed action for the reason given.

This is a formal statement of the principle, of course, abstracted from any particular case. Kant offers us four examples of the detailed application of his method of pure practical reason.

1 A man who has suffered a great deal and anticipates even more suffering before his life is over, wonders whether it would not be better if he took his own life. But he asks himself what his reason would be, and whether he could consistently will that people always act on this reason. His reason is that life holds out a greater likelihood of bad than good for him, and so the maxim under examination is this: 'Whenever the future promises more bad than good, kill yourself'. But immediately he sees (Kant argues) that this could not be a law of nature because it is precisely the fact of the future's looking bleak that provides us with a reason to work for its improvement. It is precisely because we have no food in the house (for example) that we have a reason to go out and get some. A world in which the would-be suicide's maxim held as a law of nature, would pretty soon destroy itself because everything that supplies good reason to work for the continuation of life would lead people to kill themselves. From this it follows, Kant thinks, that suicide is against the moral law.

2 A man is in debt. He has the opportunity to borrow money with a promise to repay, but knows that in fact he will never be able to repay it. He is nonetheless tempted to make the promise, a lying promise, but asks himself whether this would be morally right. Once again the categorical imperative is appealed to, and he sees that, were it to be a law of nature that those in dire financial circumstances always made lying promises, this would lead immediately to the collapse of the institution of promising since lenders would know that the money would not be repaid and would refuse to lend. It follows that lying promises are contrary to the moral law.

3 A man has a natural talent for something, but an inclination to idleness tempts him to ignore it and hence fail to improve it. He asks him-

self whether there is anything morally wrong in this. And immediately he sees, or so Kant claims, that though a world of essentially idle and pleasure seeking people is possible, it is impossible to will that such a world exist, since any rational creature will want to keep open the opportunities which different kinds of talent provide.

4   A prosperous man sees many others around him in poverty and hardship but says 'What concern is that of mine? I have no desire to contribute to the welfare of the needy. And, should I fall on hard times, I have no intention of calling upon others myself.' It is possible, Kant says, to imagine a world in which everyone takes that attitude, but it is impossible to will that, through your will, such a world come into existence. For then you would have robbed yourself of the help and sympathy of others which you are likely to want when times get hard.

These examples are meant only as illustrations of a general thesis about morality and it is to that thesis we must return. But it is worth remarking that most philosophers share John Stuart Mill's estimation of Kant's attempt to apply pure practical reason to particular examples – 'when he begins to deduce from his precept any of the actual duties of morality, he fails, almost grotesquely, to show that there would be any contradiction' (Mill 1871, 1998: 51–2). None of the examples is convincing. Take the last. It depends upon the hardhearted man wanting precisely what he says he does not mean to claim – the help of others should he himself fall upon hard times. It is certainly open to Kant to doubt that anyone would continue to hold this view once hard times were actually upon him. But if so, this is a result of the very human nature that Kant thinks has no part in pure practical reason, and does not show that the principle 'Offer and ask no help' cannot be consistently maintained, even if, as a matter of fact, it is not likely to be consistently maintained by those who hold it. It seems that Kant is conflating logical impossibility and psychological improbability.

Or consider the first example. This is supposed to show that suicide is impossible for a rational being. But it does nothing of the kind. We can consistently maintain that it is rational to commit suicide when circumstances are *very* adverse without thereby agreeing that suicide is justified in the face of any adversity whatever. It is only by equating the two that Kant's conclusion follows.

UNIVERSALIZABILITY

Still, if Kant does the job of illustration badly, this does not necessarily mean that the basic philosophy at work is unsound. What is important is whether the method he proposes for deciding what morality requires of us is satisfactory. That method consists of applying a test to every reasoned action, a test that has subsequently become known in moral philosophy as 'universalizability'. This is the procedure of seeing whether your own reasons for action could apply to everyone equally or whether they amount to nothing better than special pleading in your own case.

There are many sophisticated twists and turns that can be given to the philosophical elaboration of this test, but in fact it is not far in spirit from what is a common enough way of thinking. When some action is proposed people often ask of themselves and others – 'What if everyone did that?'. This is thought to be an important objection, but it is open to two different interpretations. Sometimes the idea is that the consequences of everyone's doing the action in question is highly *undesirable*. For example, I might object to your walking on the grass on the grounds that if everyone did so, the cumulative result would soon be no lawn. However, an alternative interpretation of the 'What if everyone did that?' objection draws attention to the fact that there are some actions which it would be *impossible* for everyone to perform, with the result that any attempt to justify performing them must involve some special pleading on the part of the individual. For example, the advantage of cheating depends upon its being the case that most people don't cheat, so any attempt to justify *my* cheating must involve special pleading.

It is in this second test of universalizability that Kant is interested, and he gives it its first formal elaboration. It is important to see, however, that in contrast to the first interpretation, he is not speculating upon what the general run of humanity would do, but rather what we could consistently will to be the behaviour of all humanity. We are not asking 'What *will* everyone do?' but 'What if everyone *were* to do it?', knowing of course that everyone will not. The test is about consistency not consequences.

Kant's illustrations offer us a number of categorical imperatives – you ought not to commit suicide, you ought not to make lying promises, you ought to develop such talents as you have, and so on – but Kant argues that these can all be derived from one basic imperative from which all the laws of moral conduct can be derived. It is this: 'I should never act in such a way that I could not also will that my maxim should be universal law' (Kant 1785, 1959: 18). What he means is this. If you want to know whether what you propose to do is morally right or not, ask yourself whether you can consistently will that everyone whenever they have the same reason as you do, should act in that way. Or to put it in philosophers' jargon, ask yourself if you can consistently universalize the maxim of your action.

Kant goes on, with an ever increasing degree of abstraction, to formulate two other versions of the categorical imperative. His argument is complex and the resulting claim is that the fundamental moral law is one which requires from us 'respect for persons'. He formulates this version thus: 'Act so that you treat humanity, whether in your own person or that of another always as an end and never as a means only' (Kant 1785, 1959: 47).

This formulation has become known as the ideal of 'respect for persons'. It has been more influential in Western moral philosophy than any other ethical idea, perhaps, and to understand it properly a great deal needs to be said about it. But it is not necessary here either to trace all the steps by which Kant reaches this ideal or to explore the ideal itself more closely. For what we want to know is not whether 'respect for persons' is a good moral principle, but whether the conception of the moral life in which it is one element is a conception that we have good reason to accept. And enough has been said about Kant's philosophy to allow us to summarize and examine this conception. First the summary.

SUMMARY OF KANT'S PHILOSOPHY

When we ask questions about 'the good life' there is built into them an ambiguity. We can mean 'the happiest life' or we can mean 'the worthiest life'. It is the latter that is more important since the best a human being can hope for is to be worthy of happiness, and to attain such worthiness is to lead a moral life. This does not consist in doing good, however, because whether the good we try to do actually comes about is not a matter over which, ultimately, we can exercise control. Between aspiration and reality misfortune may well intervene. Neither does the moral life consist in having the right sort of attitudes. Whether we are cheerful, friendly, generous and optimistic, or solemn, withdrawn, thrifty and pessimistic is a matter of the nature with which we are born, and hence also something over which we can exercise little control. Consequently our temper, good or bad, is not something which can properly attract either praise or blame.

What can properly be examined from a moral point of view is our will, the intention behind the things we do and say, because this is wholly within our control as rational agents. Be we rich or poor, clever or stupid, handsome or ugly, jolly or sad, everyone of us can aim to do what is right just because it is right, and if we succeed in this we succeed in living a morally good life.

But how do we know what is right? We know it by considering what actions are categorically forbidden or required, not because of their consequences or outcome in any particular case, but on grounds of pure reason alone. These are all those actions which match up to the test of the most fundamental categorical imperative of universalizability and respect for persons.

Kant's moral philosophy has generated a huge quantity of comment, interpretation and criticism. A great deal of this has served to show that there are complexities in his thought of which even he was not wholly aware. Moreover, however impressive his attempt to delineate a clear conception of morality pure and simple and to give it a firm foundation in reason, it is widely agreed that Kant's philosophy fails. Some of the reasons for this failure lie in quite technical philosophical issues which are difficult to explain briefly or simply. But the larger part of the failure arises from features of Kant's conception of the moral life whose unattractiveness or inadequacy can be shown without too much complexity. There are in fact three main objections. These have to do with the separation of intention and outcome, the test of universalizability, and the idea of doing one's duty for its own sake. We will consider each of these in turn.

ACT, INTENTION AND OUTCOME

Kant holds that the moral worth of an action must reside in the will with which it is performed, or as we would more naturally say, in the intention behind it. This is, as we have seen, because people cannot be held responsible for nor can they claim the merit of outcomes over which they have very imperfect control. It is both pointless and wrong to praise and blame people for things that they could neither prevent nor bring about. 'An unfortunate fate' or a 'step-motherly nature' may bring our best intentions to nothing. It is to our intentions, then, that praise and blame must be attached.

Many people find this an intuitively appealing idea, and yet it is hard to see that it can be sustained for long. We may want to confine moral merit and demerit to the intentions behind an action, but it is very difficult to deny that actions and their consequences must also be taken into account. *Intending* to murder someone is wrong, presumably, at least in part because actually murdering them would be wrong, and whether I actually murder them is a matter of consequences. If I am to murder someone, it is not enough for me to pull a trigger or plunge a knife. My victim must actually die as a consequence of what I do. Similarly, intending to save someone from drowning is meritorious, presumably because the action of saving them is, and once more this is partly a matter of the actual consequences of my intention. It is not enough for me to have reached for their hand, or pulled them aboard; they must go on living as a result. If, then, we are to concern ourselves with the moral character of intention, we are at the same time obliged to take actions into account and cannot take as indifferent an attitude to success as Kant's way of thinking would suggest.

Someone might deny this, deny in other words that actions are morally important. They might claim that what matters from a moral point of view is not what we *do* but what we *try* to do. This is indeed a common thought. Many people think that moral right and wrong is not about accomplishing things or being successful but about trying hard and doing your best. 'At least you tried' is often offered as moral compensation for failure. ('It's the thought that counts' expresses the same sentiment.) But though the belief that trying is more important than succeeding is quite widely shared, at least one important objection can be brought against it. This objection arises from the fact that genuine attempts and intentions have to be *expressed in* actions. Trying to do something is not the same as doing it, certainly, but it is still the performance of some action or other. I cannot be accused of trying to murder you unless I have succeeded in some action or other – holding up a gun, firing it, waving a knife, putting a poisonous substance in your food. If none of these actions or others like them take place, there is no substance to the claim that

I tried to murder you. And this means that *some* consequential actions must take place if we are to talk even of the moral assessment of attempts.

Similarly, I cannot claim to have tried to save a drowning child unless I have succeeded in doing something else – reaching out my hand, running for a life belt, pulling at his body. Were you to see me sitting perfectly still and accuse me of callous indifference to his plight, it would hardly do for me to reply that I had tried to save him but that an 'unfortunate fate' or a 'stepmother nature' had intervened in every one of my attempts and robbed my good intentions of any result whatsoever. I cannot reasonably say that I have attempted to do something, if absolutely none of my attempts have met with any success of any kind.

The upshot of this argument is really very simple. If we are to make a moral assessment of the lives of ourselves and others, we have to decide not only whether what we *meant to do* was right or wrong, but also whether what we *did* was right or wrong. Since doing anything whatever involves having *some* effect on the world, however small, this moral assessment cannot but be in part concerned with the success of our intentions. This means that success cannot be left out of the calculation in the way that Kant suggests. It is not enough, in short, simply to have a good will. A good will that accomplishes nothing whatever cannot 'shine like a jewel'.

THE UNIVERSALIZABILITY TEST

Of course, none of this shows that will and intention are not of great moral importance. Nor does it show that intentions do not matter. It is still the case that people who mean well, but whose good intentions do not come off for reasons quite independent of their actions, deserve moral commendation. From this it follows that at least some moral assessment is based upon considerations other than success.

It is here that Kant's most widely discussed contribution to moral philosophy comes into play, namely his formulations of the categorical imperative. Kant claims to offer us a test by which our actions and intentions can be assessed, a test quite independent of desired or actual outcomes. This is the test of universalizability. According to Kant we have to ask ourselves whether an action we propose to perform could consistently be performed by every-one similarly placed and with the same reasons. And, he argues, such a test plainly rules out many of the sorts of actions the moral consensus of his day condemned – suicide, lying promises, failure to develop one's own talents. We saw, however, that Kant's own illustrations of this principle are far from con-vincing. The fact that they do not work very well is not in itself conclusive proof that the test is a poor one, because it might be made to work better than Kant himself manages to do. But when we try to apply it more rigor-ously it turns out, in fact, that the test is *too easily* satisfied.

In the previous chapter we saw that the existentialist's 'ethics of authen-ticity' – the idea that good actions are made good by the sincerity with which they are performed – has difficulty in accommodating the case of 'the sincere Nazi'. This is the person who engages *sincerely* in behaviour widely recognized to be evil. Our intuitions suggest that this sincerity, far from making those actions good or even better than similar actions per-formed in *bad* faith, actually makes them worse. Indeed it is arguable that bad actions become truly evil when they are freely, deliberately and sin-cerely performed.

A similar objection to the Kantian ethics of intention can be found in what we might call 'the *consistent* Nazi'. Let us characterize Nazis as peo-ple who act on the maxim 'This person should be exterminated because he/she is a Jew'. Now according to Kant's moral philosophy we can put this maxim to the test by appealing to the categorical imperative – 'Act only according to that maxim by which you can at the same time will that it should become a universal law' – and we might point out to Nazis that if it were a universal law of nature that Jews were regularly exterminated, then if they themselves were Jewish, they would have to be exterminated. Now as a matter of fact it was not unknown for enthusiastic Nazis to be found to have Jewish ancestry, and if such people were to engage in some special pleading, some argument which made theirs a special case, we could indeed accuse them of failing to judge in accordance with the categor-ical imperative. We could show, in other words, that the maxim 'This person should be exterminated because he/she is a Jew' was not being universalized.

But if these people were *consistent* Nazis, who not only conceded but positively endorsed the idea that were they to be found to be Jewish they too must perish, we could not find fault with them on these grounds. To be prepared to promote political ideals that taken to their logical conclusion imply your own destruction may be a *psychologically unlikely* attitude of mind for most people. But it is certainly *logically possible* and displays consistency. However, if a policy of genocide is deeply mistaken from a moral (as well as every other) point of view, consistency in its application is hardly any improvement. And in so far as people are prepared to sacrifice *themselves* in a programme of genocide, this reveals not their moral rectitude but their fanaticism.

The same point can be made about one of Kant's own examples. Recall the man who prided himself on his independence and neither gave nor asked for charity. Kant says that such a man could hardly will that were he himself to fall on hard times it should nonetheless be a universal law of nature that no one assist him in his poverty. Now it may be psychologically unlikely that an individual in need could wish to receive no assistance (though surely we are familiar with people who are too proud to receive charity), but it is plainly not a logical contradiction. The opponents of charity can as easily apply their harsh doctrine to themselves as to others if they choose. Whilst we may remark upon their rather grim, almost inhuman, consistency, this does not make their action any better, because it does not make them any the less uncharitable. Once more, consistency does not seem to bring objectionable actions any nearer to what we recognise as moral right and wrong.

The 'consistent Nazi' objection is not merely a matter of comparing the results of universalizability with intuitive moral conviction. It can also be used to show that the test of universalizability is quite powerless when it comes to deciding between competing moral recommendations. Consider two, contradictory, recommendations. 'Never kill people just because they're Jewish', and 'Always kill people who are Jewish because they're Jewish'. The case of the consistent Nazi shows that the second of these recommendations, however loathsome, can be made to square with the demands of the categorical imperative, and it should be fairly obvious that the first can be made to satisfy it. But if contradictory proposals can both satisfy the test of universalizability, it follows that that test is unable to discriminate between good and bad recommendations. In short, it cannot tell us what to do. From this it follows that Kantian universalizability cannot provide the means by which to determine right from wrong.

The question of what Kantianism has to say about Nazism is not merely theoretical, but arises in at least one specific instance. Hannah

Arendt, in her famous book *Eichmann in Jerusalem*, records how Adolf Eichmann, who was tried and executed for his part in the destruction of millions of Jews, astonished his examining officer when he suddenly claimed that throughout his life he had been guided by Kantian moral precepts.

> The examining officer did not press the point, but Judge Raveh, either out of curiosity or out of indignation at Eichmann's having dared to invoke Kant's name in connection with his crimes, decided to question the accused. And to the surprise of everybody, Eichmann came up with an approximately correct definition of the categorical imperative: 'I meant by my remark about Kant that the principle of my will must always be such that it can become the principle of general laws' . . . . He then proceeded to explain that from the moment he was charged with carrying out the Final Solution he had ceased to live according to Kantian principles . . . . [But] what he failed to point out to the court was that in this 'period of crimes legalized by the state', as he himself now called it, he had not simply dismissed the Kantian formula as no longer applicable, he had distorted it to read: Act as if the principle of your actions were the same as the legislator or of the law of the land . . . . Kant to be sure had never intended to say anything of the sort . . . . But it is true that Eichmann's unconscious distortion agrees with what he himself called the version of Kant 'for the household use of the little man' [in which what] is left of Kant's spirit is the demand that a man do more than obey the law, that he go beyond the mere call of obedience and identify his own will with the principle behind the law – the source from which the law sprang.

Arendt then goes on to comment:

> Much of the horribly painstaking thoroughness in the execution of the Final Solution that usually strikes the observer as typically German, or else as characteristic of the perfect bureaucrat – can be traced to the odd notion, indeed very common in Germany, that to be law abiding means not merely to obey the laws but to act as though one were the legislator of the laws that one obeys.
>
> (Arendt 1963, 1994: 136–7)

We may indeed agree with Arendt that Kant had never intended to say anything of the sort, but the philosophical point this concrete example illustrates is that there is nothing in the logic of his universalizability test that rules it out.

DUTY FOR DUTY'S SAKE

So far we have seen that Kant's view of the good life as the moral life is marred in two respects. First, the emphasis he places upon moral goodness residing in our will or intention to do our duty and not in the good or bad consequences of our actions is mistaken since a complete divorce between intention, action and outcome is impossible. For this reason, there can be no question of judging an intention right or wrong without considering the goodness or badness of at least some of the consequences of that intention. This means that the moral quality of a life cannot be decided purely in terms of will and intention.

Second, even if we agree that intention must form a large part of our moral assessment, the idea of requiring the reasons upon which we act to be universally applicable, i.e. the requirement of universalizability, does not supply us with an effective test for deciding which intentions are good and which are bad. People can consistently pursue evil courses of action, and wholly contradictory recommendations can consistently be based upon the same reasoning. It follows that universalizability is not an effective test at all. Any action or mode of conduct can be made to meet it and hence no course of action can be shown to be ruled out by it.

But besides these two objections there is a third. Kant observes, with some plausibility, that it is not enough to *do* one's duty. Morality requires that we do it *because* it is our duty and for no other reason. In other words, a morally good life does not consist merely in acting in accordance with moral right and wrong, but doing so because of an explicit commitment to moral right and wrong. Those who do not steal because they never have the chance or inclination to, or because they are fearful of punishment, are to be contrasted with those who never steal because it is wrong to steal. This is what is meant by saying that they do their duty for duty's sake. And according to Kant, acting on this reason exceeds in value acting in the same way for any other reason. It is worth recalling the passage quoted earlier where he says:

> To be kind where one can is duty, and there are, moreover many persons so sympathetically constituted that without any motive of vanity or selfishness they find an inner satisfaction in spreading joy, and rejoice in the contentment of others which they have made possible. But I say that, however dutiful and amiable it may be, that kind of action has no true moral worth.
>
> (Kant 1785, 1959: 14)

Now if the moral life is the life of duty for duty's sake, and the best (in the sense of finest) form of human life is the moral life, we are led rather swiftly to the somewhat unpalatable conclusion that many happy and attractive human lives fall far short of the most admirable kind of life, and may even realize nothing of it at all. Consider for instance someone who is talented and clever and who, being naturally disposed to use these gifts for the health and happiness of others, works hard on inventing and developing an ingenious device that is of great use to the physically handicapped. The work is enjoyable, though not specially well paid; much good is gladly done, but without any sense of 'doing one's duty'. Is it really plausible to claim, as Kant does, that such a life has 'no true moral worth'?

There is, however, an even more implausible and uncomfortable conclusion to be drawn from Kant's conception of morality and that is that we must attribute high moral worth to deeply *unattractive* human lives, and hence prefer them to the sort of life just described. That this is an unpalatable consequence of the theory is brought out by the following description of one of Anthony Trollope's characters in *The Eustace Diamonds*, Lady Linlithgow.

> In her way Lady Linlithgow was a very powerful human being. She knew nothing of fear, nothing of charity, nothing of mercy, and nothing of the softness of love. She had no imagination. She was worldly, covetous and not unfrequently cruel. But she meant to be true and honest, though she often failed in her meaning; and she had an idea of her duty in life. She was not self-indulgent. She was as hard as an oak

post – but then she was also as trustworthy. No human being liked her; – but she had the good word of a great many human beings.

This rather appalling picture of rectitude which knows nothing of happiness but means to do its duty can hardly strike us as the model of the life we ought to lead. This is especially true when set beside that of happy hardworking lives in which a lot of good is done but where duty for its own sake plays little or no part. Of course, the defender of Kant's moral philosophy might use the same argument that has been employed at several other places in this book – it is not a good reason to reject a philosophy of value just because it conflicts with what we commonly think; after all what we commonly think about morality and the good life may be wrong, just as what people have thought about health and medicine has often been corrected by scientific investigation. Perhaps then Lady Linlithgow's life *is* to be admired as a good example of the sort of life we ought to lead.

But the conflict with common thought is not so easily ignored. Here we must return to the opening topic of this chapter, doing right and faring well. There a distinction was drawn between two senses of the expression 'the good life'. In one it meant 'living as we ought', what we may call 'the virtuous life', and in the other 'living as we would like to', what we may call 'the happy life'. Just as in the story of Faustus we find an attempt to abandon the constraints of virtue entirely in the exclusive pursuit of happiness, so in Kant's moral philosophy we find an attempt to divorce completely the concerns of virtue and happiness, in the belief that the most important thing is to lead a virtuous or moral life. It is this attempt at a complete separation that makes possible the construction of lives and characters like Lady Linlithgow which, though naturally repellent, we must regard as exemplary instances of the Kantian good life.

But in fact virtue and happiness cannot be held completely separate in this way. This can be seen if we consider once more the foundations of Kant's thought. His concern is to urge upon us an ideal greater than that of the happy life, namely a life worthy of happiness. There are two ways in which we might think of this as the greater ideal. On the one hand we might suppose that though a happy life is good, a deservedly happy life is better. This is, I think, the other side to our thought about the wicked who prosper – that they don't *deserve* to prosper. On this way of thinking, the good life has two aspects, virtue and happiness.

Kant takes it another way. The moral life is a superior mode of life because so long as we are *worthy* to be happy, there is a sense in which we don't need happiness itself. We have attained the most admirable life. Virtue is its own reward. This is how it is possible for those who are unhappy and unattractive to lead good lives on the Kantian model. The question arises, however, as to why anyone should aspire to such an existence. What, in other words, could motivate anyone to try to lead a moral life conceived of in this way?

To see how important this question is in the context, imagine a world in which an 'unfortunate fate' and 'a step-motherly nature' constantly held the upper hand, so that to act in accordance with the moral law was a sure-fire way of courting disaster. (There have occasionally been societies in which this condition seems to have prevailed.) In such a world virtue and happiness are not only separate but in constant competition, and people are regularly faced with the choice of doing their duty for its own sake at the cost of personal misery, or ignoring the call of duty and securing their own happiness and that of their families and friends. What should they do in such a world?

On the one side there is plainly reason to forget about duty – it will lead to misery. On the other side (if we ignore some of the objections considered earlier and assume that Kant's arguments are sound) there is the conflict with pure practical reason. But what does this amount to in the end? It amounts to this: if I act against the moral law, I will be acting irrationally, i.e. inconsistently, and contradicting myself in the reasoning upon which I act. Put like this, however, the demands of the moral law do not seem so very overpowering. While it is no doubt important to be rational and avoid inconsistency, contradiction or incoherence in what we say and do, if the cost of so doing is certain to be personal misery (as we are imagining), there is surely at the very least equal reason to abandon pure practical rationality.

Kant would probably have denied that there is a problem here. On his view, once our duty has been discerned, only those who are morally insensible will fail to 'reverence the law'. There is no further reason to be found or given for doing what duty requires of us. But what of the possible conflict between duty and happiness? If duty can require us to sacrifice our happiness, don't we need *some* basis to choose between the two? To appreciate Kant's answer here we need to see his philosophy in the context of its background belief that our duty is part of a natural harmony of purposes by which God ensures that there is no ultimate conflict between duty and happiness. Indeed, Kant thought that the best argument for God's existence arises from the fact that rational action is only possible if duty and happiness do not in the end conflict, and must therefore presuppose a God who can and will ensure this.

Something of this idea will be explored further in Chapter 9. Most philosophers, however, have not followed Kant along this theological path. They have tried to defend a non-religious conception of morality and for them the problem remains – why should I follow the dictates of duty at the expense of happiness? This is in fact the reverse of the problem that we encountered in the examination of egoism, hedonism and eudae-monism. There we saw that a reason is needed to persuade us to abandon all our customary scruples or sense of right and wrong in favour of what we want or what would give us pleasure. Here, on the other hand, we are in search of a reason to abandon all our natural concern with happiness in obedience to the demands of something called 'the moral law'. And the Kantian non-theological answer to this question – obedience to the moral law for its own sake is a requirement of pure practical reason – does not seem sufficiently weighty to override the natural considerations in favour of happiness.

It may well be argued, of course, that all the fault arises from focusing upon worthiness to be happy than upon happiness itself. In fact, some philosophers have thought that morality is centrally concerned with happiness; that the morally good person is *not* the sort of person Kant describes, who strives to obey an abstract, rational law indifferent to the welfare of human beings as we find them. Rather a morally good person is someone who seeks in all they do to bring about 'the greatest happiness of the greatest number of people'. This last expression is, in fact, the slogan of an alternative but no less influential school of moral philosophy – utilitarianism – and this is the subject of our next chapter.

SUGGESTED FURTHER READING

Original sources

David Hume, *A Treatise of Human Nature* Bk. II Pt III. Bk. III Pt I
Immanuel Kant, *Foundations of the Metaphysics of Morals*

Commentary

James Baillie, *Hume on Morality*
H J Paton, *The Categorical Imperative*

Contemporary discussion

Christine Korsgaard, *The Sources of Normativity*
Phillip Stratton-Lake, *Kant, Duty and Moral Worth*

7

UTILITARIANISM

The previous chapter concluded that Kant's conception of the best human life as one lived in accordance with moral duty pursued for its own sake encounters serious difficulties. Three of these are specially important. First, it seems impossible to disregard the successfulness of our actions in deciding how well or badly we are spending our lives. Second, Kant's categorical imperative, by means of which we are supposed to determine what our duty actually is, is purely formal, with the result that contradictory prescriptions can be made to square with it. Third, the divorce between a morally virtuous life and a personally happy and fulfilling life, and the emphasis upon deserving to be happy rather than actually being happy, leaves us with a problem about motivation. Why should anyone aspire to live morally, if doing so has no necessary connection with living happily?

If these are indeed major problems with the 'duty for duty's sake' conception of a good life, we might suppose that a more successful conception is to be obtained by giving pride of place to happiness and our success in bringing it about. This is just what utilitarianism, the major rival to Kantian moral theory, does. In order to understand the importance of utilitarianism properly, something needs to be said about its origins. We can then consider its merits as a way of thinking about good and bad, right and wrong.

UTILITY AND THE GREATEST HAPPINESS PRINCIPLE

The term 'utilitarianism' first came to prominence in the early nineteenth century but not as the name of a philosophical doctrine. It was rather the label commonly attached to a group of radical English social reformers at whose instigation many important social measures were brought into effect. The term derives from the word 'utility', meaning 'usefulness', and the social reformers were labelled in this way because they made the practicality and usefulness of social institutions the measure by which they were to be assessed, rather than their religious significance or traditional function. But the reformers' idea of what was useful and practical did not always coincide with the view or interests of those who had to live in the institutions they reformed. It was the utilitarians who were behind the dreaded institution of the workhouse which replaced the old Elizabethan Poor Law, and into which the poor and unemployed were often obliged to go. Under this new system the poor were not left in their own localities and given financial assistance by town officials, as they had been since the time of Queen Elizabeth I, but were compelled to move into large institutions where food, lodging and employment were provided under the one roof. Hence the name 'workhouse'. Throughout the early and middle decades of the nineteenth century workhouses were constructed in many parts of England and Wales. These may have served social 'utility' better than the ramshackle workings of the Poor Law, for they took vagabonds off the street and enabled financial limits to be put on the total cost of welfare. But the poor greatly feared the prospect of the workhouse, and the misery and degradation of those who lived in many of them, most famously portrayed by Charles Dickens in *Oliver Twist*, has become an indelible part of our image of Victorian England. It is this rather harsh conception of utility that lies behind the modern meaning of 'utilitarian', nowadays defined as 'concerned with usefulness alone, without regard to beauty or pleasantness' (*Chambers Dictionary*).

Both this definition and the popular picture of the Victorian workhouse, however, are quite inappropriate when we consider the philosophical doctrine called utilitarianism, because its chief concern is with general happiness rather than social convenience. Indeed the philosophical doctrine is in fact somewhat misnamed since, far from ignoring pleasure and happiness, its most fundamental doctrine is that 'that action is best, which procures the greatest happiness'. This famous expression, generally known as 'the Greatest Happiness Principle' predates the label 'utilitarianism' by several decades. It is to be found first in the writings of Francis Hutcheson (1694–1746), an Irish Presbyterian minister who became Professor of

Moral Philosophy at the University of Glasgow in Scotland (where he had the distinction of being the first professor in Scotland to lecture to his students in English rather than Latin). Hutcheson wrote a treatise entitled *Inquiry into the Original of our Ideas of Beauty and Virtue* in which the formulation of the Greatest Happiness Principle just quoted is to be found. But Hutcheson's main concern in his writings was elsewhere and he did not develop the Greatest Happiness Principle into a fully elaborated philosophical doctrine. In fact, though he provides the first formulation of its fundamental principle, the founder of utilitarianism is usually thought to be the English jurist Jeremy Bentham.

JEREMY BENTHAM

Jeremy Bentham (1748–1832) was a very remarkable man. He went up to the University of Oxford at the age of twelve and graduated at the age of fifteen. He then studied law and was called to the bar at the age of nineteen. He never actually practised law, since he very soon became involved with the reform of the English legal system, which he found to be cumbersome and obscure in its theory and procedures as well as inhuman and unjust in its effects. His whole life, in fact, was devoted to campaigning for a more intelligible, just and humane legal system. In the course of his life he wrote many thousands of pages. However, he wrote in a very fragmentary style, often abandoned a book before he had finished it, and did not bother about its publication even if he did finish it. In fact several of the few books that did appear in his lifetime were first published in France by an enthusiastic French follower. The result is that Bentham left relatively little in the way of sustained theoretical writings. Nevertheless he was the chief inspiration of the radical politicians of his day. He also founded an influential journal, the *Westminster Review*, and played a part in the establishment of University College London, where his mummified body, with a waxen head, is still on public view.

Bentham was more of a legal and constitutional theorist than a philosopher. Not only did he study constitutions, he also drew them up, and his services were occasionally sought by newly founded republics who wanted written constitutions. Bentham made the basis of his recommendations 'utility'. By this he meant not 'usefulness without regard to pleasantness' but rather that property in any object, whereby it tends to produce benefit, advantage, pleasure, good or happiness, (all this in the present case comes to the same thing) or (what comes again to the same thing) to prevent the happening of mischief, pain, evil, or unhappiness.

(Bentham 1789, 1960: 126)

Such was Bentham's influence on subsequent philosophical theory that while in common speech 'utilitarian' still means what *Chambers Dictionary* says it does, a philosophical utilitarian is one who believes in promoting pleasure and happiness. Bentham believed, as he tells us in his *Introduction to the Principles of Morals and Legislation* that 'nature has placed mankind under the governance of two sovereign masters, pain and pleasure. It is for them alone to point out what we ought to do, as well as to determine what we shall do (Bentham 1789, 1960: 125). Accordingly, the way to construct successful social institutions, i.e. institutions with which people can live contentedly, is to ensure that they are productive of as much pleasure and as little pain as possible for those who live under them. Thus expressed this is, of course, a social or political doctrine rather than an ethical one. However, we can easily extend the same sort of thinking to human actions and hold that the right action for an individual to perform on any occasion is that which will produce the greatest pleasure and the least pain to those affected by it. Bentham himself meant it to encompass both. He goes on to say:

The principle of utility is the foundation of the present work. ... By the principle of utility is meant that principle which approves or disapproves of every action whatsoever, according to the tendency which it appears to have to augment or diminish the happiness of the party whose interest is in question: ... I say of every action whatsoever; and therefore not only of every action of a private individual, but of every measure of government.

(Ibid.)

In very much the same spirit, we can extend the principle of utility to include not just actions, but whole lives. It thus becomes a general view of the morally good life according to which the best human life will be one spent in maximizing the happiness and minimizing the pain in the world.

One of Bentham's contributions to the theory of utilitarianism was the elaboration of a 'hedonic calculus', a system of distinguishing and measuring different kinds of pleasure and pain so that the relative weights of the consequences of different courses of action could be compared. In this way, he thought, he had provided a rational method of decision making for legislators, courts and individuals, one which would replace the rationally unfounded prejudices and the utterly whimsical processes from which, in Bentham's view, political, judicial and administrative decisions usually emerge.

From a philosophical point of view some of Bentham's thinking is rather primitive. The man who gave the doctrine greater philosophical sophistication was John Stuart Mill (1806–1873). Mill was the son of one of Bentham's close associates, James Mill (1773–1836). Among his many writings is an essay entitled *Utilitarianism*. It is this short work which made 'utilitarianism' the recognized name of a philosophical theory and at the same time provided its most widely discussed version. Here Mill expressly commends a divorce between the common and the philosophical uses of 'utility'.

> A passing remark is all that needs be given to the ignorant blunder of supposing that those who stand up for utility as the test of right and wrong, use the term in that restricted and merely colloquial sense in which utility is opposed to pleasure.
>
> (Mill 1871, 1998: 54)

This is, he says, a 'perverted' use of the term 'utility', and one which has unfairly discredited the 'theory of utility', which he restates in the following way.

> the creed which accepts as the foundation of morals, Utility, or the Greatest Happiness Principle . . . that actions are right in proportion as they tend to promote happiness, wrong as they tend to produce the reverse of happiness. By happiness is intended pleasure, and the absence of pain; by unhappiness, pain, and the privation of pleasure.
>
> (Mill 1871, 1998: 55)

Mill intended his work to rescue the word 'utility' from corruption, but despite his efforts, the words utility and utilitarian in common speech still mean something opposed to pleasure and only indirectly connected with happiness. But if the terminology of philosophical utilitarianism remains somewhat specialized, the doctrine itself has come to have wide appeal in the modern world. Even a cursory glance at most of the advice columns in contemporary newspapers and magazines, for instance, will reveal that their writers assume the truth of something like the Greatest Happiness Principle. Moreover, they clearly regard such a view as not only correct, but uncontentious and incontestible. Indeed, it is not an exaggeration to say that utilitarianism has come to be the main element in contemporary moral thinking. A great many people suppose that there can be no serious objection to the moral ideal of maximizing happiness and minimizing unhappiness, both in personal relationships and in the world at large. When actions are prescribed that appear to have no connection with pleasure and pain (orthodox Jewish dietary restrictions, for instance) or when social rules are upheld which run counter to the Greatest Happiness Principle (Christian restrictions on divorce, for instance) it is those actions or restrictions which are most readily called into question, not the Happiness Principle itself.

And yet, as we shall see, utilitarianism encounters serious philosophical difficulties. In order to appreciate the full force of these difficulties, however, it is first necessary to expound the doctrine more fully by introducing some important distinctions.

EGOTISM, ALTRUISM AND GENERALIZED BENEVOLENCE

Both Bentham and Mill make the principle of utility or Greatest Happiness Principle the centre of their moral thinking. Mill defines happiness in terms of pleasure and Bentham makes no distinction between the two. This focus upon pleasure may raise a doubt as to whether there is anything new in utilitarianism that has not already been discussed in Chapter 3 under the heading of hedonism. Have we not seen already that pleasure and happiness cannot be the foundation of the good life, because people may indulge in loathsome pleasures and have radically different conceptions of happiness? Why do these objections not apply to utilitarianism?

It is true, certainly, that some of the same issues as were discussed in the context of hedonism also arise in the discussion of utilitarianism. If other people have sadistic pleasures why should I promote them? This and other similar questions will be considered in a later section. But for the moment it is very important to see that, contrary to the impression Bentham's and Mill's emphasis upon pleasure may give, utilitarianism does not imply or endorse an egotistical attitude to life. It does not give any special importance to the pleasure or happiness of the individual whose actions are to be directed by it. Indeed, Bentham says that in applying the principle, each is to count for one and no one for more than one, a dictum Mill says 'might be written under the principle of utility as an explanatory comment' (Mill 1871, 1998: 105). What this means is that my pleasures and pains are not to be regarded by me as any more important than yours when it comes to deciding what it is right and wrong for me or for anyone to do. My own pleasures and pains and those of others are to be calculated and compared exactly on a par. Egotism or self-centredness (which is related to but not the same thing as the egoism discussed in Chapter 2) may be characterized as the attitude that gives pride of place to our own welfare. By contrast, utilitarians insist that everyone's welfare should be treated as equal. This ensures that utilitarianism is not an egotistical doctrine.

But neither is utilitarianism altruistic, if by altruism we mean the doctrine that the interests of others should be put before our own interests. Many people have thought altruism to be central to morality. No doubt this is largely because Western morality has been heavily influenced by Christianity, and in most Christian traditions self-denial has been regarded as a virtue. Arguably Christianity does permit a measure of concern for self alongside concern for others ('Love your neighbour *as yourself*' is one of the New Testament's injunctions). However this may be, utilitarianism certainly does allow us to be concerned with our own welfare, though not to the exclusion of others. If what matters is happiness in general, one's own happiness is as important as anyone else's. But it is not any *more* important. This feature of utilitarianism is usually called its attitude of 'generalized benevolence', a term which is to be contrasted with both altruism and egotism.

As we shall see, there remains a question whether, and on what basis, the requirement to adopt an attitude of generalized benevolence can be shown to be obligatory. Why *should* I treat my own interests on a par with others, and why *must* I treat all others on a par? Can I not reasonably favour my children over other people's? But before addressing these questions directly, there are other distinctions to be drawn.

ACT AND RULE UTILITARIANISM

Utilitarianism as Bentham defines it holds that that action is best which leads to the greatest happiness of the greatest number. (Actually, the addition of 'the greatest number' is redundant. If we seek the greatest happiness, numbers will take care of themselves). It does not take a great deal of imagination, however, to think of special contexts in which this principle would condone some very questionable actions. For instance, children often spontaneously laugh at the peculiar movements of handicapped people, and we teach them not to do so because of the hurt this causes. But from the point of view of the general happiness, it could be the case that we would do just as well, or better, to encourage their laughter. On the assumption that the handicapped are a small minority, it is perfectly possible that the pleasure given to the majority, if given full rein, would outweigh the pain caused to a minority and so accord with the Greatest Happiness Principle.

Counter-examples of this sort can be multiplied indefinitely. Imaginary cases show that the strict application of the Greatest Happiness Principle has results which stand in sharp contradiction to commonly accepted opinion. Some of the counter-examples philosophers have devised are rather fanciful, but they make the same point very clearly. Imagine a healthy and solitary tramp who leads a mundane existence and contributes nothing to the common good. If there were in the same vicinity a talented musician needing a heart transplant, a brilliant scientist needing a liver transplant, and a teenager whose life was being made miserable by a defective kidney, on anyone's reckoning the greatest happiness of the greatest number would be served by killing the tramp painlessly and using his organs for the benefit of the other three. But such an action would, of course, be wilful murder of the innocent. It follows that under certain circumstances utilitarianism would not only condone but morally require the intentional violation of the right to life.

In response to counter-examples of this kind a distinction is usually drawn between 'act' utilitarianism and 'rule' utilitarianism. Whereas the former, i.e. the version Bentham espouses, says that every action must accord with the greatest happiness, the latter says that you should act in accordance with those rules of conduct that are most conducive to the greatest happiness. Drawing this distinction enables the 'rule utilitarian' to say that, while there may indeed be occasions when an action commonly regarded as abhorrent would contribute more to the general happiness, its abhorrence arises from the fact that it is contrary to a rule which itself is most conducive to the greatest happiness. The reason for condemning the wilful murder of the innocent is indeed a utilitarian one, because the absence of such a general prohibition would greatly increase fear, pain and loss amongst human beings and hence create unhappiness. Moreover, since we cannot be sure of the consequences of each given action, and could not reasonably take time to estimate and evaluate them in each and every case, we have to be guided by general rules. And the only acceptable criterion for those rules is a utilitarian one: act in accordance with those rules which, if generally acted upon, will lead to the greatest happiness.

This amendment to the basic 'act utilitarianism' of Bentham was made by Mill. Mill regarded this apparent conflict with justice, such as is illustrated by the case of the tramp, to be the biggest stumbling block to utilitarianism. But, he claims:

> The moral rules which forbid mankind to hurt one another (in which we must never forget to include wrongful interference with each other's freedom) are more vital to human well-being than any maxims, however important, which only point out the best mode of managing some department of human affairs.
>
> (Mill 1871, 1998: 103)

It is the importance of the rules of justice for the happiness of us all, according to Mill, that commonly gives rise to a feeling of outrage when any one of them is broken. But though we have this very strong and special feeling about justice and rights, upon reflection we can see

> that justice is a name for certain moral requirements, which, regarded collectively, stand higher in the scale of social utility, and are therefore

of more paramount obligation, than any others; though particular cases may occur in which some other social duty is so important, as to over-rule any one of the general maxims of justice.

(Mill 1871, 1998: 106)

This version of utilitarianism, the rule utilitarian will say, is not vulnerable to the sort of counter-example so easily brought against the act utilitarian variety because it can explain, always in terms of utility, why some actions are forbidden in general, regardless of the finer measurements of the hedonic calculus. It can also explain the strong feelings people have about justice and injustice, because a concern with what is called justice is vital to everyone's happiness. And it can also explain why, in a few very rare cases, it may be right to overrule the dictates of justice.

In due course we will have to ask whether the distinction between act and rule utilitarianism can be sustained in such a way as to provide a defence against the sort of objection we have just considered. But before we move to a general examination of the doctrine as a whole there is one more distinction to be introduced and explained.

UTILITARIANISM AND CONSEQUENTIALISM

Act utilitarianism holds that actions should be judged directly according to their consequences for happiness. Since this seems to give rise to unacceptable applications, such as the sacrificing of the tramp for spare part surgery, rule utilitarians accordingly amend it in favour of the principle that our actions should be judged according to rules which, if followed, will have consequences conducive to the greatest happiness. But either version has two distinct aspects, usually referred to as the hedonic and the consequentialist. The hedonic aspect of utilitarianism is its concern with happiness as the ultimate criterion of good and bad, right and wrong, a point of contrast with existentialism which makes freedom more central, and with Kantianism, which gives pride of place to duty.

However, both these other doctrines can be contrasted with utilitarianism in another way; they are neither of them consequentialist. That is to say, whereas utilitarianism makes the consequences of an action the basis upon which it is to be judged, existentialism regards the authenticity or good faith with which an action is performed as the thing that gives it value, and Kantianism regards the will or intention behind an action to be what determines its moral value.

The difference between consequentialist and non-consequentialist theories shows up most clearly in the different judgements they sustain in particular cases. Take the well-known example of Don Quixote, Cervantes famous hero who pursued the loftiest ideals with the greatest enthusiasm but in a hopelessly unrealistic way. In the eyes of a Kantian, provided the ideals and enthusiasm of such a man are of the right kind, the fact that nothing of the ideal is realized, or that havoc may follow in his path, does not matter; he is nonetheless morally worthy. Or consider the actions of someone like the French nineteenth-century painter Gauguin who deserted his wife and family and sailed to Tahiti to pursue his true calling as an artist. To an existentialist his being true to himself allows us to discount the impact of his actions upon others. In neither case is happiness or unhappiness specially important. This is not just because other things are more important than happiness, but because in passing judgement on Don Quixote or Gauguin, it is not consequences that we should be judging, but the will with which, or the spirit in which, they did what they did. In taking this view both theories differ markedly from utilitarianism.

Utilitarian ethics, then, has two important aspects, the hedonic (its concern with pleasure and happiness) and the consequentialist (its focus upon the consequences of action). Moreover the hedonic and the consequentialist aspects are not only distinct; they are separate since neither implies the other. An evaluative doctrine can be consequentialist without being hedonic and hence without being utilitarian. Consider the case of Gauguin again. Utilitarians are likely to think badly of Gauguin because of the consequential pain and anguish he caused his wife and family (though a utilitarian *could* argue that the pleasure given by his paintings in the longer term has outweighed the pain he caused at first). But it is not hard to imagine another principle which, though also consequentialist, concerned itself with a different type of consequence – artistic consequences for example. Someone who took the sort of view Oscar Wilde used to espouse and defend on his American lecture tours – that the best actions are those whose consequences protect and promote beauty to the greatest degree – (a view often called aestheticism) could argue that we should think well of Gauguin because his action had good consequences for art and beauty. This sort of aestheticism is consequentialist but not hedonic. Its overriding concern is with consequences for beauty not happiness.

What this shows is that, though utilitarianism is a consequentialist doctrine, utilitarianism is not the same as consequentialism. This opens up the possibility of two different types of criticism. We might criticise utilitarians for their overriding concern with happiness or for their exclusive attention to consequences. If either criticism were found to be substantial, this would signal the refutation of the doctrine as a whole. It is especially important to mark this distinction between the two aspects of utilitarianism, because even if we think (as many do) that the importance of happiness cannot be exaggerated, it may still be the case that the consequences of an action are not all that matter. Whether there are substantial criticisms on either count is a question we shall now have to investigate. Let us begin with consequentialism.

ASCERTAINING CONSEQUENCES

Consider the nature of an action. We are sometimes inclined to think of actions and their consequences as a bit like stones thrown into a pond. The stone causes ripples that travel outwards until their force is spent, at which point the stone's effect is ended. But in reality actions are not like that. They do indeed effect changes in the world. By and large that is their point. But the consequences of an action have themselves consequences, and those consequences in their turn have consequences. The consequences of the consequences also have consequences, and so on indefinitely. The position is further complicated when we add negative consequences, that is, when we take into consideration the things that *don't* happen because of what we do as well as the things that do. One consequence of my buying a bottle of wine is that the wineshop makes money, but another is that the bookshop loses out on the purchase I might have made instead. The addition of negative consequences makes the extension of the consequences of our actions indefinite, and this means that it is difficult to assess them. It may make it impossible, since there is now no clear sense to the idea of *the* consequences of an action at all.

To appreciate these points fully consider the following example. It used to be said that the First World War was begun by the assassination of the

Austrian Archduke Ferdinand in the streets of the Balkan town of Sarajevo. Let us ignore the historical complexities which might cause us to question this claim and suppose it to be true. The assassins were successful because of a mistake on the part of the Archduke's driver, who drove up a dead end and was forced to turn back. As the car halted in order to turn, the assassins got the chance which had evaded them all day. Thus Ferdinand was shot when he would otherwise have been driven safely home, had the driver not made his fateful error.

What are we to say of the driver's action in turning the wrong way? Its immediate consequence was that the Archduke was dead. But the consequence of that was the outbreak of a war in which many millions were slaughtered. That war provoked the Russian Revolution which eventually brought Stalin to power, and it ended with a peace settlement under which Germany was treated so harshly that the settlement, far from establishing a long-lasting peace, itself became a major contributory factor in the rise of Hitler. With the rise of Hitler came the Holocaust, the Second World War, the development of nuclear weapons and their use at Hiroshima and Nagasaki. Considered from a utilitarian point of view, that one simple error must have been the worst action in history by a very wide margin.

Of course, there is something both monstrous and absurd about attributing responsibility for this vast chain of consequences to the Archduke's driver. To begin with, it must cross our minds to wonder whether most of the same events would not have happened anyway. Another equally natural response is to say in the driver's defence that his was an unintentional mistake and that it was the assassins, after all, who deliberately committed the murder. To respond in this second way is revealing. It has two distinct aspects. The first part of the defence looks beyond the consequences to the driver's intentions. The fact that this is a very natural response shows how contrary it is to deep-seated ways of thinking to assess an action solely in terms of consequences. The second part of the defence suggests that the chain of consequences may not be the same as the chain of responsibility. The assassination of the Archduke was certainly a consequence of the driver's mistake, but perhaps it does not follow from this that he is to be held responsible. The driver was responsible for the car's being halted in a side road, but it was the assassins who decided to fire. Why should the driver be saddled with responsibility for their decision?

Both these lines of thought are important, but a third objection to consequentialism observes that if we are to trace its consequences indefinitely in this way, we may as easily go back beyond the driver's action and construe it as a consequence of someone else's action. Why start the chain of consequences with him, rather than the superior officer who assigned him to that duty? And why stop there? Why not see this assignation as the consequence of the actions of whoever appointed the superior officer? And so on indefinitely.

ASSESSMENT AND PRESCRIPTION

A consequentialist might reply to these criticisms as follows: We must distinguish between the appeal to consequences in assessing an action after it has taken place, and the anticipation of consequences in recommending or prescribing a future course of action. If it really is true that most of the worst aspects of twentieth-century European history were consequences of that hapless driver's mistake, then it was indeed an appalling error. But of course consequences on this scale could not be foreseen at the time, and the driver cannot properly be accused of acting so as to bring about those consequences. In deciding to turn the car he made a fateful decision, but at the time he acted rightly if, as far as he could see, such a decision was likely to have good consequences. Concern with consequences before the event can obviously only be with *anticipated* consequences (since they haven't happened yet), whereas the concern with consequences after the event is with *actual* consequences. As a result, strange though this may sound, it can be right to perform an action which turns out to have been wrong, because 'wrong' here just means ineffectual.

If we observe this distinction between assessment and prescription, a consequentialist might argue, we do not get the absurd or monstrous results that the example of the Archduke's driver was supposed to reveal. So long as we are clear that it is an *assessment* we are making, we can ask about the actual consequences of the driver's mistake independently of his responsibility for those consequences. The reason for taking his action as the starting point of our assessment and not looking further back to the things that gave rise to it, is just that we have chosen to ask about the consequences of that action and not an earlier one. We can just as easily ask about the consequences of the assassin's action and find these to be horrific too. There is no uncertainty here provided we are clear about which action or event it is whose consequences we want to assess.

When it comes to holding people responsible, on the other hand, the position is quite different. If we enter imaginatively into the driver's situation, we have to decide what, as consequentialists, it would be sensible to prescribe as his best action at the time and in the circumstances prevailing. Pretty plainly, having made his mistake, the recommendation would be that he should turn the car in order to take the Archduke back safely. He was not to know that assassins would by chance enter the same street at that moment. Therefore, because the *anticipated* consequences were good, even though the *actual* consequences were not, he chose rightly.

This distinction between deciding how to act and assessing how we have acted is obviously of the greatest importance for consequentialism, because we cannot know the consequences of our actions before we have taken them. As a result, a doctrine restricted to assessment after the event would have no practical application. But if we cannot assess actual consequences before the event, how are we to decide what to do? The answer is that we have to rely upon generalizations about cause and effect and follow general rules. We estimate the likely consequences of a proposed course of action on the basis of past experience, and we summarize our experience in useful general rules of conduct.

Does the distinction between assessment and prescription overcome the objections to consequentialism it was intended to meet? The first objection, that any action has an indefinitely long chain of consequences which it would be impossible to anticipate or assess, raises some very deep and difficult philosophical questions about cause and effect. Fortunately, I do not think we need to get embroiled in these for present purposes. Whatever way one looks at it, we can say with certainty that shooting people hurts and often kills them, and frequently brings misery and grief in its train. We may be unsure just how far to trace the consequences of an action, or rather, which of the many consequences are relevant to moral assessment. It is plain, however, that we are indeed able to make limited judgements of this sort. Perhaps for practical purposes it is always necessary to draw a somewhat arbitrary line when estimating consequences, but so long as we can make some such estimate, we can raise the question whether it is chiefly or solely the agreed consequences of the action that matter.

Consequentialists say it is, and others like Kant say it is not. The dispute between them can only arise once the relevant consequences have been agreed upon. Thus any difficulty about estimating the consequences in a more absolute sense cannot settle that dispute in favour of either party. In short, there is certainly a metaphysical difficulty about the idea of *the* consequences of an action, but it is one which need not trouble ethical consequentialism since in practice the morally relevant consequences of an action are usually agreed upon.

The second problem is not so easily circumvented, however. This is the objection that it is unreasonable to say that people have acted badly because of consequences which were not merely unforeseen but unforeseeable. We can usefully return here to an example from the previous chapter – someone who raises money and dispatches medical supplies to some disaster stricken part of the world. The medicines are badly stored and as a result become contaminated. The consequence is that those who are given them fall horribly ill and in the end more people die than if no supplies had been sent in the first place. The Kantian thinks this sort of example shows that consequences are irrelevant to the moral merits of the action.

The consequentialist would reply, however, that consequences are relevant even to examples of this sort. What makes the action praiseworthy is that it was an attempt to prevent pain and promote health and happiness, i.e. an action whose probable consequences were good. Certainly, it is not enough for people to mean well; they must actually be motivated by an accurate estimate of likely consequences. What makes such a principle of action praiseworthy, consequentialists think, is the fact that, special cases apart, acting upon *anticipated* good consequences generally leads to *actual* good consequences.

CONSEQUENTIALISM AND SPONTANEITY

But this reply raises a further difficulty, which philosophers generally refer to as 'the problem of spontaneity'. Is it true that if in general people try to anticipate the consequences of their actions, this itself will tend to lead to good consequences? Take the case of children falling into ponds or rivers. If potential rescuers pause to take stock and estimate the consequences of any attempted rescue, in most cases the children will drown. Similarly, in the case of plane crashes or earthquakes, time taken up in consideration of the consequences will very likely increase the death toll. If more lives are to be saved in circumstances such as these, what is needed is spontaneity on the part the rescuers, a willingness *not* to stop and think but to act spontaneously. Of course spontaneous action does not always lead to the best consequences. I may save someone from death but thereby condemn them to a life of constant pain and misery. Or I might unwittingly pull a future Hitler from the flames. Had I stopped to calculate, these results might have been anticipated. This shows that sometimes it would be useful to estimate consequences. The trouble is that we cannot know these occasions in advance and so the general good is better served if we do not try to estimate the consequences of our actions.

This is a curious conclusion. Though in retrospect the moral quality of an action is to be assessed in terms of consequences, at the time of its performance what matters is the *unreflective* belief that it is the action which ought to be performed. More lives will be saved if people uncritically believe that you ought to try to save life *whatever the consequences*. In this way, it seems, consequentialist doctrines (act so as to bring about the best consequences) are worthless as guides to action. In other words, if what has been said about spontaneity is true, the very belief that it is the consequences of an action that matter ultimately, requires us *not* to be practising consequentialists.

If we extend this line of reasoning from consequentialism in general to utilitarianism in particular, we must conclude that a belief in the Greatest Happiness Principle requires us not to be practising utilitarians at least some of the time. The greatest happiness will not always be served by those who spend time and effort on hedonic calculations but sometimes by those who spontaneously follow their own best instincts.

ACT AND RULE

At this point a utilitarian will be tempted to reply that throughout the discussion of consequentialism the crucial distinction between act and rule utilitarianism has been overlooked. While an act utilitarian, it will be recalled, believes that every action should be taken so as to maximize happiness, the rule utilitarian thinks that our actions should be determined by rules which, if generally followed, would lead to the greatest happiness. So a rule utilitarian might say this: It is true that people ought not to pause on each and every occasion to ponder the consequences of their actions. For one thing we are not always able to estimate the consequences of our actions with any degree of accuracy, and for another the *general* welfare and happiness does often need people to act spontaneously and be guided by their own instincts. But all this shows is that people should follow *rules* of conduct, and should often do so in a wholly unreflective and intuitive way. It is, however, utilitarian rules that they should follow, rules framed in accordance with what is most conducive to the welfare and happiness of all.

It should now be evident that the distinction between act and rule utilitarianism is a very important one because it has been called upon to provide the means of replying to two serious objections. To the objection that utilitarianism too readily justifies the use of unjust means to utilitarian ends, (our example was the murder of a tramp to provide others with vital transplant organs), a rule utilitarian (such as Mill) replies that the rules and the deep sense of justice which this sort of counter-example appeals to, are themselves to be explained in terms of the greatest happiness principle.

Second, to the objection that it would be a bad thing if our every action was guided by the Greatest Happiness Principle, the rule utilitarian replies that our actions should be guided by an adherence to rules which are themselves justified by appeal to the Greatest Happiness Principle.

It is thus very clear that a great deal rests upon the rule version of utilitarianism. And yet some philosophers have argued that the distinction between act and rule utilitarianism cannot ultimately be sustained to the purpose for which it was introduced. The argument goes like this. Take a rule such as 'Never punish the innocent'. To many people this seems a fundamental principle of justice, but on a utilitarian account the force of this rule, whether or not we call it a rule of justice, arises from its important connection with social utility. The greatest happiness of the greatest number of people in society at large will best be served if officers of the law consider this rule inviolable. Now consider a very familiar sort of counter-example.

In a frontier town three children have been abducted, sexually assaulted, tortured and murdered. There is an enormous public demand that the local sheriff find the murderer. As time goes on and no one is arrested, public fear increases, unrest grows and confidence in the forces of law and order diminishes. A man is arrested, and such is the circumstantial evidence against him that it is widely believed that the real murderer has been found. It becomes clear to the sheriff that the man he has arrested is innocent and ought to be released, but a lynch mob has gathered and is threatening to tear down the jailhouse unless the suspect is tried and executed or handed over. There is no immediate possibility of a fair trial, but it looks to the sheriff as though serious public disorder and considerable damage and injury are likely if he tries to resist the demands of the lynch mob. Should he execute or hand over to the mob a man he knows to be innocent?

Most people would recognize this as a real dilemma. Nor should its imaginary nature mislead us. Dilemmas of this sort are common in the modern world. The following sort of case is only too familiar. Terrorists have taken innocent hostages and are about to detonate a bomb which will kill and injure many hundreds of people. The only way to stop them is to destroy their headquarters, killing the hostages at the same time. In contexts of this kind it is easy to say 'Let justice be done, though the heavens fall' (*Fiat justitia, ruat caelum*) until there is a real prospect of the heavens falling. What is of interest here, however, is not how dilemmas like these are to be resolved but how they are to be analysed. A non-utilitarian who believes that justice cannot be reduced to or even explained in terms of utility will think that what we have is a straightforward clash between the general welfare and the rights of the innocent, in short between utility and justice. It is this clash which makes these cases dilemmas.

In sharp contrast, an act utilitarian will not be able to identify any element of dilemma at all. If the balance of general good over individual loss has been properly described, then it is as clear as anything could be that we should sacrifice the innocent. From the point of view of act utilitarianism these cases are in principle no different from any other calculation about good and bad consequences, and if the good outweighs the bad then there is nothing wrong with our action. There is no dilemma to agonize over.

Few people would accept this view of the matter and are therefore inclined to reject act utilitarianism. It is rejection on these grounds that Mill and subsequent rule utilitarians have hoped to forestall. For the appeal to moral rules, it is claimed, can explain both why we think there is a dilemma in this sort of case and how we are to resolve it. The claim is that in killing the innocent in these special circumstances, though we may be acting for the best, we are nonetheless violating a firmly held rule to which deep feelings are attached. And this rule is itself based on considerations of utility. This is Mill's account of the matter. He says of cases involving the rights of innocent parties:

> To have a right ... is ... to have something which society ought to defend me in the possession of. If the objector goes on to ask, why it ought? I can give him no other reason than general utility. If that expression does not seem to convey a sufficient feeling of the strength of the obligation, nor to account for the peculiar energy of the feeling, it is because there goes to the composition of the sentiment, not a rational only, but also an animal element, the thirst for retaliation; and this thirst derives its intensity, as well as its moral justification, from the extraordinarily important and impressive kind of utility which is concerned.
>
> (Mill 1871, 1998: 98)

Cases like those of the lynch mob and the innocent hostages, then, are explained by Mill as a conflict between rational calculation of utility and a deep 'animal' attachment to a rule which is itself, in general, closely bound up with utility. But this account leaves one important matter unexplained. Why should we have the rule 'Never punish the innocent'? Mill's answer is that in general this rule serves social utility. But plainly it does not always serve it, as the frontier town sheriff's dilemma shows. So from the point of view of social utility the following rule would serve social utility better: 'Never punish the innocent unless serious social strife needs to be averted thereby'. Between this rule and the particular case, however, there is no conflict, since this more specific rule allows the handing over of the innocent man to the lynch mob.

If so, there is a very important implication to be drawn. The whole point of the rule version of utilitarianism is that it purports to offer an alternative to the unacceptable act version. But now we have seen that it does not really do so. Faced with cases like those we have been considering, act utilitarians can offer no explanation of why we think there is a dilemma. But neither can rule utilitarians. They may claim that the dilemma arises because there is a conflict between what utility demands in the particular case and what is demanded by the normal social rule governing cases of that sort. We have just seen, however, that any such conflict can readily be eliminated by carefully refining the rule to take account of these special circumstances; in other words by coming up with a different rule. It follows that on the rule utilitarian account of the matter there is no real dilemma. Thus rule utilitarianism offers no more of an explanation than act utilitarianism. To put it in philosophical language, act and rule utilitarianism are co-extensive.

SUMMARY: DOES THE END JUSTIFY THE MEANS?

We saw earlier that utilitarianism is a consequentialist doctrine, one according to which it is the consequences of actions that matter from a moral point of view. Though there is more to utilitarianism than this, this consequentialist aspect gives rise to important questions and difficulties. In the last few sections we have been exploring these difficulties in some detail, but they can be summarized around the age-old question, Does the end always justify the means? Is an action always justified if it has good consequences, regardless of the intention with which it was carried out or the kind of action it is? Consequentialists may differ over what kind of consequences they regard as good, but they must agree in thinking that, since consequences are what matter, the end *does* justify the means. The arguments we have considered suggest that this is wrong.

In the first place we cannot sensibly speak of *the* consequences of an action. And even if we agree what to regard as the relevant consequences of an action, we cannot explain responsibility simply by following chains of consequences; we also need to consider aims and intentions. Secondly, sometimes the exclusive pursuit of good consequences seems to require us to undertake courses of action that run counter to our sense of justice. In these cases we need, at the very least, an explanation of the dilemma we feel. A theory such as act utilitarianism, which takes the consequences of each individual action to be what matters, cannot do this. At best it explains why we think there is a dilemma when, in reality, there is none. This is just the objection that rule utilitarianism aims to overcome. What the argument of the last section showed is that it does not succeed in doing so. If we focus solely on the utility of the consequences, we will always have reason to prefer a rule which permits rather than forbids these objectionable actions.

Most people find these objections to consequentialism in general and utilitarianism in particular to be highly persuasive. It should be recognized, however, that they are not conclusive. Like some of the objections to other theories we have encountered, they rely upon a conflict with widely held views. To be consistent we must reject consequentialism if we are to persist with common views about responsibility, justice and so on. But we could with equal consistency hold on to consequentialism and reject commonly held views. This does not necessarily mean that we can hold on to utilitarianism, because there is another aspect of it yet to be considered, the hedonic aspect. It is to the examination of this second aspect to utilitarianism that we now turn.

THE NATURE OF HAPPINESS

Almost since the first appearance of utilitarianism, philosophers have wondered whether the idea of happiness upon which it depends so heavily can be made sufficiently clear and precise to do the job the Greatest Happiness Principle (GHP) requires of it. Many of these criticisms, it seems to me, can be answered fairly easily, others less easily and others perhaps not at all. It will be best to consider these in order.

Presented with the GHP, people often wonder what exactly happiness is. Neither Bentham nor Mill is very helpful here, because both identify happiness with pleasure and, as we saw earlier, Aristotle convincingly shows this to be a mistake. But the fact that there is some confusion in these two writers should not lead us to the conclusion that we cannot ourselves be clear about what we mean by happiness. Actually, the application of utilitarianism to everyday life does not really need an explicit account of happiness. It is enough if we are able to identify happiness and unhappiness in ourselves and others, and able to distinguish between happy or unhappy resolutions to difficulties and alternative resolutions with different merits or demerits. For instance, we can usually distinguish happy and unhappy marriages. When a marriage is an unhappy one, the question of divorce often arises. In such cases it is often said that happiness is more important than keeping marriage vows. The fact that such a claim can easily be made is evidence that, even in the absence of a general account of what it is, happiness can enter into moral deliberation.

Sometimes it is suggested that there is no *one* thing that we can label 'happiness'. Different activities and styles of life appeal to different people and what makes one person happy may make another miserable. As a result, trying to secure other people's happiness can easily go wrong, and to work for happiness in general may be impossible. Now the claim that people differ in what makes them happy is obviously true. One woman may be happiest at home surrounded by children, while to another the same style of life is stifling captivity (a theme explored in Michael Cunningham's novel *The Hours*, subsequently an award winning film). But nothing follows from this about promoting happiness. A woman for whom domesticity is the greatest source of personal happiness can readily understand that this is not true for everyone. She can regard the promotion of happiness as hugely important, and at the same time acknowledge that this does not mean prescribing the way of life that makes *her* happy as the road to happiness for *all* women. Indeed, she might expressly oppose any social convention that imposes her ideal of wife and mother, precisely on the grounds that it makes too many women unhappy.

Such differences are real but do not impair our ability to tell happiness from unhappiness and hence our ability to act on the GHP. Moreover, it is worth reminding ourselves that (as Mill observes), though there are these differences, in general there is also a wide measure of commonality in the things that make for human happiness. By and large sickness, injury, bereavement, hostility and insecurity are obstacles to happiness which anybody will find difficult to overcome. From this it follows that, though the interests and inclinations of individuals do differ, in practical deliberation there are at least some general guidelines we can follow for the promotion of happiness.

MEASURING HAPPINESS

Neither the absence of a general account of what constitutes happiness, nor the existence of differences in what makes human beings happy, presents a substantial difficulty for utilitarianism. But a critic can point out that utilitarianism requires much more than an ability to tell happiness when we see it. The theory also requires that it be measurable. Someone who accepts that we can tell happiness from unhappiness easily enough, may well deny that we can quantify it. And yet this is what we must be able to do if we are to apply the GHP. We must have some way of estimating and adding up the happiness that each individual will get as a result of alternative courses of action if we are to achieve the greatest happiness.

The idea of measuring happiness or pleasure (for to him they amounted to the same thing) figures prominently in the thinking of Bentham. As we saw earlier, he tried to think out what later became known as an 'hedonic calculus' a list of dimensions along which pleasure should be measured. In the fifth chapter of his *Principles*, he distinguishes between different sources of pleasure according to their intensity, duration and so on, and suggests how these are to be ranked in importance. We will not inquire here into the details of his scheme. One thing that is important to observe about it is that, though the name it was subsequently given – hedonic *calculus* – may be thought to imply the contrary, there are in fact no numerical calculations in it. Indeed Bentham does not use numbers at all, but only makes comparative judgements.

It is true that later utilitarians did use numbers, especially those who introduced utilitarian conceptions and ideas into economics. Indeed the principal achievement of one of the most prominent, an English economist called Jevons, was just to introduce mathematical techniques to economic theory, and one of the effects of this was the practice of representing interpersonal comparisons by graphs. The term used by the economists was not pleasure or happiness, but 'utility', and it is this term that has stuck. Economists still talk of 'marginal utility curves'. Whether what they say in this connection has much to do with the GHP is debatable, but there is no doubt that they require measurable quantities in order to theorize in the way they do. And to many who are unimpressed by the earlier objections, there really is something absurd in supposing that human happiness can be added up and represented on a graph!

But it is easy to mistake the true role of numbers here. No serious philosopher or economist has supposed that either pleasure or happiness can be measured in the way that sugar, or rainfall, or earth tremors can. Nor does anybody think we might devise an instrument of measurement.

What Bentham thought was that different pleasures could be compared in such a way as to bring out their relative importance, and there is nothing absurd about this idea. Such comparisons are being made everyday, for instance by children who have limited pocket money to spend and have to decide what purchase would give them more satisfaction, tourists whose holiday is coming to an end and have to decide which trips would be more pleasurable, or any individual choosing between a trip to the cinema or an evening at home. In general human beings have to make comparisons of pleasure in a host of different contexts, not just for themselves but for others. In choosing a surprise for your birthday I will have to decide which out of the alternatives would give you more pleasure. Even if, unlike Bentham, we distinguish between pleasure and happiness, we still find that making comparisons of degrees of happiness is something we do all the time. Parents may have to decide at which school a child would be happier. Children may have to decide whether it would make for the greater happiness of all concerned for aging parents to enter a retirement home.

Now if such comparisons can be, and regularly are made, there is no reason why they should not be represented by the use of numbers. Suppose I have three courses of action open to me and try to estimate in each case what the impact on everyone's happiness would be. I decide that course A would lead to more unhappiness than course B and that course B would lead to more unhappiness than course C. I have thus ranked the courses of action. But I might also think that course A would make people very much more unhappy than course C, whereas course B would only make them a little more unhappy. I may now represent this judgement in numerical terms, say by giving A a value of -10, B a value of $+7$, and C a value of $+10$.

To represent the matter in this way may help to make the comparative judgements clearer to myself and others. It might still be doubted of course whether, having employed numerical values, I am thereby enabled to employ the normal range of mathematical techniques, adding, subtracting, multiplying, dividing and so on. But the important point to stress is that comparative judgements can be made, and can be represented in numbers. This is all that need be meant by the phrase 'measuring happiness', and if so, another standard objection to the hedonic focus of utilitarianism falls.

DISTRIBUTING HAPPINESS

We come now to three objections to utilitarianism which are just as familiar but harder to answer than the two considered so far. The first of these has to do with distribution. The GHP tells us that every action we perform should promote the greatest happiness of the people affected by it. For the moment let us accept this recommendation. In deciding what to do with respect to any action, however, there is still a matter to be resolved. How is the happiness which I produce to be distributed?

The importance of this question is graphically illustrated in a context made famous by the Oxford philosopher Derek Parfit – population growth and economic prosperity. Sometimes governments, especially in poorer countries, have taken an active hand in what is called 'population control'. In the belief that in a large and expanding population everyone inevitably ends up with a smaller share of the national product, peasants have frequently been encouraged, and sometimes forced, to have smaller families than they would naturally choose to do. In general the rationale for this sort of policy has been some version of the GHP – the promotion of the greatest general welfare – and the idea is that though it may be beneficial to the individual to have a large family, the resulting growth in population will contribute to greater economic misery all round. So individual choice must be restricted for the greater happiness of all.

The empirical belief at the heart of this policy – that more people inevitably means poorer people – is highly questionable. After all, people, even children, are not only consumers but also producers of economic resources, and all developed countries are *both* more prosperous *and* more populous than they were in times past. But suppose, despite these serious reservations, that it is true. The relevant question here is, *if* it is true, does this imply, in combination with the GHP, that governments are right to engage in population control.

Now despite our intuitions and contrary to commonly accepted opinion, this is not an implication utilitarianism can justify, because the GHP is only concerned with *total* happiness and says nothing about how happiness (or welfare) should be *distributed*. From the point of view of the *greatest* happiness, a situation in which many millions live just above subsistence level is as desirable as one in which a much smaller number of people live in relative luxury. The use of numbers helps us to represent this very clearly.

Imagine a population of 100 million people all of whom have an average income of $1,000 a year. (Let us assume for the sake of the example that income is a measure of happiness or welfare.) The total welfare for a year may thus be calculated as one hundred billion dollars. Take now a far smaller population, say one million people. Each has an income of $100,000 a year. The sum total in a year is also a hundred billion dollars. If we were to have a choice between creating either population, the GHP would give us no reason to prefer the second to the first. More strikingly, if we imagine that in the second population each person's income falls to $80,000, the GHP now gives us reason to prefer the large population of low income earners.

It may be replied to this objection that the argument works only if we suppose that what the GHP is concerned with is total happiness, whereas nothing in the principle itself requires this, and we could interpret it in terms of *average* happiness. If we do, this odd conclusion about different populations does not follow. We have reason to prefer a society in which the average rather than the total happiness is higher, as it is in the second population described above.

This shift from total to average happiness does overcome the first version of the objection about distributing happiness. But it does not overcome all objections of this sort, because average happiness in a population is still calculated without reference to distribution within the population. This means that the GHP is indifferent on what appears to be a matter of great importance. Let us assume once more that income is a genuine reflection of welfare. The average income within one society might be $80,000 but the society be one in which many people's income fell below $1,000. In another society, the average income might also be $80,000 and no one's income fall below $40,000. The first is a society in which there is great wealth but also great poverty. The second is one in which there is no poverty, though less great wealth. Many people would think that faced with a choice we have reason to prefer the second of these societies. This is a matter for argument, perhaps. The point to be made here is that in that argument utilitarianism is silent. Since matters of distribution seem important, its silence on this score may be counted a serious deficiency.

The examples we have been considering have to do with societies and populations at large, but it is not hard to see that the same problem arises when utilitarianism is invoked in a more personal context. We can easily imagine a family in which the happiness of a favoured child is given precedence over that of every other child and contrast it with a family in which every child is treated more or less equally. The result might be, however, that total and average happiness are the same in both families. If so, most people would think that there was reason to prefer the second, and yet utilitarianism has nothing to say on this score. The fact that common sense suggests that in instances of this sort there *is* more to be said, combined with the fact that utilitarianism has *no* more to say, seems to imply that its exclusive focus on happiness is a mistake. Neither total nor average happiness gives the full story. Fairness in distribution must also be taken into account. This conclusion brings us to the second objection – that happiness is not the only or even the principal value with which we should be concerned.

MILL'S 'PROOF' AND PREFERENCE UTILITARIANISM

Why should we suppose, as utilitarianism does, that happiness is the ultimate value? This is a question which John Stuart Mill expressly addresses in the fourth chapter of *Utilitarianism* where he attempts to provide what he calls a proof of the principle of utility. His opening argument for this 'proof' is very well known.

> The utilitarian doctrine is, that happiness is desirable, and the only thing desirable, as an end; all other things being only desirable as means to that end. What ought to be required of this doctrine – what conditions is it requisite that the doctrine should fulfil – to make good its claim to be believed?
>
> The only proof capable of being given that an object is visible, is that people actually see it. The only proof that a sound is audible, is that people hear it: and so of other sources of experience. In like manner, I apprehend, the sole evidence it is possible to produce that anything is desirable, is that people do actually desire it. If the end which the utilitarian doctrine proposes to itself were not, in theory and in practice, acknowledged to be an end, nothing could ever convince any person that it was so. No reason can be given why the general happi-

ness is desirable, except that each person, so far as he believes it to be attainable, desires his own happiness. This, however, being a fact, we have not only all the proof which the case admits of, but all which it is possible to require, that happiness is a good: that each person's happiness is a good to that person, and the general happiness, therefore, a good to the aggregate of all persons.

(Mill 1871, 1998: 81)

This argument of Mill's has been much discussed. Some philosophers have thought that it fallaciously trades on ambiguity in the word 'desirable'. Whereas 'visible' only means 'able to be seen', 'desirable' can mean both 'able to be desired' and 'worthy to be desired'. Once we have been alerted to this ambiguity we can see that the fact that something is desired is evidence that it is *able to be* desired, but not evidence that it is *worth* desiring. Other philosophers have argued that, though this is a possible ambiguity, it plays no part in Mill's argument. They construe him as saying that the only evidence that something *is* worth desiring is that people *find* it worth desiring, and that there is abundant evidence of this sort for the claim that happiness is desirable.

The fact that the interpretation of Mill's argument is uncertain makes any argument for or against utilitarianism which rests solely upon its being read one way rather than another less than satisfactory. We will do better, therefore, to consider related implications of the proof, implications which Mill himself considers, and see whether or not these can lead to a more definite conclusion. One of these implications arises from the observation that, even if we accept Mill's argument as a proof of the value of happiness, nothing in it shows that happiness is the only value. This defect is important, however, because there are plainly many things besides happiness that people value as ends, i.e. for their own sake and not merely as a means to something else.

Mill's reply concedes that this is so, but he claims that anything we value for its own sake rather than as a means, we value as a constituent part of happiness. Having taken up music, for instance, because of the pleasure we derive from it, we come to value it for its own sake. Music becomes part of what happiness is for us. This reply, however, is fraught with difficulties. Mill himself provides an example which brings these difficulties to the fore. Money is valuable because it is a means to happiness. But sometimes people come to love money for its own sake. Having formerly sought money merely as a means to happiness, being rich comes to be part of what happiness means to them. Or so Mill claims. But if we think a little further on the matter, this analysis becomes very unclear. The idea seems to be that, when money is valued as a means, it is valued because of the things it can buy, whereas when it is constituent of happiness it is valued in itself. Suppose I spend money on an expensive and fashionable car. The possession of the car makes me happy. Or suppose, being a miser, I keep the money. In this case possession of the money itself makes me happy. In both cases the possession of something makes me happy. It seems a matter of indifference whether we say in the first case that the possession of the car was a means to or a part of my happiness. Similarly it seems a matter of indifference whether we say, in the second case, that the possession of the money is a means to or a part of my happiness. Either way, neither the car nor the money is valued in itself, but only because it makes me happy.

From this it seems to follow that Mill's distinction is no distinction at all. He has not actually managed to accommodate into his scheme of thinking values other than happiness which are valued in themselves. If we persist in the view that there are such values, then the supremacy of happiness has not been shown. But even if Mill's distinction between 'means to' and 'part of' were a good one, there is a further difficulty. It appears that other things that are valued in themselves can conflict with happiness, and there seems no reason to suppose that we must prefer the latter.

An example familiar to philosophers is that of the deathbed promise. Suppose I solemnly and sincerely promise a dying man that, once he is dead, I will set the record straight (so to speak) by telling his wife and family of his numerous but secret infidelities with the wives of friends and colleagues. Once he is dead he cannot be pained or distressed by my failure to keep my word. (Let us ignore complications about life after death.) On the other hand his wife and family and former lovers will all face distress and embarrassment. The happiness principle demands that I break my promise to the dying man. Yet I may feel that fidelity to that promise and to truthfulness in general is more important than happiness. What has Mill to say on the other side?

What he does say (though not in connection with this specific example) is that I desire to tell the truth because I would be happiest doing so. But this need not be the case. Perhaps the act of revealing the dead man's sins is deeply distressing to me, not least because of my former attachment to him. Mill seems to say at this point in the argument that if I desire to tell the truth, it must be the happiest course for me, because 'to think of an object as desirable (unless for the sake of its consequences), and to think of it as pleasant, are one and the same thing' (Mill 1871, 1998: 85). This is, of course, a dogmatic assertion on his part. The issues it raises, and the reasons for rejecting it, however, have already been discussed in previous chapters and so we need not labour them here. The conclusion to be drawn is that Mill has not succeeded with his 'proof' of the supremacy of the value of happiness.

The difficulty of proving the supreme value of happiness has been recognized by some philosophers who have nevertheless wanted to hold on to the general structure of utilitarianism. Acknowledging that Mill's equation of desire and pleasure is without foundation, they have suggested that we might express the whole doctrine not in terms of happiness but in terms of desire satisfaction or preferences – the right action is that which leads to the satisfaction of the greatest number of desires. This version of utilitarianism, generally known as preference utilitarianism, has been much discussed and raises many interesting issues. But here there is room to mention only one. If the shift from happiness to desire satisfaction solves any problems, it also creates them. It seems right to say that happiness is a value, and hence the creation of happiness a good thing. The question is whether it is the only, or the supreme value. But it is not obvious that desire satisfaction in itself is a value at all, just because some desires are bad. If a girl desires to sleep and a man, contrary to his own best instincts and hence to his happiness, has a strong desire to rape someone, I will maximize the satisfaction of desires by bringing the girl to him drugged sufficiently soundly to make her unaware that she has been raped. To act in this way seems unquestionably wrong, and it adds nothing in its favour to observe that at least it maximized the satisfaction of desire.

MOTIVATION AND THE LIMITLESS MORAL CODE

The preceding section concluded that Mill's proof of the supreme value of happiness does not work, and can't be rescued by appeal to the more abstract notion of 'preference satisfaction'. But even if it had, there is a third and final objection to utilitarianism still to be considered.

We have seen that both the consequentialist and the hedonic aspects of utilitarianism raise difficulties. Although it has taken some time to explore these properly, both sets of difficulties can be summarized in a similar way. The attempt to focus exclusively on consequences and on happiness fails because other things besides consequences matter and happiness is not the only value. But suppose for the sake of argument it had been shown to everyone's satisfaction that, from the moral point of view, the right action is that action whose consequences lead to the greatest happiness. We could still ask why we should go in for morality at all. In its more familiar form this is the question 'Why should I be moral?'.

To some people this seems a peculiar question. Considered in relation to utilitarianism it can quickly be made a genuine one. This is because it is not hard to show that the moral life conceived of along utilitarian lines makes demands upon us which we have every reason to resist. These demands arise from its boundlessness. This boundlessness has two aspects. First within utilitarianism moral questions and moral demands are constant. Secondly, if happiness is what matters, it cannot matter whose happiness it is. Let us consider these points in turn.

Most people think of moral questions as periodic. That is, we go about our daily lives, within a framework of law and decency no doubt, but by and large free of moral questions. Moral issues do arise, and sometimes they arise very acutely. Moral questions are *special* questions and when we are faced with them, they often require a certain amount of agonizing. The question 'What shall I have for dinner?' is not (in the normal way) a moral question, and though it requires me to choose, it would be absurd to think that choosing involved anything in the way of heart searching. In short, moral questions are occasional.

Such a view of the place and nature of morality may or may not be correct. It is however incompatible with a utilitarian view of morality. Since at every moment of my waking life I could be engaged in action conducive to the greatest happiness, I am constantly faced by moral questions. For every action I perform, at home, at work, at play, I can and must ask myself – am I doing right? Under a utilitarian regime the question 'What shall I have for dinner?' *is* a moral question, every time it arises. This seems a very demanding life to lead.

Of course a utilitarian can always say that the common view of morality as occasional is wrong, that moral questions do arise constantly, and indeed if life is to be guided by utilitarian principles, this rejoinder is correct. But it is not to the point. If moral demands are truly unremitting, this is a reason for asking very seriously 'Why should I *be* moral?'

The other aspect of the unlimited character of utilitarianism is, if anything, even more disturbing. It is illustrated by an example first discussed by the English social thinker William Godwin (1756–1836). Godwin was a convinced utilitarian and he saw that the commitment to the greatest happiness could give rise to painful choices. He imagines a case in which the house of the French Archbishop Fenelon, reputed to be a great benefactor of mankind, goes on fire, and the choice is between rescuing Fenelon or rescuing his maid. Godwin thought that the answer was clear; the right thing to do was rescue Fenelon. But a critic reading this raised a question about what Godwin's attitude would be if the maid in question were his grandmother. Godwin replied that in this case too the right thing to do would be to rescue Fenelon.

Some people were appalled at this reply, and philosophers have frequently discussed it and cases like it. But the importance of the example is not just as another counter-example to the application of utilitarianism, similar to many of those already encountered. The point rather is that the sort of morality utilitarianism comprises can give rise to occasions when we are called upon, not merely to sacrifice our nearest and dearest, but to treat them exactly on a par with everyone, and anyone, else. Since our friends and relatives matter much more to us than strangers, even those we know to be benefactors, why should we do this?

One familiar answer is that it is morally right. Assuming contrary to all the objections rehearsed so far, that the utilitarians are correct in their account of morality, this is certainly true. But once again it is not to the point, and hence not an adequate answer. The question is not: Is treating our friends and relatives on a par with everyone else the morally right thing to do? Rather the question is: Why should we do the morally right thing if this requires us to treat those who are special to us as though they were not? It has sometimes been said at this point that the moral law is overriding, something which *must* take precedence over every other consideration. But this is just another way of asserting that we must do what morality requires. The question is: Is morality overriding, and if so why?

Someone who raises this question will not and cannot be satisfied with an answer which appeals to the content of morality itself. This means that no further refinement of utilitarianism (or any similar moral doctrine) will answer this question once it has arisen. It follows that even if all the difficulties and objections we have been considering could be overcome, there would still be a question about the ground in which the demands and requirements of utilitarianism are rooted. And this applies to certain conceptions of morality as such. In fact, our examination of utilitarianism has led to the same conclusion as the examination of Kantianism. Even though utilitarianism gives happiness prime importance, we are left looking for a motivating reason to adopt it. The problem lies with morality itself. However we conceive it, whether along utilitarian, Kantian or some other lines, we can always ask what the basis of morality itself is. There are too quite different explanations that are commonly offered. The first is that the basis of morality is social agreement, and the other that morality is ultimately rooted in religion. These are the topics of the last two chapters.

SUGGESTED FURTHER READING

Original sources

Jeremy Bentham, *Introduction to the Principles of Morals and Legislation*
John Stuart Mill, *Utilitarianism*

Commentary

Ross Harrison, *Bentham*
Roger Crisp, *Mill on Utilitarianism*

Contemporary discussion

Derek Parfit, *Reasons and Persons*, Part 4
David Lyons, *Forms and Limits of Utilitarianism*
J J C Smart and Bernard Williams, *Utilitarianism For and Against*

8

CONTRACTUALISM

A recurrent problem for moral philosophy, one that we have encountered several times already, is the question of how to bridge the gap between what is the case and what ought to be the case. As we saw in an earlier chapter, philosophical egoists think that in the case of the first person no problem exists; if I want or need something, then I have a reason to try to get it, and so, rationally I ought to. The altruist, by contrast, does seem to have a problem. How could it follow from the fact that *you* want or need something, that *I* ought to try and get it for you? How can the needs of *others* provide a compelling reason for *me* to act?

The previous chapter ended with the question 'On what could the demands of morality be based?' and this question raises just the same issue. Kantians and utilitarians both assemble evidence and argument to show that impartial reason and/or the general good point towards an individual's taking a certain course of action. But what reason is there for that individual to follow their prescription, especially if it implies some measure of self-sacrifice?

THE FORCE OF AGREEMENT

At this point we are taken back to the discussion of moral rationalism in Chapter 1 – the logical force of appealing to promises. One compelling reply to the question 'Why should I concern myself with the needs of others?' would be this: 'You promised to'. Immediately, this places the onus back on the egoist who asks the question, because the appeal is not directly to the needs of others, but rather to his or her own past action. It has to be true, of course, that the person so addressed did indeed promise, but whether she did or not is a matter of fact. Indeed, that is part of the force of the appeal. The promiser can say, certainly 'Why should I keep my promise?'. Some philosophers would claim (as I suggested in Chapter 1) that such a question makes no sense, that it is like asking why two things cannot be in the same place at the same time. But however this may be, the fact remains that a promise was given and that this marks out the promiser from other agents.

This point needs to be emphasized. Suppose I need some money for some urgent purpose. The egoist's point is that my need is automatically a reason for *me* to do something about it, but not automatically a reason for *you*. Let us agree then (if only for the sake of argument), that the relation between my needs and the obligations of others is problematic. There is still an important difference between another person who has promised to help me, and one who has not. In short, promises make a difference. Furthermore, the kind of difference they make is one that generates obligations. You might say 'Why should I help you, if I don't want to?' and if you never promised or agreed anything to the contrary, I might be hard pressed to give you a reason. But if you had *agreed*, this would generate a reason, because we are not relieved of our promises just because we no longer *want* to do what we have agreed to do.

It is this basic thought upon which another, rather different theory of ethics is built, a theory often called 'contractualism'. If we could show some way in which the basic principles of morality are rooted in social *agreement*, then we would have a rational foundation for the idea that moral principles cannot simply be ignored because they have no immediate connection with the individual's desires or wishes.

Conceived in this way, morality is to be thought of as the set of rules and principles that we need to agree upon if society is to function properly. In this sense our *moral* obligations are not to be distinguished sharply from our *social* obligations, and the demarcation between politics and morality is a slightly fuzzy one. That is why the philosophers who have been most influential in developing and refining this line of thought are as often thought of as political rather than moral philosophers, including especially Thomas Hobbes (1588–1679), John Locke (1632–1704), Jean-Jacques Rousseau (1712–1778) and (much more recently) John Rawls (1921–2002).

In the history of contractualism there are two key concepts – the 'state of nature' and the 'social contract'. All the philosophers just listed employ these concepts, although they say different things about them, and sometimes call them by different names. The general strategy, however, is the same – a thought experiment is conducted in which we are invited to abstract from the world of social and political structures, and by reasoning about this 'state of nature', uncover rational grounds for a 'social contract' that will govern relations between individuals in society. Once the social contract is in place, then it forms the basis of law and morality and can be appealed to as the ground of our social obligation to recognise and accommodate the needs of others.

Though this is an interesting approach to the problems with which we have been concerned, and highly attractive to many, it faces one obvious difficulty. If appeal to 'the social contract' is to carry the sort of obligatory implications that the force of agreement gives to promises in general, it has actually to be consented to. But, though occasional historical episodes similar to this have taken place – the Icelandic *Althing* (assemblies) of the tenth to twelfth centuries centuries might be an example – there is no well documented case of a pre-political society in which all the people have at one time gathered and agreed the rules for their mutual support and co-operation. In other words, there is no clearly recorded instance of *explicit* consent to a social contract. Is there any way round this difficulty, any other type of agreement that will do the job of explicit (or to use an older term, express) consent? It has been a major part of the philosophy of contractualism to supply an answer to this question.

JOHN LOCKE AND 'TACIT' CONSENT

John Locke, perhaps the most famous of all English philosophers, was the author of *Two Treatises of Government*. The first of these, which is rarely read nowadays, was directed against the writings of Sir Robert Filmer, who had argued that the authority of the monarch to govern his subjects is derived from God through the person of the first man, Adam. Having argued at length against this claim, Locke goes on in the *Second Treatise* to elaborate and defend the converse idea, an extremely radical one at that time, that kings actually owe their kingship to the people they govern, since the authority of the ruler is rationally derived from the consent of the ruled. The powers the ruler exercises are really the rights of individuals transferred to him for enforcement and protection. And this is a contention that applies not just to kings but to any form of government.

A central point of the *Treatise*, however, is directly related to the topic of the obligation that individuals have to others. Locke wants to show that:

> Every Man, by consenting with others to make one Body Politick under one Government, puts himself under an obligation to every one of that Society, to submit to the determination of the *majority*, and to be concluded by it; or else this *original Compact*, whereby he with others incorporates into *one Society*, would signifie nothing, and be no Compact, if he be left free, and under no other ties, than he was before in the State of Nature.
>
> (Locke 1689/90, 1960: 376, emphasis original)

Though the distinction we are inclined to draw nowadays between politics and morality would not have been so sharply drawn in Locke's day, his *Two Treatises* are clearly works of political philosophy, as this passage makes clear. This is chiefly because Locke is not dealing with the foundation or content of morality, which he assumes to be established by God. He takes for granted the existence of a *natural* moral law, and his question is how this natural law is related to civil society and the laws of the state. His answer is that the laws of the state should reflect, interpret and enforce the natural moral law. He nowhere has the idea that the social compact brings those laws into being, or gives them authority.

At the same time, whether we are talking about moral or political obligations, any appeal to a 'compact' faces the difficulty already identified – the absence of express consent or agreement. And on this point there is an aspect of Locke's discussion that is of relevance here. It is his conception of 'tacit' or implicit consent.

> There is a common distinction of an express and a tacit consent, which will concern our present Case. No body doubts but an *express Consent*, of any Man, entring into any Society, makes him a perfect member of that Society, a Subject of that Government. The difficulty

is, what ought to be looked upon as a *tacit Consent*, and how far it binds, i.e. how far any one shall be looked on to have consented, and thereby submitted to any Government, where he has made no expression of it at all. And to this I say, that every Man, that hath an Possession, or Enjoyment, of any part of the Dominions of any Government, doth thereby give his *tacit Consent*, and is so far forth obliged to Obedience to the Laws of that Government, during such enjoyment, as any one under it; whether this his possession be of Land to him and his Heirs for ever, or a Lodging only for a week; or whether it be barely travelling on the Highway.

(Locke 1689/90, 1960: 392, emphasis original)

Clearly Locke's concern here is still with the grounds of political obligation, but the same sort of argument can be and often is made about our moral obligations. Those who avail themselves of the advantages of moral rules can be taken to agree to those rules tacitly. The shopkeeper can only prosper if others pay their bills. The cheat depends upon others abiding by the rules; the conman relies upon the honesty and trustfulness of others; and both reveal this fact in their attempts to keep their illicit dealings hidden.

Yet, though there is clearly something to be said about membership of society generating social obligations, tacit *consent* is a most implausible mechanism by which this comes about. The problem is this. We can only say that someone has consented to something, if they have had the chance to dissent. But if we take Locke at his word there is no such possibility. If, to put it in Locke's terms, I entered a country 'Lodging only for a week' and 'barely travelling on the Highway' for the sole purpose of registering my *rejection* of the social contract, I would, despite this, have given it my tacit consent.

Of course, for the vast majority of people, even this vain attempt is impossible. The society to which they belong is the one into which they were born, not the one they chose to join, and their continuing to belong to it is simply a function of practical necessity. David Hume was the first to make this point, in his essay 'Of the Original Contract'.

Should it be said that, by living under the dominion of a prince which one might leave, every individual has given a tacit consent to his authority, and promised him obedience; it may be answered, that such an implied consent can only have place where a man imagines that the matter depends on his choice. ... Can we seriously say, that a poor peasant or artisan has a free choice to leave his country, when he knows no foreign language or manners, and lives, from day to day, by the small wages that he acquires? We may as well assert that a man, by remaining in a vessel, freely consents to the dominion of the master; though he was carried on board while asleep, and must leap into the ocean and perish, the moment he leaves her.

(Hume 1741/42, 1963: 461–2)

In short, there may indeed be a common distinction between tacit and express consent, as Locke alleges, and it may be that sometimes we can assume a person's agreement even where it has not been expressly given. But my participation in society is not sufficient in itself to show that I have consented to the basic principles of conduct that enable that society to function.

JOHN RAWLS AND 'HYPOTHETICAL' CONSENT

Express consent derives from words that have been spoken, tacit consent from actions that have been performed. In both cases the consent is actual, and the problem is that, with respect to rules whose purpose is to determine what is and what is not acceptable social behaviour, there is virtually no one whose consent to them can be said to be actual, whether express or tacit.

A different approach to the problem of consent is to be found in the twentieth-century's most influential political philosopher, John Rawls. In his famous book *A Theory of Justice* Rawls's equivalent of the state of nature is the 'Original Position'. This is also an imaginary circumstance in which people are placed behind a 'veil of ignorance' and asked to decide about the kind of society they would be willing to agree to live in. The point of the 'veil of ignorance' is to ensure that people do not simply choose the kind of society that suits them best. So, at the point of deliberation, they do not know whether they are rich or poor, full bodied or disabled, talented or talentless, male or female, etc. The idea, of course, is to introduce impartiality into their deliberations; if the rules of social engagement are to be fair, they cannot be slanted in favour of one section of society or one type of person. But equally, it would not be rational (Rawls thinks) for someone to agree to a society in which he or she was a permanent member of an underclass, and the whole point of deliberating about the fundamental moral rules that regulate social conduct is to come up with a set of rules that can command the rational assent of all those to whom they apply.

It is this second point that is most important in the present context. The purpose of Rawls's thought experiment (at least on one interpretation) is to arrive at some fundamental principles that rational self-interested people would agree to. He comes up with two such principles in fact. The first says that we should allow individuals as much freedom as is compatible with an equal amount of freedom for all, and the second says that individual wealth should be distributed according to what is called 'the Difference principle', a principle whose purpose is to limit the possible gap between rich and poor.

Like Locke's (though perhaps less clearly), Rawls's thought experiment is about social and political principles rather than moral ones, and for that reason it would not be pertinent to explore his two principles in detail here. For present purposes, the relevant concept at work in his theory is that of *hypothetical* consent. What his thought experiment shows (if it works) is that a society that operates according to certain rules would command the consent of rationally self-interested people thinking fairly.

Many critics have argued that his thought experiment does *not* work, that there are defects in the reasoning that is supposed to get us from the original position to the two basic principles. In particular, it has often been argued that Rawls's conclusion relies upon attributing to the people in the original position a very conservative attitude to risk. He supposes that people weighing up the pros and cons of different social arrangements would always opt for a society in which though there was no chance of fabulous wealth, there was less chance of great poverty. However, we know that some people are naturally disposed to take a gamble, and anyone less averse to risk than Rawls assumes would not be rationally bound to subscribe to the principles he elaborates. Still, the chief point to be observed here is that, even if his argumentative strategy *does* work, the resulting *hypothetical* consent is not enough to bridge the rational gap between egoistic motivation on the one hand and altruistic obligations on the other.

The reason is that contractualism has to appeal to agreement. It says that you can justifiably be asked to do what the rules of morality require you to do, because whatever you may or may not *want* to do, you have agreed to those rules. Now if we try to formulate this principle using the concept of hypothetical agreement, it does not work. I can justifiably be asked to comply with rules which I have actually agreed. Appeal to the hypothetical is required only if I have *not* actually agreed. The claim is that under certain conditions I would agree; that is the force of calling it hypothetical. What are those conditions? One is, that I am a fully rational agent. Now *perhaps* it is plausible to say that I am bound by rules which, if I were fully rational, I *would* agree to (not everyone accepts this claim), but where does this leave those who are *not* fully rational? It seems that it leaves them free of any such obligation.

This point needs to be stated very carefully. In referring to people who are not fully rational, we are not referring to people with serious mental incapacity, but only to people who are unlikely to go through deliberations as complex as those Rawls offers us. It cannot be said of someone that they *would* have accepted the conclusions of a rationally valid argument if they are people unable or unwilling to follow arguments. So the binding force of hypothetical consent (if it has such force) can not be applied to them. It seems we must conclude that such people are not bound by the rules that more rational people would be bound by.

This is an unfortunate implication, because the whole point of the Rawlsian thought experiment is to establish the obligations and restrictions with respect to freedom and justice that apply to *all* members of society. His theory is supposed to provide a rational grounding for the basic social rules which everyone can legitimately be compelled to observe, and the existence of non-fully rational people implies the existence of a group who cannot be legitimately compelled to comply.

One possible response is this. So long as Rawls's principles are indeed grounded in reason, then I am rationally justified in applying them to all members of society whether they are fully rational or not. The problem with this response is that the concept of consent falls out of the reckoning altogether. Certainly, it seems reasonable to think that I am justified in getting you to agree to rationally well grounded rules of social behaviour, whether you follow all the reasoning behind them or not. And, once you *have* agreed to them, I can legitimately require you to keep to your word whether you want to or not. But this is to appeal to actual consent, and it is the general absence of such actual consent that motivates the appeal to hypothetical consent. What we have now seen is that hypothetical consent cannot make good this absence and cannot therefore secure what actual consent secures. The only further possibility is to forget consent, and appeal directly to the force of the reasoning itself.

HOBBES AND THE DICTATES OF PRACTICAL REASON

This is precisely the approach adopted by another famous theorist of contractualism, Thomas Hobbes (1588–1679). As with Locke and Rawls, Hobbes reasons from a 'state of nature' to a civilized state but with this important difference. Whereas Locke's state of nature is one governed by the laws of God and Rawls's original position is expressly designed to ensure impartiality, Hobbes's state of nature is a 'war of all against all'. In what is probably one of the most frequently quoted passages from any philosopher, he describes it as a condition where

> there is no place for industry; . . . no culture of the earth; no navigation . . . no commodious building; . . . no knowledge of the face of the earth; no account of time; no arts; no letters; no society; and which is worst of all, continual fear and danger of violent death; and the life of man, solitary, poor, nasty, brutish and short.
>
> (Hobbes 1651, 1960: 82)

Such circumstances arise from the supposition that people are naturally egoistic. This is what makes Hobbes's thought experiment specially relevant in the present context, because it is expressly addressed to an egoistic mentality. His argument, in brief, is that everyone has a clear practical reason to get out of this state of nature whatever their purposes or desires, because in the 'war of all against all' the plans of the egoist no less than the desires of the altruist will in all probability come to nothing. Consequently, everyone has a powerful reason to seek some sort of social order, and thus to agree with whatever it takes to secure that order.

One way of understanding Hobbes is to see that for him the central problem of social life is one of social co-ordination. How can people pursue their very different and often conflicting goals without constantly frustrating each other? A social order in which the strong simply dominate the weak will not do, because even the strongest must sleep and can fall ill. Nor is it the case that the cause of the difficulty is irrationality such that Plato's philosopher-king might provide the solution.

To see this, imagine the following circumstance. Some people derive their livelihood from fishing, but the stock of fish in the lake around which they live is declining. The only way to preserve the fish stock in the longer term is the introduction of individual quotas, i.e. a limit on how many fish each fisherman may take from the lake. This way the future of everyone will be secured. The alternative is that everyone loses their livelihood. The problem is that each individual fisherman can reason cogently as follows:

'Suppose that *I* stick to my quota, but others do not. In this case, the lake will get fished out, and everyone will lose out in the end, but I will lose out in the short term as well, since by observing the quota allocated to me I will suffer an immediate drop in income that others do not. Suppose on the other hand that I *break* my quota. Then, if others break theirs, the lake gets fished out, certainly, but I am not a special loser. Contrariwise, if others keep to their quotas while I break mine, the fish stocks will be preserved to my long term benefit as well as to theirs, but unlike them, I will not suffer an immediate drop in income either. So, regardless of whether other fishermen ignore *or* observe their quotas, my best strategy is to ignore mine.'

It is important to emphasize that this line of reasoning is perfectly cogent. In the circumstances described it is indeed in the interests of the individual to break the rules. The problem is that *every* individual fisherman can reason in this way with equal cogency, with the result that no one has any rationally grounded obligation to keep the quota. The curious outcome is that if everyone acts rationally, the collapse of the fishing stock is guaranteed and communal disaster ensues. How is this paradox to be overcome?

To come up with an answer we should start with the following obser-vation. It will be in the interests of each individual fisherman to *keep* to the rules if (1) every one else does and (2) he will suffer if he does not. If the chain of individualistic reason that has such a destructive effect on the gen-eral good is to be broken, individuals have to know how others will behave. Now they can only know that everyone *will* comply with the quotas if they know that everyone will be *compelled* to. This is one way, perhaps the only way, in which the potential conflict between individual rationality and the common good is overcome. It is also the heart of Hobbes's argument for the practical necessity of the sovereign state, and in my view it is a power-ful argument. It shows that human beings in society can act in ways that are *both* individually rational *and* socially destructive.

The mere existence of rules governing social behaviour is not enough to remedy this. Crucially, people must actually act in accordance with them. Nor will merely agreeing to keep them do, for if as in the imaginary sce-nario of the fishermen, each individual has a rational incentive to *break* the rules, then there is equal incentive to break any agreement to keep them. This means that consent – whether hypothetical, tacit or even express – cannot be the right concept to invoke in this context. Each indi-vidual has a rational incentive both to consent to the rules and subse-quently renege on his consent. The special power of Hobbes's argument lies in its showing that the *only* adequate solution lies in the creation of some institution with both the authority and the power to *enforce* rules and agreements. It uses coercion to advance and protect the general good by compelling individuals to act in accordance with rules whether they want to or not. And this enforcement applies to all, regardless of their rationality because the general good to be realized is in the longer-term interests of everyone.

Hobbes's conception of the state of nature is thus radically different from Rawls's conception of the original position. It is one in which individual reasoning, far from leading to moral or social rules or principles upon which all will agree, militates against any such rules and undermines the gen-eral good they are meant to secure. This is why a sovereign authority to rule over individuals and discount their reasoning is required. At the same time, it demonstrates the practical wisdom of accepting such an authority as a necessary condition of everyone's having a secure and satisfactory life and a protection against the anarchic war of all against all. Hobbes's reasoning, if sound, shows that rational egoists should accept enforceable rules of social order because these are in their own best interests even where the application of these rules conflicts with their immediate purposes and desires.

As with Rawls, many commentators have doubted whether Hobbes's argument really works. But even if it does, it will not do anything to bridge the gap between rational egoism and moral altruism with which we have been concerned. Hobbes's *Leviathan* is unmistakably a work of political rather than moral philosophy. Its purpose, and its outcome if it succeeds, is to show that the state is both essential and central to the possibility of social order. If what we call 'morality' has a part to play in this, then morality is something that the state must not only enforce, but determine. What is morally wrong, will be what the state says is morally wrong.

POLITICS, MORALITY AND RELIGION

This conclusion will be unacceptable to many people, chiefly for three reasons. First, in contrast to former periods and different cultures (Islam, for example) Western thought has come to regard politics and morality as importantly distinct. Most modern democracies are politically liberal in the sense that they believe the law ought not to be used to enforce specific moral beliefs. It is this that explains liberalizing changes in the laws relating to marriage, homosexuality and abortion. Such changes have come about because of the widespread belief that, even if adultery or homosexuality or abortion, *is* morally wrong, individual moral choice is a fundamental freedom, and it is not the proper business of the state to make its citizens' moral choices for them by forcing them to be good.

Second, there are many aspects of behaviour that we think of as immoral – telling lies, being disloyal to friends, gossiping maliciously, for example – against which, it seems, there cannot really be effective laws. Conversely, there are morally praiseworthy characteristics which legislation cannot bring about. We cannot compel people to be generous or kind, for example. So it seems that there is indeed an important sphere of conduct and evaluation beyond that of 'legal' and 'illegal'.

Third, and perhaps most powerfully, if it were indeed the laws passed by the state that determined what is morally right and wrong, this would put the state itself beyond the reach of morality. In the face of the history of the twentieth-century and the excesses of state action in Nazi Germany, the Soviet Union, Mao's China, Pol Pot's Cambodia and South Africa under apartheid (to name only the most striking examples), the idea that the state could be the *source* of moral right and wrong seems intolerable. In order to pass the right sort of judgement on the gross violations that groups and individuals suffered at the hands of these states, we have to have available a level of evaluation and criticism that transcends the laws passed by governments, whether we call this morality, or human rights, or natural law. In short, it seems certain that there can be, and that there are, unjust states and morally bad laws. Yet how could this be, if the state is the ultimate moral arbiter?

'Hobbism' was feared by Hobbes's contemporaries and by subsequent commentators and social theorists because it was thought to licence authoritarian government and to make the state (what Hobbes in fact called it) a 'mortal God'. Locke's account of the state of nature is formulated in part as an alternative to the Hobbesian, and it differs radically by making the rights of the subject, not the power of the sovereign, the touchstone of right and wrong. For Locke, the role of the state is not to establish (in the sense of 'define') moral right and wrong, but to make sure that the natural rights of the individual are formulated with sufficient precision to make their application clear, fair and consistent. When Locke refers to the office of 'Magistrate' he is thinking of someone with the special task of interpreting and enforcing natural rights that limit the actions of the state and its officers as much as they limit the actions of citizens with respect to each other. These natural rights flow from natural laws, laws which ought to govern human relationships in the state of nature no less than in political societies, and against which the actions of rulers with respect to their subjects are to be assessed. This is why Locke allows citizens the right of rebellion against tyrannical government. When the 'fundamental rights of man and citizen' as they are sometimes known, are *violated* rather than protected by the state, then in the name of those rights citizens are justified in rebelling against their rulers.

By implication, *contra* Hobbes, the source of these natural laws and rights cannot be the sovereign state. Their origins and their authority must come from elsewhere, and in Locke it is very clear where this is. Natural rights are literally God-given, and thus the authority of morality comes not from the state but from God, to whom kings are accountable no less than their subjects. This appeal to divine authority is much less plausible nowadays than it was in Locke's time. Contemporary moral and political philosophers do not often appeal to God in the course of their arguments. But even in very ancient times philosophical doubts were raised against the suggestion that the ultimate source of moral authority is God. This is the subject of the next and final chapter.

SUGGESTED FURTHER READING

Classic sources

John Locke, *Second Treatise of Government*
Thomas Hobbes, *Leviathan*
David Hume, 'Of the Social Contract' in *Essays Moral, Political and Literary*
John Rawls, *A Theory of Justice*

Commentary

D A Lloyd-Thomas, *Locke on Government*
Michael Lessnoff, *Social Contract*

Contemporary discussion

David Gautier, *Morals By Agreement*

9

ETHICS, RELIGION AND THE MEANING OF LIFE

In this final chapter we arrive at topics which many people expect philosophy, and moral philosophy in particular, to be specially concerned with, namely God, good and evil and the meaning of life. Before considering these topics directly, however, a general summary of the argument that has brought us to this point may be useful.

THE ARGUMENT SO FAR

One way of approaching some central questions of ethics is to ask: 'What is the best sort of life a human being can live?' The first answer we considered was that given by the egoist: the best life is one in which you get what you want. There are a variety of objections to this answer, but the most important is this. Egoism supposes that our wants and desires are in some sense 'there' waiting to be satisfied, whereas the truth is that we are often uncertain about what to want. We can intelligibly ask not merely about what we *do* want out of life, but about what we *ought to* want. This question, however, egoism cannot answer. It follows that egoism is inadequate as a guide to good living. Though it tells us what to do, given pre-existent desires, it cannot help us critically form those desires.

The second candidate considered was hedonism, the view that the good life is the life of pleasure. Hedonism goes one stage further than egoism since it recommends not merely the pursuit of desires in general, but a certain specific desire – the desire for pleasure. Consequently, hedonism cannot be charged with the sort of emptiness that egoism can. Moreover, it appears to enjoy an advantage in arguments about good and bad, because pleasure is a value with natural appeal, and hence a promising value upon which to build a philosophy of the good life. But hedonism is not without its own difficulties. If we interpret the life of pleasure along the lines of the Cyrenaics, a 'wine, women and song' sort of life, the facts of human biology and psychology make it impossible to pursue sensual pleasures exclusively since they nearly all bring sensual pains in their wake. This might lead us, as it did the Epicureans, to interpret the ideal life of pleasure along more refined lines, and to recommend, for instance, a life in which sampling fine wines is preferred to getting roaring drunk. But if we do make this alteration in our idea of pleasure, we lose the natural appeal that gives hedonism an advantage over other philosophies, since the Epicurean life, far from being one of self-indulgence, is actually one of considerable self-restraint.

In any case, against either version of hedonism the point can always be made that there is more to life than pleasure. Even more importantly, as Aristotle saw, there is more to *happiness* than pleasure, and it is this observation that led us to consider the claims of *eudaemonia* or well-being as the supreme value. Aristotle defines the well-being of a thing in terms of its natural function or end, which is why his moral philosophy can be described as a form of naturalism. Ethical naturalism faces this question, however. Can human beings be said to have a natural end or function? One interesting response to this question makes appeal to ethology, socio-biology and evolutionary biology, the relatively recent sciences that study human beings as evolved social *animals*.

However, the attempt to wed Aristotelian philosophy and Darwinian biology cannot be considered wholly successful. The heart of ethical naturalism is the attempt to settle questions of moral conduct by reference to our nature as human beings, but because human beings have proved adaptable to a host of different environments, it inevitably leaves many disputes between conflicting styles and modes of life unresolved. Besides, even if it settled a great many of these, it would still have one great failing, at least in the eyes of existentialists. On the existentialists' view what is distinctive about human beings is their freedom from natural determination, their ability to rise above natural contraints, and their responsibility for their own fate and conduct.

It is this freedom to transcend our nature that *eudaemonism* seems to ignore and existentialism brings to the fore. In the examination of existentialism, however, problems of a different sort emerged. The 'authentic' life that it recommends is, on reflection, a conception indifferent to specific content; it is as good to choose the life of an authentic villain as that of an authentic hero, if all that matters is freedom and authenticity.

Kant tries to show that freedom is not all that matters, that rationality matters just as much. He argues that freedom and reason can be reconciled in a duty centred conception of the moral life. Much that Kant has to say is subtle, but crucially he appears to leave out of the picture the consequences for human happiness. In doing so, he removes any basis which might motivate us to choose the moral life that he so strongly recommends. This is why he speaks of an irreducible 'reverence for the law' as the source of moral motivation, a conception which, as he himself observes, merely states and does not explain our interest in morality.

The failure of Kantian moral theory to provide an account of moral motivation led us to consider a familiar alternative – utilitarianism – a doctrine that gives pride of place to human happiness and might for this reason be expected to overcome the problems Kant's moral philosophy encounters. But in fact, a very similar difficulty emerges from a critical examination of utilitarianism. Here too we are left with this question: what reason have I to promote the general happiness at the expense of my own personal happiness or the happiness of those nearest and dearest to me? Utilitarianism cannot answer this question and as a result cannot, so to speak, assert its authority over us.

It may seem, in the light of this summary, that the argument so far has been disappointingly negative. Six ethical theories have been examined and every one of them found to be deficient. The net result appears to be that we are no further on than when we started. But in fact this is not so. From each stage of the argument something valuable has emerged and in the light of the whole we now have a much clearer conception of what it is we are looking for in the way of a successful theory of ethics. We know that we must be able to answer the question 'what *ought* I to want?'. This is what our discussion of egoism showed; that desire satisfaction is no guarantee of a happy life. The discussion of hedonism, on the other hand, showed that there is more to happiness than pleasure, and the discussion of Aristotle and sociobiology showed that even happiness is not enough as the sole constituent of a good life. As existentialists insist, we must also recognize the claims of freedom and responsibility.

The further discussion of existentialism, however, revealed that our freedom is not only the recognition of responsibility to ourselves, but to others. It is personal freedom and responsibility to others that Kant tries to reconcile in his conception of the moral law. One result of his attempt however, is his failure to take seriously personal happiness. At best Kant sketches a moral life which we only have reason to follow from the point of view of abstract reason. But why act in accordance with reason as Kant conceives it, if it makes us unhappy? Similarly, at best utilitarianism outlines a life of impartial benevolence directed at the happiness of all mankind. But again, why act impartially, if my own happiness suffers? These are of course egoistic questions, but nonetheless real for that.

What we can see as a result of the argument, then, is that some way must be found to accommodate the importance of both freedom and happiness, and a rational basis given to the moral demands of others that can satisfy the legitimate demands of egoism. It is precisely for the accomplishment of this task that many people look to religion.

THE AUTHORITY OF MORALITY

The problem faced by either the Kantian or the utilitarian conception of the moral life may be termed a problem about the authority of morality – the claims of morality in the competition between personal desire and social obligation. It is this problem that contractualism in many of its forms is intended to address. Suppose we think of moral rules not as personal ideals but as the rules that people agree to live by. This suggestion is attractive because, by putting agreement at the heart of morality, it bridges the gap between egoism and altruism, a gap that appears to dog many of the most influential ethical theories. Contractualism aims to make promising or contracting the foundation of social obligation, but closer examination shows that the most successful version of this manoeuvre subsumes morality under politics and thus in effect eliminates it. Hobbes's argument, if it works, uncovers the basis of *political* authority, but it still leaves us with a problem about the authority of *morality*.

The Kantian prescription for a good life is this: 'Always act in accordance with what rational thinking shows to be your duty'. The utilitarian prescription is: 'Always act with a view to impartial benevolence'. When either fundamental principle is questioned, there seems nothing further to say; we can only repeat the prescription. 'Why should I act in accordance with what reason shows to be my duty?' 'You just should'. 'Why should I adopt an impartial attitude and regard my own happiness as no more important than anyone else's?' 'You just should'. What appears to be needed is some prudential or egoistic reason of the form 'It's better for you if you do'. But if we do make self-interest the basis of moral obligation, this seems to imply that morality is no more than enlightened self-interest, and that moral scruples are to be abandoned when (so to speak) they get in the way of personal happiness and satisfaction. In short, abstractly moral reasons seem to lack personal appeal, and concretely prudential reasons seem to lack the right sort of authority.

To many thinkers the way out of this difficulty lies in recourse to the authoritative will of God. It is not difficult to see in outline how this solution is supposed to work. If God is creator and loves His creation, if He is both all powerful and all good, what He commands cannot fail to provide both prudential and moral reasons for action. Obedience to the will of God appeals to our rational self-interest – no one could rationally reject the commandments of such a God, because God will unfailingly prescribe the kind of life most conducive to individual well-being. At the same time, since God is perfect, His commandments must also be compatible both with justice and with the well-being of all creation. It seems then that appeal to the will of God is the way to settle the vexing questions of moral philosophy which have defeated the other lines of thought explored so far. God lays down for us the rules of a good life, and He is uniquely placed to do so since He has created the world in which that life is to be led.

Of course the matter is not as simple as this. From earliest times those who have appealed to God as a solution to philosophical problems have been plagued by doubts and difficulties. Three are specially important. First of all, is there a god who is the sum of all perfections? Second, granted a positive answer to this first question, can we ever know for certain what God wills for us? Third, if we did know the will of God, would this really provide us with a better grounded guide to life than the non-

180

religious philosophies we have been discussing and found wanting. All three of these questions have a very ancient history and have been intensely debated ever since human beings began to think about philosophical and theological questions. Let us consider each of the three difficulties in turn. For simplicity's sake, I will set out all three at their strongest and most persuasive form before considering what response it might be possible to make to them.

THE EXISTENCE OF GOD AND THE PROBLEM OF EVIL

Does God exist? It is a plausible speculation that more pages have been written on this question than any other subject in human history. Philosophers and theologians have developed several distinct arguments in favour of the hypothesis that God exists. Others have claimed the arguments to be invalid, and still others, such as Kierkegaard, have claimed that all such arguments, positive or negative, are worthless from the point of view of true religion. Some of the greatest thinkers of all time have been convinced religionists – Plato, Augustine, Aquinas, Descartes, Newton – and some have been sceptics or outright atheists – Hume, Nietzsche, Marx, Darwin. Others – Spinoza, Kant, Hegel, Einstein for instance – have, as a result of their intellectual reflections, subscribed to versions of religious belief that more orthodox thinkers have condemned as heretical. Given this long and complex history, it is impossible for an introductory text to moral philosophy to engage at any length with the issues that belief in the existence of God raises.

However, there is one aspect of this large subject that is of special significance to the connection between the existence of God and basis of ethics, namely the well-known 'problem of evil'. The problem of evil is not a problem for all religions. Eastern religions such as Hinduism and Buddhism have no place for the concept of God as the Western 'monotheistic' religions of Judaism, Christianity and Islam understand it. Even in these monotheistic religions the belief in a God whose nature is perfect and who is the source of all things good needs to be qualified. The actions of Yahweh as represented in the Hebrew Bible are often more like those of an irritable and whimsical tyrant than of a loving heavenly father. ('The

Lord, whose name is Jealous, is a jealous God', Moses is told in the book of *Exodus*.) In Islam it is the perpetual and inescapable sovereignty of Allah, rather than inexhaustible love, which is the principal focus of concern. (The opening section of the Qur'an says 'The Praise is to God, Lord of the worlds, the merciful Lord of mercy, ruler of the judgement day'). It is chiefly in Christianity that great emphasis is placed upon the love of God for His creation ('God so loved the world that he gave his one and only Son'. Gospel of John 3:16) For this reason Christian philosophers and theologians have been more concerned with the problem of evil than those of any other religion.

The problem has its practical side, and those who believe in the love of God can hardly fail to experience it from time to time. We have only to look at the suffering and destruction which the world at any place or period of history will be found to contain, to find ourselves asking 'Where is the love of God here?'. The practical problem is to trust in God's goodness in the face of human and animal suffering, suffering which sometimes seems to reach immense proportions, as evidenced by the Holocaust in which six million Jews are estimated to have died, the ravages of Pol Pot, the Cambodian tyrant responsible for the death of over a million people, or the frightful slaughter in Rwanda where, in the course of three months, the Hutus machetéd an estimated 850,000 Tutsis.

But we can also give the problem a philosophical interpretation, and turn it into an argument which generates the firm conclusion that there is no loving God. The philosophical version of the problem is given one of its best known renderings by Hume, some of whose ideas we have already considered.

> [God's] power we allow infinite; whatever he wills is executed: but neither man nor any other animal are happy: therefore he does not will their happinesss. His wisdom is infinite: he is never mistaken about chusing the means to any end; but the course of nature tends not to human or animal felicity: therefore it is not established for that purpose ... Epicurus' old questions are yet unanswered. Is he willing to prevent evil but not able? Then he is impotent. Is he able, but not willing? Then he is malevolent. Is he both able and willing? Whence then, is evil?
>
> (Hume 1779, 1963: 171–2)

If God is all loving, He will want to put an end to evil and suffering, and if He is all powerful nothing can stop him from doing so. From the fact that He always wants to eliminate evil (His omnibenevolence), and the fact that He has the power to do so (His omnipotence), it follows that there ought to be no evil in the world. But there *is* evil in the world, and from the undoubted reality of evil we are forced to conclude either that God does not want to eliminate it, in which case He is not all loving, or else that He cannot, in which case He is not all powerful. In theological language, the existence of evil demonstrates that God cannot be both omnipotent and omnibenevolent. John Stuart Mill expresses this conclusion very forcibly. 'Not even on the most distorted and contracted theory of good which ever was framed by religious or philosophical fanaticism, can the government of Nature be made to resemble the work of a being at once good and omnipotent' (Mill 1878: 389).

It is a small step from this conclusion to the non-existence of God altogether. If there is a God at all, that is to say a Being worthy to be worshipped, that Being must be possessed of all perfections, and hence must be both omnipotent and omnibenevolent. This the argument from evil has shown to be impossible. It follows that there is no God.

Some people find this argument wholly persuasive, rooted as it ultimately is in the unquestionable facts of experience. Others have tried to find a flaw in it. Whether there is a satisfactory answer or not is a subject we will leave for the moment while we consider the second of the problems outlined above.

THE PROBLEM OF RELIGIOUS KNOWLEDGE

If God does exist, can we ever know for certain what His will for us is? The world's experience of religion suggests that we can't. To begin with, we must first settle the question 'which religion?'. Arguably there is no such thing as 'Religion', only religions, and these give quite different pieces of advice. What is permissible under one religious code is quite impermissible under another, and what is obligatory under one is a matter of total indifference to another. For example, suppose we ask whether people should live monogamously or polygamously (a genuine question for people in some parts of Africa today). Leaving Mormonism aside, the Christian religion rules polygamy out, holding up monogamy not only as an ideal, but as the only form holy matrimony can take. Islam on the other hand makes polygamy not only permissible but desirable. Or take another example. Is it important how we prepare our food? Those religions with dietary laws (Orthodox Judaism, Islam, to a lesser extent Sikhism) hold that it is, though they prescribe quite different rules (indeed, the Sikh dietary laws expressly forbid the consumption of meat slaughtered in the Muslim style). For others, Christianity for instance, the manner in which food is prepared is a matter of indifference, reflecting Christ's remark that it is not what goes into but comes out of a man that defiles him. The examples could be multiplied almost indefinitely, and what they appear to show is that the appeal to religion as a guide to conduct is unhelpful, since in practice it is an appeal to a vast range of different, and often contradictory, prescriptions for the good life. If the central ethical question is 'How should I live?', appeal to religion fails by the curious route of providing an embarrassment of answers.

Of course, it can be suggested that we should try to adjudicate between these different answers, to decide which we should accept and which we should reject. But on what grounds are we to do this? In so far as each religion claims to be based upon divine revelation, through Moses or Jesus or Mohammed, or the Guru Nanak or Joseph Smith, they are pretty much on an equal footing. On this ground alone there does not seem much to judge between them since the prescriptions of *Leviticus* (the third book of the Hebrew Bible), the Christian Gospels, the Qur'an or the Guru Granth Sahib (the Sikh scriptures) seem equally likely or unlikely candidates for the mind of God.

The only plausible way open to us for judging between them, appears to lie in putting their claims to some other test whose authority we recognize. For instance, we might 'test' the Jewish dietary laws or the Sikh requirements regarding length of hair and beard against the demands of modern hygiene. We might try to assess the implications for human happiness of the Christian ideal of chastity and fidelity to a single partner in a world where contraception has created sexual freedom. Or we might examine the compatibility of Islamic codes of conduct with the free and equal treatment of women. But in each case we would be testing what purports to be the revealed will of God against some other external standard, thereby going beyond religious revelation and ultimately basing our code upon something else – a belief in hygiene, or sexual freedom or the equality of women. Religion would not be playing the fundamental role.

Our examination of the problem of religious knowledge has thus brought us in fact to the third of the questions outlined above; does religion provide a better grounded guide to the good life than the secular alternatives we have found wanting? In the examples just given we were led to try to resolve differences by appeal to non-religious conceptions of the good. That this inevitably happens if we try to appeal from good to God, so to speak, is the conclusion of the oldest philosophical examination of these matters, Plato's Socratic dialogue *Euthyphro*. The dialogue remains one of the best discussions of the issue and for this reason can still function as a focus of the argument at this point.

THE *EUTHYPHRO* DILEMMA

Euthyphro is a very characteristic Socratic dialogue. It takes its name from its central character, a man supposedly expert in the ways of religion, whom Socrates begins to question. The dialogue is set against a rather intriguing background. Euthyphro, a man of widely acknowledged religious devotion, meets Socrates outside a courthouse and it emerges from the opening remarks of their conversation that Euthyphro is engaged upon the business of prosecuting his own father for murder. On hearing this Socrates is somewhat astonished and not unnaturally supposes that the murder victim must be someone to whom Euthyphro is closely attached. But Euthyphro replies as follows:

> It is funny that you should think it makes any difference, Socrates, whether the dead man was an outsider or a member of my own household, and not realize that the only point at issue is whether the killer killed lawfully or not; and that if he did, he must be let alone, but if he did not, he must be prosecuted – that is, if he is the sharer of your hearth and table; because if you consciously associate with such a person and do not purify yourself and him by prosecuting him at law, you share equally in the pollution of his guilt. As a matter of fact, the

deceased was a day-labourer of mine; we were farming in Naxos and he was working for us there. Well, he got drunk, lost his temper with one of our servants and knifed him. So my father bound him hand and foot and threw him into a ditch; and then sent a man over here to ask the proper authority what was to be done. In the meanwhile he not only troubled himself very little about the prisoner, but neglected him altogether, considering that he was a murderer, and it would not matter if he died. And that was just what happened; what with starvation and exposure and confinement, he died before the messenger came back from consulting the expert. That is why both my father and my other relations are angry with me: because on the murderer's account I am prosecuting my father for manslaughter, whereas in the first place (as they maintain) he did not kill the man, and in the second, even supposing that he did kill him, since the dead man was a murderer, one ought not to concern oneself in defence of such a person, because it is an act of impiety for a son to prosecute his father for murder. They have a poor comprehension, Socrates, of how the divine law stands with regard to piety and impiety.

(Plato 1954: 22–3)

The case so described is an intriguing one from both a moral and a legal point of view, but Socrates chooses to light on the last sentence, and thereby leads Euthyphro to make the claim that, unlike the rest of his family, he is an expert on what the divine law does and does not require. With a strong touch of irony Socrates declares himself anxious to become Euthyphro's disciple that he may himself come to be possessed of such great and valuable knowledge, and with the questions he now raises, the philosophy proper begins. The dialogue falls into three main parts, but since it is the middle section that is of greatest importance in this context, it will be sufficient to outline the contents of the other two sections only briefly.

In the first part of the dialogue Socrates argues that it is only what all the gods agree on that could possibly be a guide to good conduct. It is hard for people in modern times to take much serious interest in talk of 'the gods', but what this section effectively shows is that talk of 'gods' in the plural is redundant, and that any attempt to give the good life a religious basis must appeal to one God.

In the third section Plato raises interesting questions about the very possibility of a devout life. If God is perfect and lacks nothing, how can we serve Him? There is nothing mere mortals can do that would be of any real value to God. At a later point something of this issue will be considered again. Here we can pass it by, because our concern must be with the second section of the dialogue.

In that section Socrates presents Euthyphro with a dilemma, that is, a question which seems to have only two possible answers, neither of which is acceptable. The dilemma (expressed in more modern language than Plato employs) is this: Is something good because God approves of it, or does He approve of it because it is good?

An example may make the question plainer. Take the relief of suffering such as is exhibited in the New Testament story of the Good Samaritan. On his way from Jerusalem to Jericho a man is set upon by thieves. He is robbed of his goods and left for dead by the roadside. A priest comes along, but passes by on the other side for fear of getting caught up in something unpleasant or inconvenient. Likewise a Levite (a very respectable sort of person) passes by. Then a Samaritan comes along. (It is important to know that the Jews of Jesus' time thought badly of Samaritans). Unlike the other two, he stops and helps the man, taking him to a wayside inn. He even leaves money with the innkeeper to cover the injured man's expenses.

This story has commended itself to generation after generation as an illuminating example of the love of neighbour Christians are commanded to show. But is the Samaritan's conduct good only because it accords with what God commands? Or is it rather that helping the injured is good in itself and this is why God commands it? Plato, writing long before this story was first told, puts the general point this way: is something holy because it is beloved of the gods, or is it beloved of the gods precisely because it is holy?

Suppose we answer 'yes' to the first alternative, and agree that there is nothing more to the goodness of an action than its being in accordance with the will of God. Then it seems that if God had required us to do the opposite of what we customarily think is right, it would be equally good; if God had commanded the Samaritan to cross the road from Jerusalem to Jericho and aggravate the victim's wounds, this would have been a good thing to do. But to think this is to think that what we take to be good and bad, right and wrong is not *intrinsically* so, but quite contingently so, that it is arbitrarily fixed by God. On this view there is nothing good about happiness and nothing wrong about suffering *in themselves*; it just so happens that God chose to declare these good and bad respectively, and might as easily have chosen to condemn those who are kind and generous and praise those who are malicious or greedy.

Most people are inclined to reject this horn of the dilemma. They think that God commands us to do what is good because it is good; that God does not act in the manner of the infamous Roman emperors Nero or Caligula, wilfully and whimsically commanding one thing on one occasion when they might as readily command the opposite on another. Rather God sees the truth, commands what is *really* good and forbids those things that are *really* bad.

But if this is so, then the things that are good and evil are good and evil, *whatever* God may think of them. It follows that they are thus independent of His will, and hence neither based upon nor determined by it. By trying to avoid making good and evil subject to a capricious will, we are caught on the other horn of the dilemma. God is not after all the foundation of good, but at best its revealer. Whatever He may will, good is good and bad is bad in reality and independently of His will.

The net result is this: We started out in search of something that would ground the claims of morality in such a way as to answer the prudentially oriented questions of the egoist. It was here that the appeal to the authority of God was supposed to help. But what Plato's dialogue shows is that either good and bad are dependent upon the will of God, in which case they are a wholly arbitrary matter, or else they are not wholly arbitrary, in which case there is no room for any appeal to God.

On three counts, then, any appeal to religion as the basis of a good life seems to be ruled out. The reality of evil in the world throws into doubt the very existence of the right sort of God. Great variety amongst the religions of the world and in the ways of life and kinds of conduct they prescribe creates a major difficulty in deciding what sort of good life the appeal to religion would underwrite. Finally, and perhaps most importantly, Plato's arguments in the Euthyphro seems to show that even if the first two difficulties can be overcome, religion cannot logically serve as a ground for morality.

RELIGIOUS EXPERIENCE AND RELIGIOUS PRACTICE

Is there any reply to these difficulties? Many philosophers and theologians have thought so, but once more it will not prove possible in the present context to enter into a detailed consideration of the many replies and counter replies that have been formulated over the centuries (though interested readers will find a much more extended treatment of the problem of evil in my book *Evil and Christian Ethics*). Here I propose only to explore one very important line of thought.

Let us begin with two striking considerations. The first is this. In the problem of evil, the reality of suffering and misery is presented as a reason for denying the existence of a loving God. In other words, the form of the problem is assumed to be one about hypothesis (A loving God exists) and evidence (There is evil in the world). It is an interesting fact, however, that it is precisely in the experience of suffering and evil – death, disease, bereavement, degradation – that most people turn to hopes of a loving God, turn indeed to religion in general. It seems that the experience of something which is supposed to count as evidence *against* God's existence very often figures as the principal cause of that belief. No doubt there are possible psychological explanations of this, but explanations of this sort often assume that people turn to religion in spite of their experience. Why should we not conclude, to the contrary, that the experience has enabled them to see something that might otherwise be missed? If this is true, the traditional construction of the problem of evil must have left something important out of the picture.

The same point may be illustrated in other ways. People are sometimes brought to religious belief by a sense of having been miraculously delivered from some disaster. In every case there is always a simple explanation of how it was that they were not crushed by falling masonry, or how it was that help came upon the scene at just that moment (or whatever). These simple explanations adequately cover the facts of the case, but the people involved very often go further and offer explanations in terms of divine agency or providential care and guidance. Sceptics rightly point out that, as explanations, these appeals go beyond the evidence and add nothing to our knowledge of the causes of the event. The truth of this is so easily acknowledged, however, that the fact that people nonetheless continue to make references to God and miracles should alert us to the possibility that the significance of their appeal may not have much to do with looking for explanations. Perhaps something quite different is going on when people turn to God or call upon Him in prayer. The philosophical 'problem of evil' assumes that what happens to us is evidence for and against God as it would be against someone in a courtroom. But when we look more carefully at how religious belief actually arises and what sustains it, the conclusion seems to be that religious experience is *not* to be thought of along the same lines as gathering evidence for and against scientific explanations.

A second important consideration is this. In what has been said so far we have assumed that religion underwrites moral values (if it does) by showing that God has issued explicit directions for the conduct of a good life. Now in one way this is true. But in another it is not. If we think, as many do, that religions lay down rules for a morally good life, or for a personally successful one, we have made an important mistake, because such a view, however common, is contrary to the facts about religious codes of conduct. Relatively little of what we find in the sacred literature of the world's religions is expressly to do with what might be called moral conduct, and even less with worldly success.

This is true of even the most familiar examples people use. Take the Ten Commandments, which are often supposed to be typical of a religious morality. The first four of these commandments concern our relationship to God, not our relationships with other people, and the remaining six take the larger part of their significance from this fact. Or consider Christ's 'Sermon on the Mount'. Though often spoken of as a piece of moral teaching, the Sermon is in fact much more concerned with how to pray and worship than it is with the details of ethical conduct. Again, the Qur'an has a great deal to say about how to keep in the right path ordained by God, but only a small part of this has to do with moral injunctions, and most of it with 'calling upon the Name'. The principal duties of the Muslim are to prayer and worship. The same is true of the Sikh scriptures. Even the Buddhist scriptures, though much concerned with how to live, are interested in the religious path to release from this world rather than rules for successful living in it. The fact is that the great religions of the world are not principally concerned with ethics at all, but with the religious life for its own sake. Their aim is not to make men and women good or successful, but to bring them into a relationship with the divine.

190

We might summarize these two points in this way. First, the springs of religion lie in experience which is not to be thought of as merely adding more to the general accumulation of evidence and formulation of explanations. Second, the sort of life religion recommends, though it may contain elements having to do with moral right and wrong and with personal happiness and achievement, is a distinctive sort of life. What both points suggest is that religious experience and conduct provides a context in which other sorts of human endeavour are to be assessed and understood. In religion we do not have a simple expansion of other concerns – scientific, moral or personal – but a change of perspective. Religion, in a phrase of David F Swenson's is a 'transforming power of otherworldliness'.

Neither of these considerations in itself provides convincing answers to the three major problems outlined. What they may do, however, is set us upon a line of thought that will eventually supply the means of answering them. We shall have to see. But in the meantime we can conclude that the importance of religion, if it has any, is not to supply better explanations of natural phenomena or underwrite the principles of morality more securely, but to provide a context in which these things are given *meaning*.

THE MYTH OF SISYPHUS

That religion is principally concerned with the meaning of life is almost a commonplace. But philosophers have found it difficult to determine just what is meant by 'meaning' in this context. 'Does life have a meaning?' is a question the meaningfulness of which may itself be doubted. One useful way of exploring the issues involved lies in thinking about the story of Sisyphus – a classical myth from the ancient world made famous in recent times by Albert Camus' existentialist essay about the meaning of human life, to which he gave the title *The Myth of Sisyphus*.

Sisyphus was a legendary king of the ancient Greek city of Corinth. He was reputed to be exceedingly cunning, and amongst the most fantastical deeds attributed to him is the story that, when Death came to take him, Sisyphus managed to chain it up, so that no one died until Ares came and released Death again. In the end Sisyphus was condemned to eternal punishment for, amongst other misdeeds, betraying divine secrets to mortals. It is the form of his punishment that is of interest here. Sisyphus had to roll a large stone up a hillside. But things were so arranged that, just as the stone reached the top, it would tumble down to the bottom and he had to begin all over again. And so it would continue for ever.

It is important to see that the labours of Sisyphus are not objectionable because they are difficult or tedious, but because they encapsulate a perfect image of pointlessness. Sisyphus's life, spent in the way the myth describes, is a meaningless one; this is what makes it a punishment. And the meaningless arises from the fact that he is trapped in an endless cycle of activity where what he does at one time (pushing the stone up the hill) is completely undone shortly afterwards (when it rolls down again). It is the fact that nothing enduring is accomplished or attained that makes the whole thing pointless. Yet, having seen that in this way Sisyphus's life is indeed meaningless, we are at the same time usefully placed to ask what would give it meaning.

For Camus, the importance of the story lies in the fact that all our lives are like this. In a famous opening passage he says

> There is but one truly serious philosophical problem and that is suicide. Judging whether life is or is not worth living amounts to answering the fundamental question of philosophy. All the rest . . . comes afterwards.
>
> (Camus 1942, 2000: 11)

The question of meaning arises because the human condition is one in which 'absurdity, hope and death carry on their dialogue'. Camus sketches a number of possible responses to this absurdity. In most of them, the absurdity of existence is acknowledged, but that acknowledgement can take different forms. One, the least admirable, is resignation, the simple acceptance of our 'thrownness' (to use a term from Heidegger), that we occupy a world in which we simply find ourselves. But another form of acknowledgement seizes upon the absurdity of existence with a kind of gusto and relishes to excess the things available for experience and consumption, a life marked perhaps by the old motto *carpe diem* – 'seize the day'. A third form of acknowledgement is the 'absurd hero' who is in revolt against the contingency of existence. 'You have already grasped', says Camus in the final chapter of his essay, that Sisyphus is the absurd hero. He is, as much through his passions as through his torture. His scorn of the gods, his hatred of death, and his passion for life won him that unspeakable penalty in which the whole being is exerted towards accomplishing nothing... Sisyphus, proletarian of the gods, powerless and rebellious, knows the whole extent of his wretched condition; it is what he thinks of during his descent. The lucidity that was to constitute his torture at the same time crowns his victory. There is no fate that cannot be surmounted by scorn. If the descent is thus sometimes performed in sorrow, it can also take place in joy. . . .

One does not discover the absurd without being tempted to write a manual of happiness. . . . There is but one world, however. Happiness and the absurd are two sons of the same earth. They are inseparable. It would be a mistake to say that happiness necessarily springs from the absurd discovery. It happens as well that the feeling of the absurd springs from happiness.

(Camus 1942, 2000: 108–10)

Camus wants to distinguish between attitudes to absurdity, but it is unclear what the criterion of discrimination is, because in the end, it seems that the scornful attitude here described is to be commended and valued because it issues in a kind of happiness. On his analysis, this is a subjective state of mind, and the trouble is that it is a state of mind that can be achieved in other ways.

This point is well brought out by Richard Taylor, an American philosopher who has also discussed the myth of Sisyphus at length. Taylor suggests two possible modifications to the story. Suppose that, while doing nothing to alter his task and conditions materially, the gods in their mercy inject him with a substance that has the curious property of giving him a desire to roll stones. As a result, whenever he is rolling the stone, however pointlessly, he is happy, and as the stone rolls down hill again, he grows restless and eager to begin his labours once more. This odd desire on Sisyphus's part is of course non-rational; it is after all merely the result of a substance injected into him. But for all that, it gives his activities a value for him, since the existence of the desire allows him a measure of satisfaction with the life to which he has been condemned. We might describe the position in this way. Sisyphus's life has *subjective* value; it contains something that matters *to him*. However, it still has no meaning. The endless rolling of a worthless stone remains pointless. Nothing about the activity itself has changed. The only thing that has changed is Sisyphus's attitude to it. And we might express this point by saying that, objectively speaking there is no more meaning to his life now than before.

But Taylor also invites us to consider a second modification in the story. Let us imagine that Sisyphus rolls not one stone but a series of stones to the top of the hill. This in itself does not alter the pointlessness of the activity, but suppose we add that the stones which Sisyphus rolls have a key part to play in the construction of a gloriously beautiful temple. In this case all his efforts have a point beyond the satisfaction of chemically induced desires. They contribute to a project independent of his own personal satisfaction. We could express the difference by saying that on this second modification of the story, Sisyphus's activity comes to have *objective* point or meaningfulness, because the facts about the activity, and not merely about Sisyphus, have been changed.

SUBJECTIVE VALUE AND OBJECTIVE MEANING

The distinction between subjective value and objective meaning is similar to one that we have encountered already, in the first chapter in fact, but its application to the topics of this chapter needs further investigation.

We can see that in the case of Sisyphus subjective value at best renders his activity meaningful in a very limited way. Given the life to which the gods have condemned him, having the strange desire he does may make him happier, and this no doubt is why Taylor describes it as an act of mercy on the part of the gods. But though the fact that he is pursuing his own happiness makes his activity more intelligible, the things he finds his happiness in still seem fruitless and silly. Indeed, given other modifications to the story, we can intelligibly pity this Sisyphus more than the first. Suppose he not only enjoys rolling stones, but believes it to be of the greatest importance.

In this he is unlike Camus's Sisyphus, who, though condemned, can at least shake his fist at the gods in recognition of what he had been condemned to. Taylor's new Sisyphus is not only condemned but deluded. He is not aware of the full extent of his condemnation, of just how pointless his life is. Yet does Camus's 'absurd hero' really surmount his condition by scorn? Not in the right way. How can it be that I make my life meaningful by the recognition of its ultimate meaninglessness? Perhaps it is the case, as Camus alleges, that scornful recognition brings a kind of happiness, but the alternative Sisyphus is happy too.

Now consider objective meaning. Suppose it is true that the stones Sisyphus so laboriously pushes to the top of the hill are indeed incorporated into an architecturally spectacular building. But suppose at the same time that Sisyphus does not know this. Then, though there is indeed a point to his labours, he himself cannot see it. His existence and activity remain *subjectively* valueless. He can take no satisfaction in them and life will be, for him, as pointless a round of drudgery as it was before.

If this is a correct analysis, it seems that neither the provision of subjective value, nor objective meaning is alone sufficient to redeem the lot of Sisyphus. What is necessary is *both* that some purpose or point is served by what he does, *and* that he knows and desires that this be the case. Only under these conditions can it be true that he has a fully meaningful existence.

What is true of the story of Sisyphus replicates a conclusion we have arrived at several previous points in this book. We saw that egoism is defective in part because it rests upon a divorce between the subjectively desired and the objectively desirable. Similarly, pleasure is insufficient as the touchstone of good because it too admits of the possibility that subjective pleasure and objective good are completely divorced. So too with existentialism which tries to find objectivity in pure subjectivity. With Kantianism and utilitarianism the fault lies in the other direction. Both erect systems of objective good and bad, right and wrong, but offer no explanation of how they might generate subjective value, i.e, value for those to whom they apply.

If this is correct, any adequate account of a meaningful life, and by extension, a good one, must provide a basis for both objective meaning and subjective value. Some philosophers have denied that this is possible. For instance, the American philosopher Thomas Nagel, in a widely discussed essay entitled 'The Absurd', contends that the objective and subjective points of view are mutually exclusive. From this it follows that we cannot reasonably look for any means of uniting the two. But, Nagel goes on to argue, the felt need to do so is in any case a sort of confusion. Being creatures who are able to adopt a point of view which is objective with respect to subjective involvement, human beings are prone to a sense that life is absurd or meaningless. But we should worry about this only if we insist on mistakenly applying the objective point of view to things that can only admit of subjective value. Not surprisingly they fail to meet the test. According to Nagel, what is important to human beings cannot be shown to be important in some other more objective sense. But he also thinks that it does not *need* to be shown to be objectively important, since it is important in the only way that matters, namely subjectively. (These are themes on which Nagel has written at greater length in *The View from Nowhere* and *The Last Word*.)

Richard Taylor, whose amplification of the Sisyphus myth we have been following, does not think that objective and subjective meaning are in principal mutually exclusive. But he does think that subjective meaning is better, because objective meaning is unobtainable. To see why he thinks this we need to look at the story once more. On one modification Sisyphus remains condemned to repeat an operation that results in nothing and is made to feel happy with his lot. On the other modification, his activity is given a point, its causal contribution to a magnificent building. But if we think about this further, Taylor says, we see that, though of longer duration, such buildings are also subject to destruction. No matter how great a human achievement we consider – the Egyptian pyramids, Chinese civilization or the Roman empire – we know that the passage of time has eventually reduced them to nothing. Agade, the ancient imperial capital of Akkadia, for example, was 'one of the most magnificent cities ever built by the hand of man . . . [It] boasted the widest canals, the largest gate, the most people and a pyramid like temple two hundred feet wide at its base. Yet of this city not one brick stands . . . [and] archeologists cannot guess within ten miles where the king's palace stood' (Pelligrino 1994: 128). In reality, then, those activities we are inclined to rank as most valuable and enduring are no less part of a cycle of repeated creation and decay and what truly makes them valuable is not anything other than the fact that we, whose activities they are, take a pride and satisfaction in them.

If this is true, than the two modifications of the Sisyphus myth we have been exploring do not really present us with an alternative between subjective and objective value. Both make Sisyphus's life valuable and mean-ingful in subjective ways. Neither could lend it objective value, on Taylor's view, because nothing does endure for all eternity. Of course Taylor does not deny that the striving for objective meaning and value is a marked part of human life. He quotes the well-known Christian hymn:

> Change and decay in all around I see;
> O Thou, Who changest not, abide with me

but he contends that though a longing for unity with the eternal is a marked characteristic of human beings, it is ultimately in vain. Its satisfac-tion would have to lie in a world where 'there is neither pain or grief' but where, too, all seeking, striving and creating had ceased, and where, con-sequently, total boredom would overwhelm us. If there is one life worse than Sisyphus's, it is the life in which we do nothing whatever.

THE RELIGIOUS PERSPECTIVE

Camus, Taylor and Nagel, in different ways, reject a common aspiration that religion can provide a perspective within which we might hope to combine both objective meaning and subjective value. It should be noted straight away, however, that whether they are right or wrong in this, not all religions could provide such a perspective. The possibility of just such a perspective is precisely what Buddhism, for instance, denies. In common with other eastern religions, Buddhism thinks of human beings as caught up in an inexorably turning wheel of existence to which we are chained by the constant desire to be doing, making, achieving. But this human desire or craving can never be wholly satisfied since with desire necessarily comes the possibility of privation and frustration. Everything we do is necessar-ily impermanent.

The secret of religious enlightenment, revealed to the Buddha as he sat beneath the Bo tree, is the suppression of desire, a systematic elimination of all our attachments to the world. In such turning away comes *moksha* or release and eventually, for it may take more than one life to achieve it, entry to Nirvana – a term which captures both the idea of nothingness and of heaven. The Buddhist ideal, then, finds supreme value in personal extinction. (Whether this amounts to *total* extinction is a further matter.) In so doing it wholly discounts subjective values because it is these, after all, that keep us chained to the unending cycle of birth, death and rebirth. It is of great interest to note that, while Western minds are accustomed to think of religious faith as entailing the belief and hope that we will be saved from eternal death and live for ever, the belief of Eastern religions is that, other things being equal, we *do* live for ever and it is from this dreadful fate that we must look to spirituality to save us.

It is only certain religions, then, that are likely to provide the sort of perspective for which we are looking, and chief among these are the great monotheistic religions of the West – Judaism, Christianity and Islam. All three have a common root, namely the religion of the ancient Israelites. The essence of ancient Judaism is to be found in the Hebrew scriptures and these begin, as is well known, with the book of *Genesis*, a name that actually means original creation.

It is very clear from the opening chapters of this book that above all else its author(s) meant to attribute to God the creation of everything; His creation was *ex nihilo*, from nothing. Accordingly, we are told, before creation began everything was 'without form and void'. It is also clear that as things come into existence the test of their adequacy is whether God regards them as good from the point of view of His creative purposes. God in effect *creates* good. A parallel with human creativity may be instructive here. When an accomplished artist paints a picture, or a gifted composer writes a piece of music, the whole context of their work makes each part of it 'right' for the place in which it appears. Part of their genius is that they are able to construct sequences of sound and visual patterns that are perfect in their place. But this perfection is not something independent of the work. It arises from the contribution that each part makes to the whole.

A similar account can be given of divine creation. Any piece of God's handiwork takes its value from its place in the whole story and pattern of creation. When it comes to the creation of human beings we are told that man is made 'in the image of God' and thus able to appreciate and use the good things that have been created. But, as is well-known, creation is followed by the Fall and the effect of this event is to rupture the unanimity between God and man, to introduce the possibility of divergence between the fundamental principles of creation and the mentality of human beings.

The subsequent development of the three great monotheistic religions may plausibly be interpreted as an attempt to understand how this rupture might be repaired.

Whatever way we regard the creation story and its relation to contemporary science, whether as spiritual myth or primitive cosmology (or both), it is not difficult to see how it relates to the topics of this chapter. If God creates good *ex nihilo*, there is no sense in which it can be independent of His will. On the other hand, if human beings have the freedom to diverge from the principles of creation we can easily conceive of circumstances in which they subjectively desire something different to what God's creative act intended for them. There is thus a sense in which what is *objectively* good and what is *subjectively* good can come apart. The ideal condition, of course, is one in which human beings want for themselves what, by their very creation, God has ordained for them, and bringing this to pass is what talk of salvation and redemption is all about.

We need not concern ourselves here directly with the difficult issue of just what sense we can make of this cosmic story and of what truth there is in it. (Interested readers will find some further discussion in my book *The Shape of the Past*.) Our purpose has been to sketch in outline a religious perspective in order to see whether in principle it can solve those problems in the philosophy of value which the appeal to religion is meant to solve. To decide this question we need to look again at the three difficulties set out earlier.

THE THREE DIFFICULTIES RECONSIDERED

These three difficulties were: the problem of evil, the problem of religious knowledge and the Euthyphro dilemma. To see how the sort of religious perspective just outlined might provide ways of overcoming these difficulties it needs to be stressed at the outset that the fundamental conception of good at work is itself a religious one. From a religious point of view the ultimate aim of all human thought and activity must be to return us to our proper place in creation and hence to a harmonious relationship with God, the source of everything.

For those who adopt it, this way of thinking throws a different light on the problem of evil. To begin with, though the things which we commonly describe as evils – pain, degradation, death – are indeed bad, evil properly speaking must now be thought of as those things which present obstacles to restoring the relationship with God. Pain and death can be evils for they may indeed create obstacles of this sort. People are often made bitter and resentful by their sufferings and the frustration of their hopes. But this is not necessarily so. As we noted earlier, it is a striking and important fact that calamitous events, far from destroying religious belief can *strengthen* it, often by engendering a sense of total dependence. Sometimes, too, we can overcome the evil things that happen to us by gracefully accepting them. Literature is full of stories whose point is to show how the same material suffering (war for instance) while destroying one person raised another to an almost superhuman level of grace and courage.

Secondly, if we adopt the religious perspective, we have to understand the idea of the love of God somewhat differently from the idea assumed by the normal version of the problem of evil. What it means to say that God is infinitely loving is that He wants and is always ready to grant a relationship of communion – literally 'being at one' – with His creatures. To question the reality of God's unfailingly love, then, is to doubt whether He really does want such a relationship with His creation. But if the first point about evil is correctly taken, we cannot properly conclude that the existence of evils in the ordinary every day sense is indeed evidence against the love of God. No doubt it is not easy to secure a proper relationship with the divine, but to show that God does *not* love us we would have to show that there are contexts and occasions on which this is simply impossible, and this is what the existence of death, degradation and suffering on their own cannot show. So long as it is true that these things can be overcome, they do not constitute evidence against the love of God.

From a religious perspective the problem of evil, then, is not what it is commonly made out to be. This does not make death, destruction and so on, any easier to tolerate, of course. The question 'Where was God in the Holocaust?' is still an important and deeply troubling one from a religious point of view in so far as we cannot imagine how God might be sought and found by the victims or perpetrators. But the answer to the problem, if there is one, could not consist in any kind of mitigation or explaining away of that horrendous period of history. Rather, religious reflection must show, if it can, how even horrors of that magnitude may be overcome.

An appeal to the religious perspective also casts a different light on the problem of religious knowledge. Certainly it is true that the prescriptions for human conduct which religious teachers have made differ considerably. But it seems broadly correct to say that they are all to be characterized as the removal of obstacles to restoring a right relationship with God. They thus share the same aim. About just how this aim is to be accomplished they differ, but their differing in this respect is philosophically speaking no more significant than are the differences between scientists and historians over which research methods to use.

It is true that in many instances religious differences are much more fundamental than this parallel suggests, but then, presumably, the religious quest is a much more ambitious one than the scientific. There is not space here to go into the matter fully, but before we can assume that religious differences (unlike scientific ones) are ultimately irresolvable, it needs to be shown that there has been no progress in religious understanding in any way comparable to that in scientific understanding, and that we never have good reason to abandon religious doctrines and prescriptions which were formerly widely accepted. For my part I do not think this can be shown. If that is right, we can say that the great variety of religious doctrine and prescription, though it presents practical difficulties, does not in itself represent a philosophical objection to the idea of religious knowledge.

The problem of religious knowledge led on to the Euthyphro dilemma by suggesting that in trying to sort out the competing claims for different religions we have no choice but to turn to other more familiar standards of good and bad. Now we can see this to be a mistake. There is indeed a religious standard by which they are to be judged, namely the adequacy of each religious prescription to remove real obstacles to a relationship with the divine. There is, however, a problem of another sort here. We can state this test in the abstract. But how are we to know when it has been satisfied? To my mind, the answer to this question can only lie with an appeal to the religious experience of humankind. The proper test for recommendations for the religious life must take the form of assessing whether they properly encapsulate what both ordinary believers and religious mystics have said and felt and whether they really do open up avenues to such experiences. It needs to be said at once, of course, that many people think religious experience to be illusory and the believer and mystic to be deluded. These are important claims and need to be investigated, but once more this is not a topic that can be entered into further here.

What is important for present purposes is to see that the appeal to a religious perspective does not answer the Euthyphro dilemma by providing a reason to opt for one horn rather than the other. Rather, it supplies a different conception of good in the light of which the relative importance of those things which we generally regard as good and bad may be assessed. Consider again a parallel with human creativity, this time the writing of a play. Imagine a play of which there survive, apparently, only fragmentary portions. The play as a whole is lost, but people nevertheless perform and enjoy the fragments and have their own estimates of the respective merits of the characters and events they contain. From time to time another fragment is discovered, but one day the text of the whole play is found. This throws a completely new light upon our understanding of the fragments we already possessed. Moreover, it changes our perspective in a different way to that in which the acquisition of one more fragment would make a difference, because it reveals the plot to us and hence the *meaning* of the play. In turn this brings about a re-estimation of the older fragments. They do not lose the capacity to give enjoyment, but this enjoyment is now tempered by an understanding of their *relative* importance in the work as a whole.

The parallel is this. We have seen that in thinking about the good life there is a sort of fragmentation between the claims of personal happiness and fulfilment and the claims of impartial respect for the good of others. We can see that both matter, but cannot quite see how they can be put together. The problem with secular philosophies we have been examining is that none of them seems able to supply an answer. Within the religious perspective, however, we can see how one might be provided. Both personal happiness and morally decent conduct towards others have their part to play in re-establishing communion with the divine. Neither, however, is to be identified with that aim, and neither is to be regarded as good independently of the contribution it makes to that communion. In what theologians call 'the divine economy', both personal happiness and respect for others are important, but they take their importance, and their *relative* importance, from their place in the task of redemption.

THE UNITY OF THE OBJECTIVE AND SUBJECTIVE – 'WHERE TRUE JOYS ARE TO BE FOUND'

It is now possible to explain how the appeal to religion can overcome the tension between subjective value and objective meaning. If the broad outlines of certain religions are true, then there is a divinely ordained purpose that explains both the nature and the objective meaning of the cosmos. But it is also true that, while fulfilment of God's purpose is possible only with the willing co-operation of human beings, their freedom in this respect allows them to diverge from God's ordination if they so choose. Ultimately, the most satisfactory world is one in which human beings want to follow the divinely prescribed order, and hence find greatest subjective value in the divine purpose. In this way, to use a traditional phrase, the service of God is perfect freedom. Within the religious perspective total subservience to God is the condition of human freedom from sin and death. Religious subservience of this sort is the whole aim of Islam, a word actually meaning 'submission', whose devotee is called a 'Muslim', the one who follows 'the straight path'. It is also a religious aspiration expressed in this old Christian prayer.

> Almighty God, who alone canst order the unruly wills and affections of sinful men: Grant unto thy people, that they may love the thing which thou commandest, and desire that which thou dost promise; that so, among the great and many changes of the world, our hearts may surely there be fixed, where true joys are to be found.

Such at any rate is one view of the religious perspective and of the way in which it overcomes some of the difficulties encountered in earlier chapters. Unfortunately if it does solve some problems, it brings others no less serious in its wake. One of these is the sheer difficulty of religious thought and language. For many, religious 'insight' is accomplished only by trading in mystery mongering. Religious theorizing for them is a good case of *obscurum per obscurius* – explaining the obscure by means of the more obscure. This is not always so, but even when religious language does not seem impossibly difficult to attach sense to, religious thought necessitates a great amount of metaphysical theorizing, about the relation of God to the world for instance, and it calls into play whole worlds beyond our ordinary perception. Consequently, the appeal to religion as a means of resolving problems in the moral philosophy of the good life may be offset by the even greater problems it raises.

More importantly, religious belief arises not merely from intellectual inquiry and speculation, but from religious feeling and experience. It is rarely, if ever, that people are argued into religious conviction. Without this crucial element, religious ideas remain, so to speak, inanimate, and the theoretical problems they engender seem little more than intellectual curiosities. The appeal to religion, therefore, cannot be successful on the basis of philosophical argument alone. Moreover, the philosophical exploration of religious ideas is very unwelcome to many religious people, who would rather rely upon the authority of a church or on personal 'faith'. It is true that the origins of much contemporary intellectual inquiry lie with the Christian religion, but it is also true that the history of religion, including Christianity, contains a good deal of hostility to intellectual criticism. From both points of view, that of secular scepticism and of unreflective religion, the ideas of this final chapter do not present viable solutions. For those who take either view, religion cannot and should not be expected to complete a philosophical task.

For some then, religious faith may provide further avenues of exploration for the issues we have been concerned with. For others it cannot. But if we were to return to the end of the previous chapter and stop there, a serious problem remains. How are the egoistic demands of personal happiness and the altruistic demands of morality to be squared? To ask this question is to ask whether there is a good life. Is it not rather the case that the morally virtuous life and the personally happy one are radically different conceptions of the good life? But if so, which should we choose, and how are conflicts between them to be resolved?

The recourse to religious ideas is intended to overcome such conflicts, but it brings with it ideas that are difficult to make sense of. If we do take the view that the ideas invoked by religion are too abstruse and perplexing to offer much illumination, the following choices present themselves. First, we could somehow learn to live with the dichotomy. This is what the majority of people do, in fact. They pay most attention to personal concerns and some attention to what they perceive to be moral demands. Such people get by, but their mode of existence is unsatisfactory from a philosophical point of view, since it is deeply incoherent. But then, they may not worry about philosophy.

For those to whom philosophical reflections matter, a second option presents itself – to opt for one conception or the other, in the way that Kant opts for the dictates of pure practical reason. The objection to this alternative, however, is that all the arguments appear to have shown neither option to be wholly satisfactory in itself.

The arguments appear to show this, but is it true? This raises a third possibility, that the arguments be examined all over again, that we go back to the start and reconsider the questions of moral philosophy as critically as we can. To arrive at the end of a book and reach this result may initially be dispiriting. Can the whole thing have been worthwhile? Yet this third option is in fact the properly philosophical one, and the one best warranted by the book itself. Those who have been caught up in the arguments will have seen very clearly that there are countless issues here which need to be explored again and again. Philosophy is a large and ancient subject. Though the book is full of conclusions, it is properly described as an introduction.

SUGGESTED FURTHER READING

Classic sources

Plato, *Euthyphro*
David Hume, *Dialogues Concerning Natural Religion*
John Stuart Mill, *Three Essays on Religion*
Albert Camus, *The Myth of Sisyphus*

Commentary

David O'Connor, *Hume on Religion*
Richard Taylor, *Good and Evil*

Contemporary discussion

John Cottingham, *On the Meaning of Life*
Gordon Graham, *Evil and Christian Ethics*
John Haldane, *An Intelligent Person's Guide to Religion*
Thomas Nagel, *The Last Word*
Julian Young, *The Death of God and the Meaning of Life*

BIBLIOGRAPHY

This bibliography contains all the works discussed or referred to in the text, together with those listed in the suggestions for further reading. Where two dates of publication appear in brackets after the author's name, the first refers to the original date of publication and the second to the date of the translation/edition that has been used and/or is recommended.

Aristotle (2002) *Nichomachean Ethics* (translation, introduction and commentary by Sarah Broadie and Christopher Rowe), Oxford, Oxford University Press.

Arendt, H (1963, 1994) *Eichmann in Jerusalem: A Report on the Banality of Evil*, New York, Penguin.

Baillie, J (2000) *Hume on Morality*, London and New York, Routledge.

Bentham, J (1789, 1960) *A Fragment of Government* and *Introduction to the Principles of Morals and Legislation* (edited by Wilfred Harrison), Oxford, Basil Blackwell.

Camus, A (1942, 2000) *The Myth of Sisyphus*, London, Penguin.

Cottingham, J (2003) *On the Meaning of Life*, London and New York, Routledge.

Crisp, R (1997) *Mill on Utilitarianism*, London and New York, Routledge.

Danto, A (1975) *Sartre*, Fontana Modern Masters, Glasgow, Collins.

Dickens, C (1838, 1966) *Oliver Twist*, World Classics, Oxford, Oxford University Press.

Foot, P (2001) *Natural Goodness,* Oxford, Clarendon Press.

Gardiner, P (1988) *Kierkegaard*, New York, Oxford University Press.

Gautier, D (1986) *Morals By Agreement*, Oxford, Clarendon Press.

Geach, P (1969) *God and the Soul*, London, Routledge.

Godwin, W (1793, 1971) *Enquiry Concerning Political Justice* (edited and abridged K C Carter), Oxford, Clarendon Press.

Gosling, J C B (1982) *The Greeks on Pleasure*, Oxford, Clarendon Press.

Graham, G (1997) *The Shape of the Past: A Philosophical Approach to History*, Oxford and New York, Oxford University Press.

—— (2001) *Evil and Christian Ethics*, Cambridge, Cambridge University Press.

Haldane, J (2003) *An Intelligent Person's Guide to Religion*, London, Duckworth.

Hanfling, O (1988) *The Quest for Meaning*, Oxford, Basil Blackwell.

Harman, G (1977) *The Nature of Morality: An Introduction to Ethics*, New York, Oxford University Press.

Harrison, R (1983) *Bentham* (The Arguments of the Philosophers series, edited by Ted Honderich), London, Routledge & Kegan Paul.

Hegel, G W F (1821, 1991) *Elements of the Philosophy of Right* (ed. Allen Wood, translated by H B Nisbet), Cambridge, Cambridge University Press.

Hibbert, C (1988) *The Personal History of Samuel Johnson*, Harmondsworth, Penguin.

Hobbes, T (1651, 1960) *Leviathan* (edited with an Introduction by Michael Oakeshot), Oxford, Basil Blackwell.

Hollingdale, R J (1985) *Nietzsche: The Man and His Philosophy*, London, Routledge.

Howells, C (1992) *The Cambridge Companion to Sartre*, Cambridge, Cambridge University Press.

Hughes, G J (2001) *Aristotle on Ethics*, London and New York, Routledge.

Hume, D (1779, 1966) *Dialogues Concerning Natural Religion*, in *Hume on Religion* (selected and introduced by R Wollheim), London and Glasgow, Collins.

—— (1739, 1967) *A Treatise of Human Nature* (reprinted from the original edition in three volumes and edited with an analytical index by L A Selby-Bigge), Oxford, Clarendon Press.

—— (1741–2, 1974) *Essays Moral, Political and Literary*, Oxford, Oxford University Press.

Hutcheson, F (1725, 1973) *Inquiry into the Original of Our Ideas of Beauty and Virtue* (edited by Peter Kivy), The Hague, Nijhoff.

Kant, I (1785, 1959) *Foundations of the Metaphysics of Morals* (translated, with an introduction, by Lewis White Beck), Indianapolis, Bobbs-Merrill Educational Publishing.

Kaufman, W (1968) *Nietzsche: Philosopher, Psychologist, Anti-Christ* (third edition), Princeton, Princeton University Press.

Kierkegaard, S (1938) *The Journals of Søren Kierkegaard* (translated by Alexander Dru), New York, Oxford University Press.

—— (1843, 1983) *Fear and Trembling / Repetition* (edited and translated with an introduction and notes by Howard V Hong and Edna H Hong), Princeton, Princeton University Press.

—— (1843, 1992) *Either / Or: A Fragment of Life*, Harmondsworth, Penguin Books.

—— (1846, 1992) *Concluding Unscientific Postscript to Philosophical Fragments*, Volume I (edited and translated with an introduction and notes by Howard V Hong and Edna H Hong), Princeton, Princeton University Press.

BIBLIOGRAPHY

—— (1846, 1992) *Concluding Unscientific Postscript to Philosophical Fragments*, Volume II (edited and translated with an introduction and notes by Howard V Hong and Edna H Hong), Princeton, Princeton University Press.

—— (1846, 1964) *Concluding Unscientific Postscript to Philosophical Fragments* (edited and translated with an introduction and notes by David Swenson and Walter Lowrie), Princeton, Princeton University Press.

Korsgaard, C (1996) *The Sources of Normativity*, Cambridge, Cambridge University Press.

Laerteus, D (1925) *The Lives of the Philosophers* (translated by R D Hicks), London, Heinemann.

Leiter, B (2002) *Nietzsche on Morality*, London, Routledge.

Lessnoff, M (1986), *Social Contract*, London, Macmillan.

Lippitt, J (2003) *Kierkegaard and Fear and Trembling*, London, Routledge.

Lloyd-Thomas, D A (1995) *Locke on Government*, London and New York, Routledge.

Locke, J (1690, 1960) *Two Treatises of Government* (a critical edition with introduction and notes by Peter Laslett), New York, Cambridge University Press.

Long, A A and Sedley, D N (1987) *The Hellenistic Philosophers* (Vol. 1), Cambridge, Cambridge University Press.

Lorenz, K (1963) *On Aggression*, London, Methuen.

Lyons, D (1965) *Forms and Limits of Utilitarianism*, Oxford, Clarendon Press.

MacIntyre, A (1967) *A Short History of Ethics*, London, Routledge.

—— (1971) *Against the Self-Images of the Age*, London, Gerald Duckworth & Co. Ltd.

—— (1981) *After Virtue*, London, Gerald Duckworth & Co. Ltd.

—— (1999) *Dependent Rational Animals: Why Human Beings Need the Virtues*, London, Gerald Duckworth & Co. Ltd.

Mackie, J L (1977) *Ethics: Inventing Right and Wrong*, Harmondsworth, Penguin Books Ltd.

Manser, A (1966) *Sartre,* London, Athlone Press.

Mill, J S (1969) *Three Essays on Religion* (Collected Works, Vol. 10, edited by J M Robson), Toronto, University Press.

—— (1871, 1998) *Utilitarianism* (edited by Roger Crisp), New York, Oxford University Press.

Moore, G E (1903, 1960) *Principia Ethica,* Cambridge, Cambridge University Press.

Nagel, T (1970) *The Possibility of Altruism*, Oxford, Clarendon Press.

—— (1979) *Mortal Questions*, Cambridge, Cambridge University Press.

—— (1986) *The View From Nowhere*, New York, Oxford University Press.

—— (1997) *The Last Word*, New York, Oxford University Press.

Nietzsche, F (1895, 1889, 1968) *Twilight of the Idols* and *The Anti-Christ* (translated by R J Hollingdale), London, Penguin Classics.

—— (1887, 1994) *On the Genealogy of Morality* (edited by Keith Ansell-Pearson), Cambridge, Cambridge University Press.

—— (1887, 2001) *The Gay Science* (edited by Sir Bernard Williams), Cambridge, Cambridge University Press.

—— (2003) *Writings from the Late Notebooks*, Cambridge, Cambridge University Press.

O'Connor, D (2001) *Hume on Religion*, London and New York, Routledge.

Pappas, N (1995, 2003) *Plato and the Republic*, London, Routledge.

Parfit, D (1984) *Reasons and Persons*, Oxford, Clarendon Press.

Paton, H J (1947) *The Categorical Imperative*, London, Hutchinson.

Pelligrino, C (1994) *Return to Sodom and Gomorrah*, New York, Random House.

Plato (1955) *The Republic* (translated by Desmond Lee), London, Penguin Classics.

—— (1960) *The Gorgias* (translated by Walter Hamilton), London, Penguin Classics.

—— (1973) *Euthyphro*, in *The Last Days of Socrates* (translated with an introduction by Hugh Tredennick), Harmondsworth, Penguin Books.

Rand, A (1989) *The Virtue of Selfishness,* New York, Signet Books.

Rawls, J (1973) *A Theory of Justice*, Oxford, Oxford University Press.

Sartre, J-P (1943, 1957) *Being and Nothingness* (translated by Hazel Barnes), London, Methuen.

—— (1946, 1973) *Existentialism and Humanism* (translated by Philip Mariet) London, Methuen.

Searle, J (1964, 1967) 'How to derive "ought" from "is"' in *Theories of Ethics* ed. P Foot, Oxford, Oxford University Press.

Smart, J J C and Williams, B (1973) *Utilitarianism For and Against*, Cambridge, Cambridge University Press.

Smith, M (1994) *The Moral Problem*, Oxford, Blackwell.

Stratton-Lake, P (2000) *Kant, Duty and Moral Worth*, London and New York, Routledge.

Taylor, R (1970) *Good and Evil*, New York, Prometheus.

Williams, B (1985) *Ethics and the Limits of Philosophy*, London, Collins.

Wilson, E O (1975, 2000) *Sociobiology: The New Synthesis*, Cambridge, MA, The Belknap Press of Harvard University Press.

—— (1978, 1995) *On Human Nature*, London, Penguin Books.

Young, J (2003) *The Death of God and the Meaning of Life*, London and New York, Routledge.

INDEX